HOUSE STORIES

House Stories

THE MEANINGS OF HOME
IN A NEW ENGLAND TOWN

Beth Luey

BRIGHT LEAF
AMHERST AND BOSTON
An imprint of University of Massachusetts Press

Bright Leaf is an imprint of University of Massachusetts Press.
Copyright © 2017 by University of Massachusetts Press
All rights reserved
Printed in the United States of America

ISBN 978-1-62534-311-6 (paper); 310-9 (hardcover)

Designed by Jack Harrison
Set in Adobe Garamond Pro with Garamond Premier Pro display
Printed and bound by The Maple-Vail Book Manufacturing Group

Cover design by Jack Harrison
Cover art: Detail from *Historic Fairhaven* by Kevin Cormier.
Used by permission of the artist.

Library of Congress Cataloging-in-Publication Data
A catalog record for this book is available from the Library of Congress.

British Library Cataloguing-in-Publication Data
A catalog record for this book is available from the British Library.

Contents

Preface

In 2005 my husband and I visited the house at 31 Middle Street in Fairhaven, Massachusetts, with a realtor. It was love at first sight. When we moved in the next year, arriving late at night and sleeping on a new bed that was the only furniture in the house, I immediately felt safe and at home. The house, built in 1800, is in the Federal style, with a central hall. From the outside, it is symmetrical and balanced: a door in the middle, with a window above it, and two windows on either side on each floor. Indoors it's less evenly divided, with the rooms on the south side somewhat larger than those on the north to accommodate the hall and stairs. But its layout is predictable: you always know exactly where you are. Its symmetry creates a sense of calm. The design of the house matches my mind: I'm organized, rational, and even-tempered. Traditionally, home is where the heart is. For me, it's also where my head is.

As I walked around town, I began wondering whether other people's houses reflect their mentalities. Fairhaven, like most towns, is full of old houses where people lived interesting lives. I read about those people and looked at the houses they lived in. I couldn't be sure whether they matched, but I became increasingly convinced that houses often help us understand the people who lived in them. That's where this book came from.

I began to explore the history of my own house when, soon after I moved in, I met a local historian. In the direct fashion of New Englanders, she asked, "You're new. Where do you live?" When I said, "Middle Street," she asked, "Which house?" And when I answered 31, she said, "Oh! The Weston house. You should look at the church records." When I did, I found the core of the first story in this book.

Fairhaven is an exceptionally fruitful place to study local history because of the pride the residents take in its past. Few towns of its size (roughly 16,000 people) can boast an archivist, a curator, a town committee to care for historic buildings, four voluntary associations that promote the town's history, and an unusual number of stories of interest beyond its borders. Although these stories are rooted in individual houses, they connect in ways that illustrate the growth of a community from isolated villages that were little more than extended families to a town with national and eventually international connections and importance.

Fairhaven also has been home to many dedicated historians whose work has been helpful to me. We sometimes disagree about emphasis, interpretations, and details, but I would be remiss if I failed to thank Natalie Hemingway, Cynthia McNaughten, Chris Richard, and the late Myra Lopes. I also wish to thank the Millicent Library and its welcoming staff; Debbie Charpentier, the town archivist, and her volunteers; the Boston Public Library, with its abundant electronic resources; the Claire T. Carney Library at the University of Massachusetts Dartmouth; the New Bedford Whaling Museum Research Library; the Rhode Island Historical Society Research Library; the Bancroft Library; and the Mystic Seaport Research Library.

Every town has houses with stories. I hope that reading these will inspire you to discover those in your neighborhood.

HOUSE STORIES

INTRODUCTION

House and Home

> . . . our endless and impossible journey toward home is in fact
> our home.
>
> —David Foster Wallace, "Some Remarks on Kafka's Funniness"

Fairhaven, Massachusetts, which calls itself "a small town with a big history," was founded in 1812, when it separated from New Bedford, the larger
city across the harbor. The area, long occupied by Native peoples, had been
settled by Mayflower passengers and their descendants in the seventeenth
century. The residents were farmers and fishermen, and the fishing industry added Norwegians and Portuguese to the mix. Later, French Canadi-
ans and English immigrants came to work in the textile mills. Its present
population of about sixteen thousand is the largest it has ever been. What
sets Fairhaven apart from typical New England towns is its architecture.
Two small neighborhoods next to the harbor boast Federal houses, some
built in the 1770s. The section to the east of the original village has street
after street of Greek Revival homes built beginning in 1830. But the most
striking architectural features are the public buildings in the town center.
Built at the turn of the twentieth century, and all designed by the architect
Charles Brigham, they look like they were imported from Europe—brick
and stone, Tudor and Gothic, French and Italianate. They were the gifts
of Henry Huttleston Rogers, a local boy who made his fortune from Standard Oil.

Fairhaven has been home to more historically significant people than
its size would predict. This book tells some of their stories, along with the
stories of people less well known but equally interesting. What ties them

together is their houses, the places where their stories happened. All of the houses are still standing and occupied, within less than a square mile, and all played important roles in their owners' lives. In doing so, the houses became homes.

A *house* is simply a building where people live. As physical objects, houses exhibit the architectural styles of the times in which they were built, the skills of their builders, and the status, means, tastes, and aspirations of those who have lived in them. They manifest advances in construction technology and materials. They appear in town maps, tax rolls, and other legal records, as well as in family photographs. They have places in the landscape, in their communities, and in the memories of their residents. A *home* is more complicated. In imagination, a home provides the warmth of the hearth, the intimacy of space shared with loved ones, the security of walls, roof, and doors, the comfort of a favorite chair and familiar bed, the domesticity of our own belongings and the cozy kitchen, the privacy secured by controlling who enters the house, the memories created within its walls, and the rootedness of a place to which we can always return. In reality, it may also be the scene of conflict, insecurity, even violence.

The houses in this book are both settings and actors in very human stories. People's experiences in them and feelings toward them were important in their lives, though often not in straightforward or traditional ways. A single house shelters different people who may view it—and one another—differently. Masters and servants may think very differently about the homes they share: to Isaiah Weston, 31 Middle Street was his castle, a place of comfort and pride; to his nursery maid, Phebe Jenney, it was something quite different. Husbands and wives, too, may see their homes differently. As Joseph Bates's religious convictions grew, a house became something to discard in preparation for a heavenly home. His wife would have preferred some security. Alexander Winsor enjoyed his brick and stone fortress as a place of safety on dry land between his clipper ship adventures, but his wives were left behind, and at least one of them wished to share his voyages. Sometimes, though, a home unites a family: the Zeitz family's palatial, multigenerational house was the capstone of hard-earned prosperity achieved through shared effort.

Feelings about home may also change as we age. Young Joseph Nye enjoyed the time he spent at home helping his father build his oil business, but as an adult he needed a very different house to live his life and express his individuality. And although Manjiro Nakahama appreciated the friendship and opportunities that Captain William Whitfield's home offered him, he soon longed for his real home, seemingly unattainable at a distance of thousands of miles. Martha Coggeshall's home, designed as a place to enjoy her retirement and entertain friends, became a burden as deaths left her alone and without heirs.

Sometimes homes fail to serve their purpose. Arthur and Mabel Small's lighthouse home, a cozy beacon of safety for ships, became a place of danger in storms. And not everyone *wants* a home: Joshua Slocum chose to live on the sea—a place that offered little safety, security, intimacy, or permanence.

People who live in small towns are especially likely to view the larger community as their home. In the eighteenth and early nineteenth centuries, Fairhaven was almost literally a family. Many people who lived here were related by blood or marriage, and the same surnames appear again and again. Even today, the town has only one high school, and its annual "homecoming" resembles a family get-together. The stories of houses, then, become community stories that help define who we are. What happens within a house quickly becomes public knowledge that shapes public opinion and public behavior. The story of Henry Huttleston Rogers, the town's revered native son and benefactor, is the story of a community as well as an individual. Appropriately, his homes and the other buildings he funded are scattered throughout the town.

The houses I have written about are typical of their times, but not representative of the whole community. We see no common sailors here, partly because they left few records but also because they often had no homes on land. Nor do we see the homes of the landless laborers on the farms outside the town center. The less substantial homes of the poor have not survived. Nor are people of color represented. The only Native person whose story is known in Fairhaven after the initial European purchase of the land was Hannah Sogg, a Wampanoag woman who was a housekeeper for Benjamin West and his two sons. When the British arrived in Fairhaven in 1778, a loyalist directed them to the West home at the corner of what is now Adams Street and Howland Road. "While looting the house they informed the Wests that they intended to burn it and refused the request of Miss Sogg to remove the old man to a place of safety," a New Bedford historian later wrote. "She, like a true heroine, carried him out herself and placed him on a feather bed against a wall in the orchard. The house was burned to the ground."[1] Although New Bedford offers a wealth of well-documented African American history and homes, Fairhaven does not.

Many books tell stories that take us on long voyages. This book, though, is a walking tour, an invitation to look through windows, cross thresholds, and learn what home has meant to men and women of one town in two centuries. The chapters are arranged so that one could walk from house to house and see all of them, as well as the public buildings mentioned, in a little over an hour. If you are not in Fairhaven, you can take the tour on Google Earth. Search for the street address (for Joshua Slocum's work yard, use "Capt. Joshua Slocum monument") and, when you arrive, click on the street view icon and drag it to the house. Except for some paint colors, the houses look much as they did at the time of the stories.

1

The Minister and the Maid

31 MIDDLE STREET

Proclaim the truth and do not be silent through fear.
— CATHERINE OF SIENA

Most Americans live in cities, and our imaginings about small-town life veer from *Our Town* to *Peyton Place*. But at the turn of the nineteenth century, most Americans lived in small towns and villages or the rural areas that surrounded them. They lived among people they had known all their lives, often related by blood or marriage. Most days were marked by the absence of drama, or even event. Yet *Peyton Place* moments did occur, and they reveal both the tensions beneath the dailiness and the ways that neighbors sought to resolve them. This is the story of one such moment in Fairhaven Village in the early 1800s.

Fairhaven was one of several villages that grew within Old Dartmouth along the south coast of Massachusetts. At the time of this story, it was still part of New Bedford, across the harbor. Oxford Village lay to its north. In 1790 Fairhaven was home to fewer than a hundred families, almost all descendants of the English settlers who had bought the land from the Wampanoags in the previous century. Its houses were clustered along Water, Middle, Main, and Center Streets near the harbor. By 1794 Fairhaven was large enough to build its own Congregational church—the Second Church of Christ in New Bedford—and the residents began to search for a minister. In August they offered the post to Ephraim Briggs Jr. Born in 1769, Briggs had graduated from Harvard College in 1791 and was the son of a noted minister in Halifax, Massachusetts. Four of his brothers were also in the ministry. Briggs chose a different pulpit, and the Fairhaven church turned to Isaiah Weston.[1]

Isaiah was the son of Zachariah Weston Jr. and his second wife, Sarah Pomeroy Perkins. He was born in Plymouth in 1772 or 1773 and graduated from Brown in 1793. He became the minister of the First Church in Middleborough, Massachusetts, that year and in November 1794 accepted the appointment in Fairhaven. He bought a house on Water Street near Center. Isaiah was a large man: quoting from a poem by William Cowper, the *New Bedford Mercury* described him as "burly, and big, and studious of his ease." In 1795 he married Sarah Dean of Raynham, Massachusetts, the nineteen-year-old daughter of Josiah and Sarah Byram Dean. Josiah was a successful businessman, the owner of an ironworks and a shipbuilding firm. He was a deacon of the Raynham Congregational Church, prominent in town and state politics, and would serve as a Republican in the U.S. Congress from 1807 to 1809.[2]

The Westons' first child to survive, Grenville Dean, was born in 1797. Two years later they moved to a small house at 33 Middle Street, a block east, where their second son, Franklin, was born. To accommodate their growing family, the Westons hired master builder Solomon Williams to construct a house on the lot next door, at 31 Middle Street. It was completed in 1802.[3] It was clearly the home of an affluent family. In the Federal style, it has a central hall and staircase, with a large parlor on the right as you enter and a smaller dining room on the left. Behind the dining room and hall is the kitchen. The parlor, hall, and dining room have oak floors, carved chair rail and crown moldings, and high ceilings. The house has chimneys at the north and south ends, so that both the parlor and the dining room have fireplaces on their outside walls. The woodwork in the parlor is elaborately carved, with dentil-work moldings and urn-and-swag cornices. The mantel is also carved in a dentil pattern, with a marble surround.

The second floor has four rooms. The south front bedroom, where Isaiah and Sarah slept, is as large as the parlor and has two closets and a fireplace with a geometrically carved mantel. The north front room was the nursery, also heated by a fireplace. The back rooms, reached by a narrow back stairway and hall, were heated only by the kitchen hearth below. The upstairs rooms have wide plank floors. The walls are of horsehair plaster, and each of the windows has twenty-four small panes. All the rooms are larger and the ceilings higher than was usual at the time. It is unlikely that a young minister of a small, new congregation could have built the fanciest house in the neighborhood without funds from his family, or his wife's. And the house's elaborate decoration was out of tune with the determinedly plain Congregational aesthetic.

The Westons probably had several servants, but I know the identity of only one: the nursemaid, Phebe Jenney, who took care of Grenville and Franklin. Phebe was born in July 1788 in Dartmouth. Her father, Jethro, was a shipwright who died in 1802. Such a position in the home of a clergyman would have been very attractive to her. I do not know when she came to work for the Westons or how long she stayed, but she was living in the house in 1802. She had probably left by October 13, 1805, when she married Franklin Tobey, a sea captain born in Sandwich. Franklin Tobey died in 1807, and after his death Phebe joined the Fairhaven church and was baptized by Isaiah Weston. On February 11, 1809, she married Elisha Tobey, a farmer and carpenter, and a cousin of her first husband. Their first child, Celia, was born later that year.[4]

The Church

Isaiah Weston's newly built church stood on the northeast corner of Center and Main Streets, just a block east of his home. It was a graceful frame building one and a half stories high, and its bell had been cast by Paul Revere.[5] The church records from 1794 to 1808 reflect the dailiness of village life. Adults joined the church; children were baptized.[6]

The only bit of controversy in those early years involved Joseph Damon, one of the founders of the church, who in 1802 suddenly stopped attending services. When Weston called on him in March for an explanation, the church records note, "the reason he assigned was that a cursed fidle was brought into the house of worship by which the pastor understood that he alluded to the Bassviol which the singers sometimes make use of." When Weston asked Damon to attend a church meeting to discuss his behavior, "he said he might come or he might not." Two church members then spoke with Damon, who told them "that if we could remove the Bassviol he would return but that he was injured and abused by two members of the Church in particular whose names he would not mention & also that the pastor had abused him & turned him out door." The church members could not act on a complaint against unnamed people, and once Weston had described the circumstances under which Damon left their meeting, they felt no need to act on that complaint either. They referred the problem of the bass viol to the church members, who chose to keep the instrument.

The membership then decided that because Damon had "pretended to scruples of conscience the Church do not proceed to criminate him but leave the door open for him to act as is most agreable to him." In November, several church members complained of Damon's failure to return and of his using bad language. Damon "promised that he would reform, that he would return to the meeting & to the communion & fellowship of the Church & although he could not approve of the use of the Bassviol in divine service yet he would return and take it upon him as a burden." By March, however, he had not returned and denied having made such a promise. In June, after two suspensions, "the Church voted unanimously to withdraw from Joseph Damon their fellowship and care."

Weston and the church members had spent an entire year trying to reconcile Joseph Damon—who appears at best to have been unpleasant and stubborn—without success. The bass viol was not an important theological issue, but the pains taken to restore good relations to this small community were significant. Although the church could have fined Damon for nonattendance, the only punishment threatened or employed was suspension or expulsion, and that seemed to be more painful to the church than to Damon.

Weston had ambitions beyond his small church. In 1804 he wrote to President Thomas Jefferson asking for the post of collector of the port of New Bedford. His father-in-law wrote in support of the idea, telling Jefferson that Weston had the backing of New Bedford merchants. Dean described him as "a Gentleman every way qualified to execute the duties of a Collector, [and] he is an undeviateing Republican and a firm Supporter of the present Administration." Nevertheless, he did not receive the appointment.[7]

Over the next five years the church continued to grow. The years 1806 and 1807 brought in many new members, some from the First Church and some from the Baptist Church. But in 1807 the church also began to suspend and expel members, either for nonattendance or because they had joined another church. Then, on July 19, 1808, "at a church meeting noted that the Pastoral relation between Isaiah Weston & this Church be & hereby is dissolved by his Dismission." No cause was given, but in all likelihood it was Weston's wish: in that year, through his father-in-law's political influence, he succeeded in being appointed collector of the port of New Bedford and moved across the harbor to a house in New Bedford.[8]

The Accusation

Less than six months later, Phebe Tobey made a shocking charge. A committee of eight men—John Alden, Benjamin Church, Barnabas Hammond, Gamaliel Church, Ruben Jenne, Elias Torrey, Lemuel Tripp, and Nathan Bates—was appointed in January 1809 to investigate, and they reported to the church on February 10:

> After a consultation of knowing our duty and what way & manner we should proceed we found it proper to send for Sister Phebe Tobey who agreable to our request came with Brother Gamaliel Church and Brother Lemuel Tripp we then thought proper to ask Sister Tobey if there was then an aggrievance with her against any of our Church . . . Sister Tobey answered there was an aggrivance with but one viz: Brother Isiah Weston we then askd her how long she had bin aggrieved She said for some time previous to Brother Weston being dismissed from the Ministry we then askd her if there had not been any Reconcilation between them since she had the occasion of this aggreviance as we understood that aggrievance bore date with her being at Brother Westons Sister Tobey answord that she had thought she had bin reconsiled with Brother Weston when she found Religion & joined our Church and mentioned some conversation that then passed between them in confesions—but for some time she thought she was not Reconciled we then askd her if she had taken the Step of the gospel for a Reconsilation Sister Tobey said she had not we then admonished her of the Impropriety of her conduct Sister Tobey then acknowledged that she had conducted improperly we then exorted her to her duty and askd her if she now felt free to proceed in the steps of the gospel Sister Tobey said she was intirely willing we then further Exhorted to make no delay and try in the steps of the gospel for a Reconciliation with the Brother alone and if there would be no sattisfaction then to take the next step and then we parted.

The committee was following the advice for reconciliation in Matthew 18:15–17: "Moreover if thy brother shall trespass against thee, go and tell him his fault between thee and him alone: if he shall hear thee, thou hast gained thy brother. But if he will not hear thee, then take with thee one or two more, that in the mouth of two or three witnesses every word may be established. And if he shall neglect to hear them, tell it unto the church: but if he neglect to hear the church, let him be unto thee as an heathen man and a publican."

Phebe Tobey did as she was told. She spoke alone with Isaiah Weston and then again with him in the presence of three other church members. No reconciliation was made, and the report continues with the accusation made to the committee on February 2:

> About six years past last fall Mrs Weston being from home watching with the sick and that about day light in the morning Mr Weston came up into the Chamber without his clothes on while she the sd Phebe lay in bed with Mr Westons son Granville that Mr Weston got into bed with her and his son that after Mr Weston got into bed he behaved indecently and offered to lift her linnen and took her hand and put an indecent thing into and Mr Weston asked her age and she replied fourteen years old and then Mr Weston left her bed and had no more conversation at that time. this above being read before the parties Brother Weston denied Sister Tobeys accusation being just and requested her to prove her assertions. and Sister Tobey replied that it was not possible for as she had no Evidance but she would inform us the Committee that she had communicated what she had accused Mr Weston with to two of her Confidence the same day that she received the Treatment in her presented Charge.

The committee sent for Phebe Tobey's confidantes "to see if the same storey had been added to or diminished . . . and found them to agree in the particulars." Weston asked whether she had further evidence and she said she did not. Weston asked the committee to report the matter to the church, but the committee was not ready to do so. They met a week later with Weston and Tobey and "for our direction implored divine assistance by joining in prayer we thus exerted and laboured hard with both of them for a reconsilation in as pressing a manner as we were able but we must inform you Brethren that all has been Ineffectual and we still remain in the dark."

The members of the committee were troubled and puzzled. They did not know who was telling the truth, but that was not the main source of their distress. Their goal was not fact-finding but reconciliation, which seemed impossible. Neither Sister Tobey nor Brother Weston would back down. No pastor had yet replaced Weston, so they had no clergyman to advise them. Beyond the guidance of St. Matthew, they had no procedure to follow. They then took a decidedly secular path: "by a motion of Brother Lemuel Williams to chose two of the Brethren to apply to Som Justice of the peas and call Sistr Phebe Tobey to make Sollem Oth to the accusation she had braught against Brother Isiah Weston."

No record remains of Phebe Tobey's sworn testimony. The committee reported to the church on February 10 and the results were discussed, but neither the report nor the discussion was entered into the church records. She presumably swore to the truth of her story; had she not, it would have been the end of the affair. Isaiah Weston was not asked to take a similar oath. But something did happen at that meeting: "There was laid before the Church a communication from Brother Isiah Weston & Sister Sarey Weston, wife to Brother Weston declaring themselves no more belonging to the 2d Church of Christ in New Bedford & withdrawing their fellowship & communion from sd Church."

The members of the church had not resolved the disagreement or reconciled the parties. If anything, the situation had deteriorated: now the Westons as well as Phebe Tobey were alienated. The committee decided to consult the pastors and members of some nearby churches. They drafted a letter to two nearby churches, one in Rochester and one in Wareham, that did not provide any details of what had happened but asked the recipients to come to Fairhaven to meet with the committee and advise them. Three clergymen and five laymen came to Fairhaven and met on March 9 at John Alden's house, a block away from the Weston house. No record remains of the evidence presented to the group, of the arguments made in their discussions, or even how long the group deliberated. We have only their conclusions, drawn up the same day:

> That the Church in accepting the Report of the Committee which advised Phebe Tobey to take the steps pointed out in the 18th Chapter of St Matthew, Before she laid her Complaint before the Church conducted with strict propriety.—That when the sd Phebe Tobey brought an accusation against Isaiah Weston, Which was not Supported by evidence, Said Accusation ought to have been dismissed.—That the Oath taken by the said Phebe Tobey in the case and that too when she was the Complainant were not Consistent with the beautiful simplicity of the Gosple "Let your communication be yea, yea, nay, nay."—Therefore, that the conduct of the Church in Recommending this measure is Reprehensible.—That the Conduct of Isaiah Weston & wife in withdrawing themselves from the Church cannot be supported by Reason nor Scripture and that his Declaration in the Case savours of an unchristian Spirit.—And that

if the Church & their Brother Isaiah Weston & wife recinde from that part of their Conduct towards each other which cannot be Justified: & in a Spirit of Christian love accommodate the Differences which at present Subsist it will be a source of happiness for many years to come, and probably will facilitate the Resettlement of the Gosple Ministry among Them . . .

The Council give it as their opinnion that no member of a Church is Justifiable in bringing an accusation against another member without expecting to support the charge by other evidence besides *his* or *her* declaration.

The next day, March 10, the members of the church gathered at the meeting house at noon and accepted the visitors' judgment.

The Aftermath

Despite his attempted resignation from the church, Isaiah Weston remained an active member as long as he lived in New Bedford. He served on the church committee that sought to replace him—an effort that did not succeed until 1813, when Abraham Wheeler became the minister. He and Sarah had two more sons and a daughter, born in 1804, 1810, and 1812, all baptized in the Fairhaven church. The church records listed him as a member, residence unknown, in 1820.

Weston's tenure as collector of the port of New Bedford did not run smoothly. He had the misfortune to hold the job at the time of the Embargo Acts—measures severely restricting imports and banning exports to other countries. Understandably, New Bedford shipowners and merchants opposed the embargo, and many tried to circumvent it. In fact, the embargo was so divisive that it became one of the main causes of the separation of Fairhaven (which supported the president) from New Bedford in 1812. The impact on the port—and on Weston's income—can be seen by the fall in duties collected: from $40,000 in 1807 to $1,800 in 1808.[9] Weston had replaced Edward Pope, a well-liked and respected figure, and his appointment was thought to be based on politics rather than ability. The *New Bedford Mercury* reported on August 8, 1808, that the "Young Federalists of *New-Bedford*," at a banquet in honor of Pope, offered a toast to "*Our new Collector*—Unless he studies the revenue laws more faithfully than he studied his Bible, 'Father Abraham and the Pope' will not be the only couple at loggerheads." The paper went on to explain that Weston had "*modestly,* and *learnedly,* and *chronologically* observed from his pulpit, that Abraham was called the Father of the Faithful, because the Lord raised him up to purify religion from the corruptions introduced by the Pope of Rome!"

Weston's tenure ended in 1813, after residents petitioned the federal government for his removal. According to some, he had been too zealous in enforcing the law. The *Mercury* noted that "when Mr. Weston was appointed to the office which he holds, we did not consider him qualified to discharge its duties . . . ; but by long practice, the business has become familiar to him . . . Mr. Weston's vigilance in detecting and bringing to justice some of his political brethren who had evaded the laws of their country, is the cause of their dissatisfaction; and they are influenced in their conduct by the spirit of revenge, which is said to be the sweetest luxury that barbarians can enjoy." Others accused him of being corrupt. Weston laid out the charges against him and his defense in a letter to President James Madison in which he accused his detractors of seeking revenge for his investigations of their lawbreaking and of wanting the office for themselves. Weston was replaced by John Hawes, who had been his main rival for the position in 1808. Weston moved to Dalton, in western Massachusetts, in 1814 and founded a textile mill. Sarah died in 1818, and Isaiah married Mary Wright the same year. When he died in 1821 at the age of forty-eight, he was designated as Isaiah Weston, Esq., rather than as the Reverend Isaiah Weston.[10]

Phebe Tobey and her husband moved to Acushnet, then the northern part of Fairhaven. In November 1810 she asked to be dismissed from the church and "recommended to some other church." The Fairhaven church denied her request because she failed to name the church to which she was to be dismissed. On September 11, 1814, with a new minister in place, the church did some housecleaning and "Voted, That, whereas, our Brother Joseph Church, & our sisters Phebe Tobey, Susannah Wilson, & Sally Tripp, Have, for a long time, forsaken our gospel ordinances, & refused to meet with us, walking contrary to their covenant engagements, & whereas, the brethren have watched over them, with much entreaty, in order to gain them, but without any prospect of success, the Church no longer consider them in fellowship, & under their watch & care, untill they manifest a disposition to return & give christian satisfaction."

Phebe Tobey never did return. She and her husband had nine children, none of whom were baptized in the Fairhaven church, all of whom lived to adulthood. Her husband died in 1866; Phebe died two years later at the age of eighty.[11]

The years from 1808 to 1820 brought turmoil to the church. Many members deserted it for the Third Church of Christ; theological differences weakened the fellowship and made it difficult to find a minister; and members were dismissed for causes ranging from nonattendance to drunkenness and adultery. In 1820, however, the second and third churches reunited. In 1845 the First Congregational Church of Fairhaven (the name the church adopted when Fairhaven seceded from New Bedford in 1812) moved to a new brick building just east of its original home. It remains an active participant in town life. Its original building, now the second floor of a newer building, remains a graceful and well-maintained landmark.

The house at 31 Middle Street has modern plumbing and wiring but otherwise is little changed. It has had thirteen owners since the Westons, and from 1884 to 1946 it was the parsonage of the Center Methodist Church, whose building, recently converted to a private home, is two blocks east of the First Congregational Church.

Ambiguity and Community

What really happened at 31 Middle Street on that November morning two hundred years ago? We cannot know. The only remaining witness is the house, and on this question it is mute. But more important than resolving the "he said, she said" puzzle is understanding what this story tells about small-town life in the early 1800s. Class mattered: Isaiah Weston—well educated and well connected—knew that Phebe Tobey could have no evidence against him that the church would accept. He was confident that his congregants would give him the benefit of the doubt, and their actions proved him right. They did not ask *him* to take an oath before a justice of the peace and, by continuing to welcome him, they implicitly accepted his story. The New Bedford newspaper, although critical of Weston's politics and abilities, did not mention the accusation, although it must have been widely circulated.

Gender mattered: All of the church members involved in this case, and all the outsiders they consulted, were male. Phebe's two friends were female, and their testimony was ignored. We have no idea what the wives of the committee members, or Sarah Weston, thought or said. Neverthe-less, Phebe's accusation was not dismissed out of hand.

Yet neither class nor gender trumped the desire to maintain community. The church wanted to keep both Phebe Tobey and Isaiah Weston in the fold. More than two people were involved: in the unrecorded conversations over supper tables, on street corners, and in bedrooms, all the congregants and townspeople would have taken sides. Everyone needed to believe that both parishioners had been treated fairly. That their efforts at resolution failed is less significant than the fact that they tried so hard.

2

Mister Rogers' Neighborhood

39 MIDDLE STREET

He did a great many things, including a number that he ought not to have done.

—*Harper's Weekly* on Henry Huttleston Rogers

As you drive over the bridge from New Bedford, a palace rises on your left: Fairhaven High School. Signs pointing to the right direct you to Fairhaven's town center. If you follow them, you come to a place that looks nothing like the New England town green of Christmas cards. There is no green. A Victorian Gothic town hall of red brick and stone dominates the north side of Center Street, facing a Romanesque library of granite, with elaborate terra-cotta details and stained-glass windows. A granite and limestone cathedral with a bell tower—the Unitarian Memorial Church—graces the next block, along with its Tudor parsonage. Two blocks further east sits an Elizabethan inn converted to a nursing home. All of these buildings date to the turn of the twentieth century, after the decline of the whaling industry that had been the source of the town's wealth. Whale oil didn't build the town center; Standard Oil did. A native son, Henry Huttleston Rogers, became one of the world's wealthiest men, a principal in the Standard Oil trust, and he used a substantial part of his wealth to build and endow the buildings, institutions, and landscape he wanted the town to have. The *Boston Globe* proclaimed that he "made a new town of his native place and finished it in oil colors."[1]

Henry Rogers' boyhood home, at 39 Middle Street, is a simple Cape

Cod house of clapboard and weathered shingles, built by his great-grandfather Stephen Merrihew around 1770. Enlarged in 1888, the house is still lovingly maintained. The home Rogers owned when he died was an eighty-five-room mansion with elaborate gardens, magnificent architectural detail, and every imaginable convenience. It was built in 1895 and torn down twenty years later, after his death. His houses, though, were a small part of his presence in Fairhaven during his life and in the present. The whole town was his home, and he shaped it to his liking. As a turn-of-the-century promoter of free enterprise wrote in his brief biography of Rogers, "We find the model town of Fairhaven molded and fashioned by her First Citizen. Everywhere are the marks of his personality, and the tangible signs of his good taste."[2]

Boyhood

Rogers was born to Rowland and Mary Eldredge Huttleston Rogers in 1840. After a single voyage on a whaling ship, his father held a variety of jobs and always earned an adequate income. Their home was small for a couple with three children, but it housed a large collection of books. Rogers was a good student, though not always well behaved: he was the first student in the new high school to be flogged. He may also have been a bit restless. He left high school to become an apprentice to an architect, but he soon returned. While still in school, Rogers earned money delivering the New Bedford and Boston newspapers and began taking orders for advertisements and writing as the New Bedford paper's Fairhaven correspondent. After graduating from high school he got a job at the Union Grocery Store, taking orders and delivering merchandise to customers. Accounts of his earnings vary. According to his friend Elbert Hubbard, his beginning salary of $3 a week was raised to $5 plus commissions after six months, and by the end of the year he was earning $20 a week. His next job was as baggage master and brakeman for the Fairhaven Branch Railroad, earning—according to another source—$40 a week.[3]

A magazine profile of Rogers reported a story current among "the older residents of Fairhaven" that he quadrupled his savings in one day. In 1857 or 1858 Rogers was at the train station waiting for the Boston newspapers he was to deliver. When the papers arrived, he noticed a headline announcing that the ship *Nancy James* had sunk with her entire cargo of sperm

whale oil. He knew that Bartholomew Taber, a Fairhaven merchant, was
expecting five hundred barrels of oil from that ship to fulfill a contract
with Charles H. Pratt, a New York oil dealer. "He hurried at once to Bartholomew Taber and imparted the news, at the same time offering to sell
him the entire consignment of morning papers provided he be permitted
to invest his $200 in Mr. Taber's oil deal. It would be fully three hours
before another delivery of papers could arrive . . . The shrewd oil merchant
quickly saw and grasped the opportunity to suppress the news . . . and to
purchase enough oil at current prices to fill his contract."[4] However much
he earned, and however he earned it, a year later Rogers had saved enough
money to make a significant investment in a different kind of oil.

A Tide of Fortune

By the time he was twenty-one, Rogers was looking for new opportunities.
His friend Charles Ellis had gone to Titusville, Pennsylvania, where Edwin
Drake had drilled the first commercially viable oil well in 1859. Ten years
after the gold rush, an oil rush began. In 1861 Rogers joined Ellis in the oil
fields and invested $600 of his savings to build the Wamsutta Oil Refinery.
Rogers apparently felt his future was secure. He returned to Fairhaven to
marry his schoolmate and childhood sweetheart, Abbie Palmer Gifford.
Abbie, a year younger than he, had grown up a few blocks away, at 36
Green Street. For $1,000 they bought "a little white house with a high
peaked roof" on a hill in Titusville, across a ravine from the home of the
Tarbell family. The journalist Ida Tarbell remembered the Rogers cottage as
"the prettiest in the world," her "first recognition of beauty in a building."
Rogers, she reported, recalled the house and its setting: "How beautiful it
was. I was never happier."[5]

The Wamsutta Refinery prospered, but the oil business—like its
products—was volatile. In 1867 the partners were unable to meet their
obligations. Rogers went to Brooklyn to meet with their principal creditor,
Charles H. Pratt. Pratt hired Rogers as the foreman of his Astral Oil Works
at $25 a week, and Rogers soon became Pratt's partner.[6] Astral grew into a
large and profitable concern, but the partners faced the challenge of competing against John D. Rockefeller's monopolistic ambitions. Rockefeller
at that time sought to drive his competitors out of business by contracting
with railroads to carry his oil at lower prices, provide other preferential

treatment, or refuse to carry other companies' oil at all. In 1872 Rogers became the spokesman of independent producers and New York oil interests in negotiating with the railroads against the Rockefeller companies.[7]

Rogers and Pratt held out for two years but realized the cause was lost. In 1874 they joined the Standard Oil trust. Rogers' earlier outspoken opposition may have served him well. Rockefeller accepted terms favorable to Rogers and Pratt, but the merger was kept secret for several years, "giving the public and smaller oil producers the illusion that they were doing business with the independent Pratt, rather than with the detested Standard Oil."[8] Rogers became chairman of the Manufacturers' Committee of the Standard Oil Company, with $100,000 of Standard Oil stock. By 1890 he was a vice president. Like others who joined the trust early on, he was "engulfed by a tide of fortune."[9]

When Rogers went to work for Pratt, he and Abbie and their two young daughters, Anne and Cara, had moved to Brooklyn. With prosperity came a Manhattan townhouse at 26 East 57th Street, along with a garage and stable one block north. There three more children—Millicent, Mary, and Henry Jr. (known as Harry)—were born. Social prominence accompanied Rogers' growing wealth. He was a member of the New York Yacht Club, Union League Club, Metropolitan Club, Century Association, Lotos Club, and Engineers Club, and he was a patron of the Metropolitan Museum of Art and the American Museum of Natural History. He enjoyed the theater and spending time with creative people. He met Mark Twain in the early 1880s, when Twain's financial situation was precarious. With Twain's power of attorney in hand, Rogers renegotiated contracts and sorted out legal tangles. The two became lifelong friends.[10]

In 1884 Rogers bought a home in Fairhaven, too, at the corner of Fort and Cedar Streets, where the family vacationed for ten years. His mother's house—even with the rooms he would add in 1888—was far too small to accommodate a family of seven.[11]

As Rogers prospered, he began reshaping his hometown. He had returned frequently, visiting his now-widowed mother and attending school reunions. In 1882 he purchased land east of Union Street between Pleasant and Chestnut, where it was rumored he was going to build a factory. The rumors ended when the *Fairhaven Star* reported that "Mr. Rogers proposes to erect upon this square a building of brick and stone creditable to himself and the town"—a school planned to be large enough to accommodate all the town's students for years to come. The economies of monopoly would be brought to the town's school system as the new school replaced the four small schools then in service. Rogers hired the architect Warren R. Briggs, who had designed a well-regarded school in Connecticut, and ground was broken in August 1883.[12]

Despite some opposition from neighbors who objected to the siting of the surrounding streets, work went forward. When the building was deeded to the town in 1885, the *New York Times* reported that it included eight large classrooms, with steam heating. Rogers provided all the furniture and books for the school as well. At the dedication on September 3, Rogers explained: "My motion was two-fold: first, that I wanted to do something which would fittingly express my gratitude and the fondness I have for my birthplace, with all its time-honored family associations; second, that I wanted to benefit you and give proof of the interest I have in the boys and girls of this town." He may also have been moved by a memory he shared with friends in later life. He told them that he had always felt cramped by the seats in his Fairhaven schools: "'If I ever get rich,' he told the teacher one day when he was more uncomfortable than usual, 'I'm going to build a schoolhouse in which the boys can be comfortable.'" Five years after the dedication Rogers noticed that the school's brick facade was becoming discolored, so he had it replaced. The *Star* reported that "the schooner A. E. Rudolph arrived with 120,000 pressed bricks for wall replacement." While the new bricks were being installed, the town's Select Board added a plaque reading "Rogers School." It is the only one of Rogers' gifts that bears his name.[13]

Rogers did not limit his philanthropy to Fairhaven. He made large donations to neighboring towns—schools in Acushnet and Mattapoisett, a building and financial support for St. Luke's Hospital in New Bedford, and a building for the Old Dartmouth Historical Society. He also gave generously to the New York Post-Graduate Medical School and Hospital in Manhattan, of which Abbie was a director.[14] When Mark Twain sought funds to pay for Helen Keller's college education, he turned to his old friend. Rogers had met Keller, and he agreed not only to pay for her education but to provide her with continuing financial support. He also provided moral support, encouraging her to continue her education. Keller was a frequent guest at Rogers' home, and she dedicated her autobiography to him.[15]

Much of Rogers' philanthropy was not made public. When Booker T. Washington spoke at Madison Square Garden to raise funds for the Tuskegee Institute, Rogers arrived late and had to stand at the back of the hall. The next day, Washington later recalled, he received a telegram inviting him to visit Rogers in his office. "He remarked that he had been present at the meeting the night previous and expected the 'hat to be passed,' but as that was not done he wanted to 'chip in' something. Thereupon he handed me ten one-thousand-dollar bills for the Tuskegee Institute," with the condition that the gift not be mentioned. Rogers continued to fund the Tuskegee Institute with a monthly gift as well as responses to special requests. One favorite cause managed by Washington was small rural schools in the south, to which Rogers contributed $500 every month—a gift that his son continued after his death. "When I was in need," Washington wrote, "I held H. H. Rogers in reserve until all others failed me, then I went to him and frankly told my needs. He always heard me through, and then told me to state the figure. He never failed me."[16]

Rogers made smaller, anonymous gifts in Fairhaven, too. "Houses were painted, mortgages were lifted, taxes paid, . . . bathrooms installed," Elbert Hubbard reported. Fairhaven friends helped with his charitable work: "Mrs. W. P. Winsor . . . worked days and months overtime on the bidding of Mr. Rogers, caring for emergency cases; where girls and boys were struggling to get an education and care for aged parents and invalid brothers and sisters; or where Fate had been unkind."[17]

Building Boom

Rogers' next major gift to Fairhaven was inspired by sorrow. In 1890 his daughter Millicent died of heart failure at the age of seventeen. Her father explained: "The germ of the Millicent Library had its origin in the darkness of a great grief and pressed its tendrils into our hearts through a little story that was told us of the dear girl whose memory we adore and desire to perpetuate. The story was expressive of what was in her thoughts a few weeks before her death and coupled with the love she held for books, there came to our children a common desire to erect a library in tribute to her memory." Like many small towns, Fairhaven lacked a proper library. Theirs was small, housed in a room over the offices of the Fairhaven Savings Bank at Main and Center. Andrew Carnegie was building free public libraries all over the nation to remedy the problem, but Rogers had something more grand and personal in mind. He acquired land on Center Street in 1890—an acquisition that required demolishing one house and moving another, along with its fruit trees, plants, and shrubs. He hired a prominent Boston architect, Charles Brigham, to design a worthy memorial.

The resulting structure of granite, terra cotta, and red tile is magnificent. The interior of carved oak and stenciled brick is embellished with fireplaces, plaster ornaments, and stained glass. The stained-glass window to the left of the entrance includes an image of Erato, the muse of lyric poetry, with the face of Millicent Rogers. It is much more than a functional library. As Rogers noted, "If we have built better than was required by the measure of practical needs, it was because we were working to an ideal that we desired should stand for the best in worth and beauty. We have tried to give the library an individuality in harmony with the character and personality, as we cherish them, of the loved one whose loss we mourn." Though Rogers' library was more luxurious than the Carnegie libraries, it was identical in purpose: "The future will reveal the good of the library, the purpose of which is to promote education and good fellowship. We want it used. We want every man, woman and child who is entitled to its privileges to feel that it is in part his own property. It is our hope that all will be interested to give the largest possible circulation to the books, that the rooms will be freely used by the people, and that there will never be permitted to grow the feeling that it is intended for the few rather than for the many."[18]

Establishing a pattern for his gifts, Rogers acknowledged that free public libraries are not self-sustaining. He continually added books to the collection and provided an endowment of $100,000, but he went further. Fairhaven did not have a town water system, and Joseph K. Nye, a young engineer, had been trying for some time to start one. In 1892 Rogers invested in the project and became the sole owner. Artesian wells were drilled, trenches were dug, and the system began to bring water to the town's homes. According to the *Fairhaven Star*, the water works were "a complete success . . . The only objection that can possibly be made to it is that its taste is so seductive, families are wasting much valuable time by hanging over the faucets and incapacitating themselves for their daily duties by becoming waterlogged." Rogers then donated all the shares to the library as a means of supporting it—a system that continued until 1968, when the town assumed responsibility for both the water system and the library.[19]

Fairhaven was also in desperate need of a town hall. Meetings had been held in churches and other auditoriums since the settlement's earliest days. A "town house" built in Oxford Village in 1843 was destroyed in a suspicious fire in 1858. Around 1900 citizens allocated $1,500 to build a new hall—a modest amount that would have financed at most a small building. Rogers had other ideas. As early as 1889, before Millicent's death, Rogers was planning to build a town hall on Center Street between William and Walnut Streets. There were three houses on the site: a double house known as the Fish-Bradford house, the Atwood house, and the Grinnell house. Rogers purchased the double house in 1889 and then had it sold at auction with the understanding that it was to be demolished because moving it would require destroying desirable shade trees. Both halves (minus furnaces, moldings, and other parts) were sold to a local farmer named D. W. Deane, who used the woodwork and windows to build poultry houses.[20]

The Atwood house was sold in March 1891 to Abbie Rogers. She had it moved one block to the southeast corner of William and Union Streets and then deeded it back to Mrs. Atwood. The town hall was to be Abbie's project, and subsequent negotiations were all in her name.[21]

The Grinnell property was more problematic. According to a local historian, Henry F. Grinnell, who had inherited the property from his father in 1852, was living in San Francisco. In 1891 Rogers sent two agents to persuade him to part with the house, but he named a price "so high that I knew there was no danger of my getting it," because "I really did not want to sell." He asked for $10,000—about four times the appraised value. Rather than pay it, Rogers encouraged the town to take the property by eminent domain. The *Star* noted that this would have been "the first time in the history of the Commonwealth that a town has taken advantage of the statute permitting the seizure of land for a town building." To move the process forward, Abbie Rogers sent a letter to the selectmen promising to take financial responsibility in case of lawsuits and to give the building to the town when it was completed. On April 25, the town offered Grinnell $4,000 for the property, and a month later he accepted the offer. In December, Mrs. Rogers gave the house to the Congregational Church, and it was later moved.[22]

Rogers again turned to Charles Brigham to design the town hall. The

Abbie Gifford Rogers. *From the collection of the Millicent Library.*

massive red-brick and granite building, with its clock tower, peaked roofs, and arched windows, serves a multitude of purposes. The ground floor houses town offices and a banquet hall now used for meetings. For many years the town's post office, police department, and jail were also located there. The second floor has some additional offices, but it is dominated by an auditorium that, with its balcony, seats eight hundred. The ornamented gambrel ceiling is divided by oak beams, and stained-glass windows illustrate the town's history: a Native settlement, the *Mayflower,* a clipper ship, the capture of a whale, Fort Phoenix (the fortification at the mouth of the harbor where the first naval battle of the Revolution was fought), a stage coach, a locomotive, and a view of Fairhaven from the New Bedford bridge. Massive electric chandeliers provide lighting, and the stage was originally draped with hand-painted curtains and stocked with ten ready-made sets, including a parlor, a prison, a landscape, a garden, a wood, and a mountain pass. The floors and woodwork in most of the building are of polished oak, but the auditorium has maple floors better suited for dancing. Most of the original custom bookcases, chairs, and tables are still in use.[23]

Abbie Gifford Rogers presented the town hall to Fairhaven on February 22, 1894, at a ceremony attended by the governor of Massachusetts, the presidents of the Massachusetts Senate and House of Representatives, and officials of nearby towns. Every Fairhaven resident received a free ticket to the ceremony, but they were so much in demand that scalpers were getting as much as $7 apiece. William Crapo, a local politician, spoke for Mrs. Rogers: "Love of Fairhaven prompts this gift. A warm-hearted attachment for the town, which is endeared to her by many associations, and a desire to benefit those who dwell therein have moved the donor to this act. Her wish is that this town house may prove a substantial benefaction to this people by bringing them together for closer union, for higher and broader culture, and for concerted philanthropic endeavor, that it may become a village center." Mark Twain offered a lesson for philanthropists, telling them they should "build these things while they are still alive, not wait till they are dead. If you do it while you are alive, it is really done and well done; but if you wait till you are dead, there is but a barren result and a divided profit—you get credit for the intention, and the lawyers get the money." Clearly, Henry Rogers shared Twain's opinion.[24]

Three months after the dedication, Abbie Rogers died in New York and was buried in Fairhaven's Riverside Cemetery. Rogers would not focus his energies on Fairhaven's town center again for five years.

"We are not in business for our health"

Rogers' philanthropy was rooted in a sincere desire to improve other people's lives, but it was financed by money earned from quite different

Henry Huttleston Rogers, 1896, portrait by J. Wells Champney.
From the collection of the Millicent Library.

motives. Rogers was a gambler who played for high stakes. He confided to Ida Tarbell, "I always play poker when the market is closed . . . I can't help it."[25] He was smart and successful, but he was also acquisitive, ruthless, controlling, and arrogant. His interests were expansive: oil, railroads, natural gas, coal, copper, electric power—even the Staten Island Ferry. No matter what the business, however, he was guided by the same principles. He always drove a hard bargain: "No man has done his business properly who has missed a single dollar he could have secured in the doing of it."[26] One admirer wrote that "he thoroughly enjoyed a battle and never relented nor let up," and another said, "He often did to others what they were trying to do to him, and he did it first." Lengthy accounts of litigation over his natural gas and copper interests show him fighting fiercely for every penny of profit. He recognized no authority with power to alter the way he operated: "We'll see Standard Oil in hell before we will allow any body of men on earth to dictate how we shall conduct our business."[27]

Rogers, like the Rockefellers, had made his fortune by monopolizing commodities and services. By the turn of the twentieth century, the legality of monopoly was being challenged. Rogers responded with contempt. When in 1906 the state of Missouri sued Standard Oil, the hearing was covered by newspapers throughout the country, most of them hostile to the trust. All of the company's officers were called to testify, but Rogers' outrageous behavior received the most attention. The *Fort Worth Telegram* reported one day's testimony under a four-deck headline: "Rogers Sneers at Inquisitor / Treats Standard Oil Hearing as Great Joke / Makes Hearing Farce / Cracks Silly Jokes at Prosecutor Hedley and Ignores Many Questions." The article offered a scathing account of "the most amazing spectacle that any law court ever witnessed": "For three hours he exhibited a monumental disregard for law and legal exactions. Sneering and cynical in speech, insolent and defiant in retort, he lolled in his chair in an attitude of amused tolerance of the proceedings apparently serenely confident that no law of state or nation could reach him or his company."[28]

Even before that hearing, Rogers and Standard Oil had been the subject of two highly critical books. The first was Ida Tarbell's two-volume history of Standard Oil, published in 1904. The second was *Frenzied Finance,* by Thomas W. Lawson, who had joined Rogers in forming Amalgamated Copper. Tarbell and Lawson (in later life) were sworn enemies of monopoly capitalism, but they painted the same admiring portrait of Rogers as a human being. Tarbell said he was "the handsomest and most distinguished figure in Wall Street. He was tall, muscular, lithe as an Indian. There was a trace of the early oil adventurer in his bearing in spite of his air of authority, his excellent grooming, his manner of the quick-witted naturally adaptable man who has seen much of people . . . The more we talked, the more at home I felt with him and the more I liked him." This liking survived Rogers' evasions during interviews. Once Tarbell lost her temper and said of a mutual acquaintance, "He's a liar and hypocrite, and you know it!" Rogers responded, "I think it is going to rain."[29]

Lawson, who found Rogers "despotic," described him at sixty-five as "one of the most distinguished-looking men of his time; tall and straight, and as well-proportioned and supple as one of the beautiful American elms which line the streets of his native town . . . When he walks, the active swing of his figure expresses power." Looking into Rogers' eyes, Lawson wrote, "there is such a kindly good-will in those eyes when they are at rest that the man does not live who would not consider himself favored to be allowed to turn over to Henry H. Rogers his pocket-book without receiving a receipt. They are the eyes of the man you would name in your will to care for your wife's and children's welfare . . . Away from the intoxicating spell of dollar-making this remarkable man is one of the most charming and lovable beings I have ever encountered." And Mark Twain claimed that "Mr. Rogers's face would destroy any harsh evidence that had ever been brought against him, he wouldn't need to say a word; those men would look at him and would recognize and realize that if he was a villain there wasn't anybody left in the country that wasn't."[30]

Fairhaven saw mostly the likeable man, the neighbor you would trust with your pocket-book, wife, and children. They saw the man who, when giving a humorous address at his high school reunion, "was dodging spitballs thrown by the girls on the back seats" and enjoyed a debate over whether a syndicate was "a lot of men entirely surrounded by money" or "a pile of money surrounded by men."[31] But there was only one Henry Rogers, and his love of power and control were in evidence in Fairhaven as well as on Wall Street. Henry Grinnell, for one, learned that it was pointless to oppose his intentions, or to expect him to miss a single dollar in a business deal. The town was fortunate in agreeing for the most part with Rogers' vision of its future. It is unlikely that he would have countenanced dissent.

The Tycoon Turned Town Planner

Abbie's death was not the only loss that Rogers suffered in 1894: the family home on Fort Street had burned down just days before the town hall was dedicated. Rogers decided to rebuild, and the new home would be on the grand scale he had adopted for the town buildings. Charles Brigham's design incorporated eighty-five rooms, including eighteen bedrooms.

There were playrooms for the children, bowling lanes for all, vast kitchens, and a well-stocked wine cellar. The house had its own power plant, as well as cold storage. Stables, gardens, and greenhouses surrounded it. The woodwork was beautifully carved, the staircases sweeping, the glass leaded. Verandas and copper-topped turrets ornamented the exterior. From the house, Rogers could see the harbor and Buzzard's Bay, where the *Kanawha*—the steam-powered yacht he bought in 1901—was moored. Named after a West Virginia river where Rogers had extensive coal and railroad interests, the yacht transported the Rogers family and friends along the coast, to the Caribbean, and across the Atlantic. She was said to be "the speediest yacht of her size afloat."[32]

Rogers next made an entirely new kind of investment in Fairhaven. Young people needed schools, but they also needed employment—a scarce commodity in the area when whaling had ended and textile mills began moving south. In 1895 he acquired the American Tack Company on Fort Street and combined it with eighteen similar businesses under the name Atlas Tack. He built a new factory on Pleasant Street, near the elementary school. With more than five hundred employees working around the clock, Atlas became the town's largest employer.[33]

In 1896 Rogers married Emilie Augusta Hart, a widow with no ties to Fairhaven. He began to support causes of interest to her, including the Messiah Home for Little Children in New York City, to which he donated $300,000 for a building designed by Charles Brigham.[34] His commitment to his hometown did not change, though, and Rogers began to reshape Fairhaven in fundamental ways. He decided that the town needed better roads, and in 1896 he campaigned successfully for the office of superintendent of streets. His salary was $3 a day, and the annual budget was $3,000. Delegating the work to an assistant, Rogers ordered the laying out and paving of streets and sidewalks. Granite curbs were installed, and two thousand trees were planted along the new streets. When the bills exceeded the budget, Rogers paid the difference. He drove around his new roads in an Electric Victoria.[35] The state was building a new bridge across the harbor, and Rogers lobbied to have it sited at Huttleston Avenue (now Route 6), rather than at the location of the old bridge. When bridge construction threatened the historic Academy building, Rogers had it moved.[36]

In 1899 Rogers' mother died, and his desire to build a memorial turned his attention back to the town center. He purchased the block east of the library and moved or demolished the houses standing on it. Charles Brigham was commissioned to design a Unitarian church, parish house, and parsonage. The result is not a typical New England church, but a gothic cathedral—elaborately carved limestone and granite embellished with saints and gargoyles, stone tracery, a bell tower, and heavily decorated bronze gates and doors. The parish house, connected by a cloister, is in the same style. The Elizabethan parsonage reflects the domestic architecture of the sixteenth century. Occupying an entire block, with lawns and trees, it is meant to evoke Renaissance England.

The interior of the church is an astonishing blend of traditional cathedral details and Unitarian theology. The carved bog-oak altar and pews would be at home in Europe (and, indeed, were created by nearly fifty Bavarian carvers brought to town to do the work) but depict Unitarian history and beliefs. The angels in the rafters represent subjects of study, reflecting Rogers' commitment to education. Italian stonemasons carved the walls and laid the floors made of marble from France, Italy, Switzerland, and the United States.[37]

Robert Reid, whose murals adorn the Massachusetts State House, designed the windows, his first and only work in stained glass. Dr. Robert Collyer, pastor of the Church of the Messiah in New York City, which Rogers attended, advised him on appropriate subjects, and Rogers asked that the Nativity and the Beatitudes be included. The east and west windows (the Sermon on the Mount and the Nativity) were created with a technique using several layers of glass. Reid was a painter, and the faces in the windows, some of which are thought to depict Rogers, Millicent, and Dr. Collyer, are unusually realistic and natural. The clerestory windows illustrate the Beatitudes. The aisle windows depict Fairhaven families, each accompanied by the symbol of an apostle.[38]

The parish house, with its oak paneling, beamed polygonal ceilings, and massive stone fireplaces, is decorated with Craftsman-style ornamentation. Dr. Collyer suggested verses to be used under the stained-glass windows. A large stage, kitchens, large meeting rooms, and small salons provide for a variety of uses. The parsonage is of stone on the first floor, with a second story of timber and plaster. The teak beams are rough-finished with carved figures.[39]

When the buildings were dedicated on October 4, 1904, ceremonies began at 9 a.m., when the largest of the eleven bells was rung for twenty minutes. The bells then tolled religious and secular music until 11:00, when services began. Prayers, hymns, a sermon, and an address were followed by lunch in the parish house. At 7:30 parishioners returned for vespers and two more addresses—one by the minister of the New Bedford Unitarian Church and another by Dr. Collyer. A dominant theme of the day was permanence and longevity—something that may have been on Rogers' mind as he recalled his mother's long life and his own advancing age. In his evening address, Dr. Collyer told the history of the small country church in the Yorkshire village where he had been raised, a church that had stood for a thousand years. "The church stands on the hill, and as the memory touches me this evening in this strong and stately pile, I ask: 'What of the thousand years to come, if you in this generation and those who come after you in this Fairhaven are faithful to the trust placed in your hands this day, and the high and sacred purpose of the giver?' Then I say, what has been shall be."[40]

At the time of the dedication, work had already begun two blocks to the east on the Tabitha Inn, which Rogers built to accommodate visitors to the town. Charles Brigham modeled it on Elizabethan inns: it is U-shaped, like the buildings where Shakespeare's plays were performed in courtyards, with external beams and plaster. It was a commercial venture, not a gift, and Rogers leased it to Catherine M. Price, who had operated an inn at Cooperstown, New York, for nine years. A *Boston Globe* reporter wrote that it "cannot be equalled in attractiveness and thoroughness of workmanship by any similar building in any town, and probably in no city in the country. An experienced builder told a Globe correspondent that he never saw anything like it!" The Tabitha Inn, named after one of Rogers' maternal great-grandmothers, offered the anticipated "first class patronage" a spacious lobby, parlor, library, two dining rooms, and a billiard room. The twenty-two bedrooms on the second floor were individually decorated, and the third floor provided slightly more modest accommodation.[41]

Work had also begun on a new high school, a project that Rogers considered especially important. His belief in the benefits of high school tells as much about his own experience as about his expectations for the graduates of the new school. The high school graduate, he told a reporter a few years later,

> is master of the ordinary implements of business life, whether it is mechanical or commercial—that is, he can read, write, spell, and figure.

He has at least a foundation of general knowledge. Our American high schools, too, cultivate a sense of the greatness of the country which inspires him with confidence in her future and hence in his own . . . The high school boy has had set for him a standard of manliness, of personal honor, of good conduct, and that give-and-take which is the necessity of all civilized social conduct . . .

The high school graduate is proud enough in his way of what he has accomplished in getting his class standing, but he does not bring his pride with him when he is going to work or looking for a job. On the other hand, the college man who is not entering one of the professions, is apt to have more pride than the situation warrants, and that is a hampering thing. He is expecting the world to come to him rather than he should set out with eager heart to discover the world . . .

[The high school graduate] is equipped for the absorption and assimilation of further knowledge.[42]

As he had done with the library, Rogers again "built better than was required by the measure of practical needs." He asked Thomas Tripp, chairman of the Fairhaven school board since 1900, to make recommendations for a new school, based on the latest facilities and ideas, and commissioned Charles Brigham to design the building, again without concern for costs.[43]

The result was a school that incorporated all the latest technology into an Elizabethan palace. Built of granite, limestone, and brick, its three stories are ornamented by carvings, balconies, gables, and a clock tower. The school had its own plants for gas and electric lights, and an apartment for the custodian. It offered fully equipped, up-to-date laboratories and classrooms for home economics and manual training; a library with bog-oak paneling and bookcases; an octagonal gym with a basketball court, showers, and lockers; an elegant auditorium; and classrooms with ornate plaster ceilings.[44] The athletic field, with concrete bleachers, was constructed by town employees assisted by fifteen students who, according to the *New York Times,* reaped a "three-fold benefit. Their toil goes toward the completion of the new athletic field . . . ; they are paid [a dollar a day] for what they do, and the vigorous open-air work is adding to their health, muscle and Summer tan." Rogers was pleased: "I thought that the old-time spirit of work and hustle had left the modern school boys, but the way in which these boys take hold and handle the shovel goes to prove that the spirit of work is still in existence."[45]

Rogers' interest in the schools extended to the teachers. In 1905, and possibly in other years, he gave each of Fairhaven's twenty-five teachers

$100, "allowing the teachers to have a good vacation without drawing on their savings." The money, "all in gold," was distributed by Thomas Tripp.[46] And to further beautify the area around the high school, Rogers had eight "cottages" built along Huttleston Avenue to the east. Said to be "of the most modern style," the houses are three stories high, with five bedrooms and three or four rooms on the first floor. Although all are about the same size, they differ in design and exterior finishes. They are set back from the street to allow for lawns and gardens. Construction began in September 1908, and the last of the houses was completed after Rogers' death in 1909. They were sold at cost, "on easy terms at a fair price."[47]

Rogers made another foray into Fairhaven politics in 1906, when he campaigned against the sale of liquor. "All day long he sped about the town in his automobile urging voters to go to the polls and vote against drink," the *New York Times* reported. "He took many citizens to the polls. While Mr. Rogers was working, the preachers of Fairhaven and women of the temperance societies were praying for his success in a room above the polling place." Fairhaven remained dry. In that year, too, Rogers complained that his town tax bill was too high.[48]

Finally, Rogers began to reshape the land itself, with an engineering project that took six years and an undisclosed amount of his money. South of Huttleston Avenue, just east of the New Bedford bridge, a wetlands area known as Mill Pond had become an "odoriferous and slimy mud hole." It was fed by a tidal creek that ran between Spring and Bridge Streets and by the Herring River, a stream running south to Huttleston Avenue and then continuing underground. There had once been a wharf and winter storage for ships, as well as a water mill. But by the turn of the twentieth century it had become unattractive and unhealthy, in part because of bridge construction. Rogers decided that it needed to be filled in to enhance the entrance to the town. He hired Joseph K. Nye, the engineer who had built the water system, to manage the project.[49]

The first step, which took one hundred laborers a year to complete, was to divert the Herring River into the harbor by constructing a six-foot-high concrete conduit. Next, Bridge Street, which lay under the high-water mark, was raised two to three feet. This entailed lifting twenty-five houses onto new foundations. Then the pond and wetlands needed to be filled in. A temporary narrow-gauge railroad was built between the site and a gravel pit on Bridge Street. Fifty men were employed on this project, which took far longer and cost much more than anticipated. Warren Delano donated land between Middle and Main Streets to expand the park. With the filling completed, the train was dismantled. Then loam was spread, trees and grass planted, and entrances and pathways paved.[50]

Finally, at a special town meeting on October 28, 1908, Rogers gave the park to the town and asked that it be named after Robert Cushman, an English Puritan who had planned to emigrate to America on the ill-fated *Speedwell* but never made the journey. He did, however, help many others to reach America and was an ancestor of both Rogers and Warren Delano.[51]

A Large Footprint

Henry Rogers died in 1909. Services were held in New York and Fairhaven, and he was buried in Riverside Cemetery. Standard Oil and his other monopolies were disbanded soon after. But nearly everything that Rogers created in Fairhaven is still in place. The town hall, library, and church complex remain in the town center, altered in their exterior only by a seamless addition to the library. The Tabitha Inn is now a nursing home and has been enlarged. The high school has an addition and some rooms have changed in purpose, but its elegance is untouched. Cushman Park is less ornamental and more utilitarian, and the Delano addition was sold. The streets and water company—expanded and modernized—still serve the town's residents. The endowments have shrunk, but various public funding sources have maintained the buildings. The Unitarian Memorial Church is planning a capital campaign to conserve the windows and repair water damage to the fabric. The Rogers School, however, is vacant and its future uncertain. Atlas Tack closed and became a Superfund site, now cleaned up but not in use. Rogers' boyhood home is happily occupied, but his mansion was demolished after Emilie Rogers' death. Part of the mansion and some of the furniture were shipped to Boston, to be incorporated into Mayor James M. Curley's Jamaica Plain mansion. Two main wings were purchased and moved elsewhere. The power plant and laundry wing are now private homes, one on Doane Street and the other on Center Street, east of the town hall. The mansion's library was incorporated into a house on nearby Phoenix Street. Town residents bought chandeliers, doors, mantels, and cabinets.[52]

Another significant contribution to the town was made after Rogers' death by his daughter Cara Rogers Broughton, later Lady Fairhaven. Fort Phoenix had been decommissioned after the Civil War and had fallen into disrepair. In 1926 she bought it and gave it to the town in memory of her father.[53] It is a town park, where the Fourth of July is celebrated with a reading of the Declaration of Independence and the firing of five cannon.

Fairhaven remains the home of Henry Huttleston Rogers. Most of us limit our renovations and redecorating to our houses. Rogers remodeled a whole town.

3

The Apple and the Tree

142 AND 146 MAIN STREET

The world is made more interesting by having every sort of person in it.

—ANDREW SOLOMON, *Far from the Tree*

On Main Street, a few yards north of the bridge to New Bedford, two houses enjoy a view of the harbor. The first—no. 142—was built in 1799 for a shipping merchant, Reuben Jenney. It is a large L-shaped three-story traditional clapboard house with a yard sloping down to the river. Jenney was one of the founders of the New Bedford Academy, a block away, and the next owner was Galen Hix, the boys' teacher and principal of the Academy. Hix sold the house to Captain John A. Hawes, a selectman, member of the school committee, state senator, and commodore of the New Bedford Yacht Club. Hawes also bought the Academy building after it ceased to be used as a school. In 1865 the house was sold to a newcomer, William Foster Nye, for $2,500. The house next door, at 146 Main Street, looms over it. Built of large randomly shaped stones, with a twenty-three-foot cylindrical tower that houses its staircases, it looks nothing like any house in town. It was designed and built by William Nye's son, Joseph Keith, in 1891. Each house is typical of its owner, and together they hint at a relationship that was close, despite differences in interests and temperament. Joe left home, but—unlike his father—he never traveled far.[1]

Apprenticeship and Adventure

William was born in Pocasset, in the southern part of Sandwich, Massachusetts, in 1824, the third of eight children of Ebenezer and Syrena Dimmick Nye. His father was a sea captain, and two of William's brothers also went to sea. William, though, had other plans. When he was sixteen, he moved to New Bedford, a city brimming with wealth and opportunity. He apprenticed himself to the city's oldest master builder, Prince Weeks, and then worked for the firm of Braddock Gifford and Timothy D. Cook.[2] With his apprenticeship complete, in 1845 he moved to Taunton, Massachusetts, to work for William Mason. Mason was an inventor in the cotton industry, and in 1842 he had bought a mill. In 1845 he decided to construct a factory building of his own design where he could manufacture the machines he had invented or improved. A company publication described the Mason Machine Works as "the largest and most complete plant for the manufacture of Cotton Machinery in this country" at the time. It was later used to build railroad cars and, during the Civil War, rifles.[3]

When his work at Mason's factory was finished, William moved to Boston, where he worked for the Appleton Organ Company. This position suggests that he was both extremely versatile and highly accomplished. Organ historians note that Appleton was "the Boston organbuilder who brought the hand-made organ to the zenith of craftsmanship," whose products "could be found along the eastern seaboard from South Carolina to Maine." The firm would have had its pick of employees.[4]

William's next job was an adventure: he went to work for the Frederic Tudor Ice Company, which transported ice from New England to southern cities, the West Indies, and India. The need for a carpenter arose on board the ships and at their destinations. Tudor had pioneered the shipment of ice to tropical climates. He had developed efficient ways of cutting ice from frozen freshwater ponds (including Walden, where Henry David Thoreau mused that "the sweltering inhabitants of Charleston and New Orleans, of Madras and Bombay and Calcutta, drink at my well," and "the pure Walden water is mingled with the sacred water of the Ganges"). He had figured out how to pack the ice tightly into the holds of ships, under the water line, and insulate it with sawdust. Other goods could be carried on top of the ice, including produce that required refrigeration. On the return voyage, the ships could carry goods back to Boston. The key to profits, though, was the ability to store the ice at its destination. He needed carpenters to build ice houses—"massive double-walled houses, which are covered by four or five separate roofs." William Nye spent three years working for Tudor, ample time to learn the Ice King's business methods.[5]

Tudor was a fierce competitor. At home, he at first hired Irish immigrants to cut the ice but later adopted the horse-drawn ice cutter invented by Nathaniel Wyeth. In addition to reducing labor costs, the cutter created uniform blocks that could be tightly packed. He bought exclusive rights to certain ponds, patented the designs for the ice house and cutter, and ensured that local landowners did not allow his competitors to use their horses. As he put it, the farmers "will learn to whom they are obliged." His tactics were so effective that he declared, "All opposition has been met and overthrown—the field is won." Tudor reduced costs in the cities to which he shipped ice by getting his customers or the local government to pay for building ice houses and eliminated competition by winning the exclusive privilege to sell ice in a given market.[6]

In Indian ports, he lobbied successfully to have ice excluded from import duties and inspection. He created demand by selecting a popular bar in each city and giving the barkeeper free ice for a year. Cold drinks became so popular with the English residents that the other bars were forced to buy his ice to compete. He offered discounts for volume purchases and "daily subscriptions." But his surviving business records show that his most effective tactic was "to cut prices drastically to force his competitors out of business. For example, Tudor would price his ice for a penny a pound until a competitor's supply had melted at the docks; then he would raise [his] prices to profitable levels."[7]

Tudor was trying to destroy his competitors, and he came close enough that he was said to be America's first monopolist. He justified his market dominance as the reward due to an innovator: his competitor in Savannah, he said, "will get about $5.00 in all for what must have cost him at least $100 . . . This business is mine. I commenced this business, and have a right to rejoice in ill-success attending others who would profit by my discovery."[8] In Tudor, William Nye found not just an employer but a model.

William next traveled to San Francisco in 1850, joining the hordes heading west in the Gold Rush. In December 1849 a massive fire had destroyed a large part of the city, and builders were much in demand. Rather than take his chances in the gold fields, he worked as a carpenter, earning $10 a day.

He then moved to Stockton, California, where he worked as a contractor and settled into the community. He arrived there at what a historian in 1880 described as "the darkest part of Stockton's history . . . , when *vice* was king and *virtue* a slave." Siding with virtue, Nye became the city recorder, acting at times as a magistrate. On June 2, 1851, he was hearing the case of five accused horse thieves. The owner of the stolen horses, a Mr. Owens, "addressed the throng of ruffians who had assembled for the purpose of convicting the prisoners, guilty or innocent, and moved that they proceed to hang them . . . In an instant fifty or more revolvers and bowie knives were drawn ready for action; the Recorder, City Marshal, and his deputies were seized and held. All the pent up animosity of the crowd was turned loose, and rushing over tables and chairs they started for their victims." The accused men managed to outrun their pursuers and reached the jail, where the sheriff locked them up and convinced the mob to disperse.[9]

In 1851 William returned to New Bedford long enough to marry Mary S. Keith, but he returned to Stockton to work. Their first child, Martha Elizabeth, was born in 1852. William left Stockton for good in 1855, returning to New Bedford and opening a store on North 2nd Street, where he sold wholesale fruit and vegetables. In this rare quiet period of his life his son, Joseph Keith, was born (in 1858) and his second daughter, Mary Athalie (1862), was conceived. He didn't stay around for her birth, though, because the start of the Civil War sent him on another adventure.[10]

William did not enlist but became a sutler, selling supplies and provisions to the soldiers in the Fourth Massachusetts Cavalry. The post, a civilian appointment often gained through political connections, would have had great appeal. "The possibilities of enormous profits and the monopolistic nature of the positions," one historian writes, "made sutlerships the aim of many individuals, scrupulous and unscrupulous." When armies were posted away from cities—or in enemy territory—the sutler was the only source of clothing, tobacco, razors, and food to supplement the often unappetizing army rations, and he offered credit when soldiers' pay was late in arriving. For most of the war, sutlers were allowed to place liens on soldiers' pay, and there was no control over what they could charge for their goods. Of course, the sutlers were taking enormous risks. They were often in physical danger, forced to abandon their goods and wagons in the face of enemy advances. They were robbed and attacked by Confederate raiders. They were extending credit to men who might not live long enough to pay their debts. For William Nye, the risks paid off. Local historians recounted his success: "His resources seemed ever to bring him out upon the winning side financially, much to the chagrin of competing sutlers in other divisions who would 'skedaddle' with loaded teams at any demonstration of the enemy. Mr. Nye oftener stood his ground and never but once [had] to leave his goods and run." He was fortunate in being attached to the "advance guard which entered Richmond April 5, 1865 . . . For many days he was the only tradesman on the streets of Richmond." He remained with the army until his regiment was mustered out in November 1865. When he returned to New Bedford, he had enough money to buy the house at 142 Main Street and to start the business that would make his fortune. Buying a large, traditional, well-sited house that had belonged to prominent Fairhaven figures was a statement about himself, his prosperity, and his prospects.[11]

A Self-Made Man

It isn't clear what made William Nye decide to enter the oil business. By 1865 whaling had long ceased to be a viable industry. The stock of whales had been seriously depleted, and petroleum had replaced whale oil for most uses. Whaling ships were in so little demand that during the Civil War about three dozen of them had been consigned to the so-called Stone Fleet of vessels loaded with rocks that were sunk to block Confederate ports and shipping channels.[12] Nevertheless, whale and other marine oils were superior for some specialized uses.

One such use was to lubricate clocks, watches, and chronometers. Because accurate timekeeping was essential to navigation on the ocean, chronometers were routinely regulated and oiled when ships called at a port. The mechanics who did this work would put a note in the clock case with their name and the date of service. "It soon became evident to these various watch tinkers that Ezra Kelley had a specially good oil," a later account noted. Kelley, a New Bedford watchmaker, began selling his oil and found the business so profitable that he gave up watchmaking. His oils became world-famous and won awards in international expositions. The oil made from the jaws and "melons" (masses of fatty tissue above the jaws) of porpoises and blackfish didn't gum up machinery and performed very well at low temperatures. It didn't corrode brass or rust iron and steel. The market, at first small and scattered, grew dramatically when the manufacture of clocks and watches was mechanized in the middle of the nineteenth century. Kelley could then sell his oil in large quantities to a growing number of factories producing thousands of watches. Kelley had a monopoly on these specialty oils: only he knew how to refine them.[13]

William Nye thought he could compete in this growing market. In the kitchen of his Fairhaven home, he began experimenting with all kinds of oil: sperm, petroleum, neat's foot, olive, castor, and thirty-two kinds of fish oil. He attracted customers among manufacturers and repairers of sewing machines, typewriters, guns, bicycles, and adding machines, and his oils began to win awards. By 1877 he was making enough money to purchase a factory on Fish Island, in the New Bedford harbor, and in 1890 he added another building and an electrical generating station. He advertised in trade journals, illustrating his sales pitches with images of bottles whose labels looked a lot like Kelley's, and offering testimonials from customers:

Jan. 12th, 1896
Dear Mr. Nye,

William F. Nye Chronometer Oil. I have been in the watch repairing business for the past four years, and have used your oil on every watch I have cleaned, which has been about 3,000, and have never had a customer say his watch stopped from freezing weather. I enclose you a weather report of this place, so you can see for yourself 50° below zero, which is very cold, and it has been lower still.

A. L. H. Brown, Watchmaker
Calgary, Alberta, N.W. Ter., Canada[14]

Nye advertised each of his products to its own market. When Americans started riding bicycles, Nye introduced his "Lily White" oil. According to a company history, "He exhibited it to rave reviews at the first national bicycle show in Madison Square Garden in 1897, where he offered a reward of '$1,000 to anyone producing an oil equal in every essential quality to his own.' No one accepted the challenge."[15] His oil may not have been much better than Kelley's, but he was a far better salesman. He also used the lessons he had learned from the Ice King, waging price wars against the competition. It was a long war of attrition, but in 1896 Kelley died, and Nye took over his company, establishing "an unbroken line to the 1844 origin of this specialized business," and "by year's end he had tripled the size of his factory, cornered the market on raw materials, stockpiled nine-tenths of all fish jaw oil in the world—and captured the world market."[16]

William Nye's politics were not what we have come to expect from hard-driving businessmen. According to a contemporary, "he ever maintains a daring independence of thought on all progressive movements and we find him in touch with all advance thinkers, even from his boyhood, avowing his detestation of anything short of a literal definition of the Declaration of American Independence, that all men (and women too) are alike 'free and equal.'" Before the Civil War, "he heartily joined in the early anti-slavery crusade with Garrison, Phillips, Parker Pillsbury, and others, as often as they . . . visited and lectured in our city."[17] He supported the presidential candidacy of Belva Lockwood, who ran on the ticket of the National Equal Rights Party in 1884. The party's platform included planks supporting women's suffrage; equal justice "without distinction of color, sex, or nationality"; temperance; citizenship for Native Americans; pacifism; civil service reform; and opposition to monopoly—a plank that Nye apparently was willing to overlook. Lockwood and her supporters were frequently ridiculed, most notably by "Mother Hubbard clubs" of young men parading in drag, orating and singing. But Nye lit lanterns in his windows during a parade of her supporters nevertheless.[18]

What most set William Nye apart from his neighbors, though, were his religious beliefs. He was, as the *Fairhaven Star* reported, "an outspoken advocate of modern spiritualism," the belief that the soul is immortal and that the living can communicate with the dead. Nearly every American had lost a family member or friend during the Civil War, and the idea that it was possible to reach those loved ones comforted many survivors. Though often ridiculed, Spiritualism in the late nineteenth century was linked to the more mainstream progressive movements that Nye embraced, including women's suffrage and equality of all races. Because Spiritualists believed they could communicate directly with supernatural forces, they rejected the hierarchy of traditional religions. Nye had little respect for Christian churches and did not consider Spiritualism a religion, but "the philosophy of life"; he maintained that "the most ignorant people are those who attend church," and that "as a people we are growing wiser, and as time advances more people had rather stay home reading and improving their mind instead of going to a church and sleeping or listening to a lot of folderol."[19]

Spiritualism was essential to William's view of life. His ancestors were very much with him, no matter where he went. At the second reunion of the Nye family, held at Sandwich in 1904, he spoke of the Nyes who had come before them: "We can but think they still live with us as we journey afar, even amid the golden wealth of the Pacific coast, and have helped us to penetrate the frigid arctic seas for their abounding wealth."[20] Nye confirmed his commitment to Spiritualism in his will:

> When the event of the departure of myself from mortal form takes place, I desire my body to be retained until unmistakable evidence of disintegration has taken place; then I desire that it be taken to the nearest crematory and there incinerated, feeling that this disposition of the form assists the spirit in more completely eliminating itself from its past environments . . . Immediately friends or neighbors may scatter my ashes . . . along the old homestead field [in Sandwich] overlooking the pond and the stretch of woodland, where I spent my boyhood trapping the wild game. That is the last kind act . . . that one can bestow upon dear Mother Earth in her overburdened conditions, with diseased and decaying mortal forms so contaminating the well springs of the fountains of life to the living.[21]

In the late nineteenth century, some Protestant churches (notably the Methodists) began founding summer communities where like-minded people could attend services, hear lectures, and be strengthened in their faith. Spiritualists did the same thing. In 1876 Nye joined a group of Spiritualists from various parts of Massachusetts in buying 125 acres on Buzzards Bay in Onset, about twenty miles northeast of Fairhaven in the town of Wareham, and establishing the Onset Bay Grove Association. The association was chartered by the state in 1877 and held a formal dedication ceremony. William was the largest shareholder. They "laid out streets, parks, and more than 700 building lots" arranged not in the Methodists' rectangular grid but in curving streets and variously shaped parks. Like the rural cemeteries being built at the time, one historian observes, "the winding paths and wooded parks of these pastoral landscapes provided a fitting forum for the Spiritualists' romantic reunions with the dead." Although the area has changed greatly, it still has winding streets and parks, with some of the original cottages still standing.[22]

The Grove was a haven for urbanites. "Coming as most of us here now do, from the heat and dust of city life, everyone seems to have left all care behind and to enter heartily into the semi-gypsy life of Onset, to hold communion with nature and the spirit-world," one woman wrote. The importance of nature was reflected in the names residents gave their cottages: "Forest Flower," "Forest Lodge," "Sunset."[23]

Some names hint at the residents' other interest. Cottages named "Wamsutta" and "Weetamoe" spoke of the Spiritualists' felt connection to the spirits of the long-dead Native peoples of the region.[24] The On-I-Set Wigwam Co-Workers sought to enhance this connection by building a structure resembling a wigwam adorned with the motto "Liberty Throughout the World, and Freedom to All Races, Erected to the Memory of the Red Man 1894." This octagonal building, 96 feet in circumference, seated two hundred people and was furnished with an organ.[25] The decor was a mixture of Native emblems and implements and contemporary decorating trends. Along with the war clubs and moccasins there was "a strange nod to the trend of decorating with a Japanese influence": "a plethora of paper fans that adorned the upper walls and continued to climb to the high ceiling."[26] Portraits on display included William Penn, Pocahontas, and King Philip.[27] Unlike the commercial events with visiting mediums, services in the wigwam were free. The morning was devoted to healing, and in the afternoons white mediums spoke with the spirits of Native Americans in their own languages—or at least not in English. According to an early account, many of the residents believed that "a message from an Indian control, unlettered though it may be, is far preferable to one from an alleged Thomas Paine, Henry Ward Beecher, or some so-called ancient spirit; the language of which, in many instances, is inferior to that of the representatives of the 'untutored' Red Man." To twenty-first-century sensibilities, the wigwam and its activities seem condescending and even offensive, but they were not meant to be. "The first object of the wigwam was to acknowledge and recognize in this land of boasted freedom the rights of the Indian race as children of the Great Spirit Father, who knew no race distinction, and to plant on American soil for the first time the red man's standard"—a sentiment not far removed from the platform of the National Equal Rights Party that Nye supported.[28]

Onset Bay Grove was also a real estate investment—one of many that William Nye had acquired over the years. It was important that it thrive for material as well as spiritual reasons. The Old Colony Railroad line connected Onset to Boston with a two-hour ride, and in 1901 a street railway from New Bedford to the town began transporting passengers in ninety minutes for 25 cents each way.[29] In 1894 a water system was installed, so that the cottages could have up-to-date plumbing, and the opening of a Western Union office provided telegram service. Some of the "cottages" required substantial investment, including an "$11,000 residence of magnificent proportions now approaching completion on South Boulevarde for Charles C. Whittemore of Boston and a fine new cottage on Shell Point for Mary Pierce of Savin Hill," as the *Boston Post* reported.[30]

The Grove offered a variety of entertainment—boating, dancing, music, and even roller skating—that would appeal to nonbelievers as well as the faithful. Promotional articles in popular magazines informed prospective visitors that "those who seek renewed health can find, regardless of creed, no better place than Onset for a summer vacation, for the air is lifegiving, being impregnated with the healing balm of the pine forests of Plymouth."[31] Of course, the organizers also hoped that those who did not believe in Spiritualism when they arrived might change their minds after a visit. Mediums who were offering their services in Onset also advertised, appealing to believers and the curious. The beauty of the setting and the village itself, as well as the extensive offerings of spiritual and secular activities, made the Grove a success, drawing thousands to the more popular lectures. When Almon B. French, a noted Spiritualist and medium, spoke, ten thousand people flocked to the Grove.[32]

The first cottage was built for Elvira S. Loring of Fitchburg, Massachusetts—a two-story Victorian gingerbread house. Simeon Butterfield of Chelsea, Massachusetts, built his elaborately landscaped cottage "upon the spot where once stood the wigwam of an Indian chief," and Helen Berry Robinson's garden featured a lily pond. Most of the houses were in Gothic Revival, Stick, or Queen Anne styles.[33] A history of the Nye Company describes the bungalow designed by William Nye's son Joe, which featured a dramatic variant on current design trends: "A huge Japanese fan, fringed with tiny electric lights, hovered from the living room ceiling." It was also innovative in practical details. "Floors throughout the house were made of cement, so they could be hosed down for easy cleaning." The garage "had doors at front and rear, so Joe could drive his car in and out without backing up."[34] Joe was not merely a summer resident, however. He made important contributions to the development of the Grove, building on a successful engineering career in Fairhaven.

Son and Heir

William's son was born in 1858, and Joe was only three when his father left home as a sutler for the Union Army. They would have started getting to know each other in November 1865, when William returned from the war and moved his family to the house on Main Street. Since William was working at home, Joe probably learned quite a bit about his experiments with oil as he was growing up. Joe attended Fairhaven schools, which prepared him to apply for a two-year program at MIT, then located in Boston's Back Bay neighborhood. He passed entrance examinations in arithmetic, geography, spelling, punctuation, English composition, English and American history, and beginning algebra; and in 1876 he joined twenty-one other students in a two-year course called Practical Mechanism. The course catalog explained that the program was designed "for those who wish to become Master Mechanics rather than engineers." It claimed to be unique because it offered shop work in metal, along with math, mechanical and freehand drawing, rhetoric and composition, English literature, and French. Tuition was $125 a year, and Joe lived in Boston while studying. It was a wise investment.[35]

Joe returned to Fairhaven and began to work for his father. A company history reports that in addition to office work, he invented devices to improve the production line: a machine to fill bottles and another to insert corks. The bottling machine "filled either one, two or three ounce bottles—a gross at a time. Untouched by human hands, the oil passed from tanks on the third floor through pipes directly into the machine, which could fill nearly 4,400 bottles an hour. Spillage from broken bottles was caught in a tray and pumped automatically up three stories to the holding tank."[36]

He also made an important innovation in the refining process in 1891, when he set up a plant in St. Albans in far northern Vermont, where refining in the frigid winter temperatures produced a purer oil that functioned down to 50 degrees below zero. At the same time, though, he left his father's company to begin working for Henry Huttleston Rogers, the Standard Oil millionaire who was remaking Fairhaven (see chapter 2). Rogers made Joe the local agent for Standard Oil and also gave him the challenging assignment of building a water system for the town. Joe had been thinking about such a plan since 1885, when he had heard the elderly Captain Alexander

William Foster Nye (*left*) and Joseph Keith Nye (*right*). *From the collection of the Millicent Library.*

Winsor telling his friends at the drugstore that he "had to go home to pump a tank full of water." Until Rogers came along, Joe had been unable to raise the money. Rogers paid for the project, with future revenues going to support the library he was giving the town, and Joe was the company's president for two decades.[37] Joe later applied what he had learned to establish water companies in Onset and nearby Wareham, as well as Edgartown on Martha's Vineyard.[38]

Joe also applied his engineering and managerial talents to transportation. He became president and general manager of the East Wareham, Onset Bay and Point Independence Street Railway and a director of the New Bedford and Onset Street Railway Company and the Onset Street Railway.[39] He built a steam-powered car that he drove from Fairhaven to New Hampshire's White Mountains and back. The greatest challenge of his engineering career came in 1903, when Rogers hired him to fill in the Mill Pond and surrounding wetlands south of Huttleston Avenue and east of the New Bedford bridge, a multimillion-dollar project that occupied him for nearly six years. At the same time, he continued to take an interest in Nye Oil. As the fisheries they had relied on became depleted, he opened new ones, in 1906 at the mouth of the St. Lawrence River and the next year at Cape Hatteras, North Carolina.[40]

Joe took an active part in Fairhaven life. When he built his house on Main Street in 1891, the *Fairhaven Star* called it "a novel structure . . . sure to attract the attention of passers by." If the exterior was unusual, the interior decoration was even more eccentric, featuring a stuffed tortoise and peacock, a giant sombrero, swords, a machete, and "enormous spears with human hair dangling from them."[41] He was a candidate for state representative in 1889 and served on the Fairhaven Schools Committee. He spoke to town groups about telegraphy and about hunting porpoises for oil. The company historian reports that "in 1904, he made local news when he acquired a grain of uranium, brought from London in a microscope tube, which he showed to friends and to students at Fairhaven High School." Joe led the grand march at Old Home Week and attended charity balls. His status in the town was confirmed when he was chosen as a pallbearer at Henry Huttleston Rogers' funeral in 1909.[42]

An avid sailor, Joe bought a thirty-foot sloop in 1885, sailing from Chelsea to New Bedford "in sixty hours' sailing time, with heavy fog and head winds," according to the *Boston Globe*. The reporter added that the sloop "will be enrolled in the New Bedford Yacht Club"; Joe became a director of the club in 1891. In 1901 he bought a twenty-eight-foot yawl, *Curlew*, for $2,000. He sailed her from Onset in October 1903, with two friends, and was expected back on October 12. The *Globe* reported: "The Curlew is an old catboat that was originally built for Snell Robinson of Wareham and has been rigged with a yawl sail by Mr. Nye. It is thought that the party touched at New Bedford on the way out and that they would have reached the neighborhood of Cuttyhunk at about the time the boat was reported dismasted and going out to sea, with little hope of it being intercepted in its course over the shoals." There was no further coverage of the incident, but Nye survived, as did *Curlew*, which he advertised for sale in 1908 for $800. He traveled to the Panama Canal, British Honduras, Jamaica, and Cuba. As one historian noted, Joe "always seemed to find management positions that did not interfere with his love for sailing and travel."[43]

Joe also had literary pretensions. He managed to be elected to the New York Press Club, though his only published writing was some poetry and reports of sailing adventures published in the *New Bedford Mercury*.[44] Even more mysteriously, he became a member of New York's Lotos Club. The club was founded in 1870 by a group of writers, but it included, according to the *New York Times*, "not only members of the artistic, literary, and musical world, but men of all professions, businessmen, men of leisure, the admirers, judges, and promoters of literature and art, frequenters of the theatre, and buyers of paintings and books, as well as artists and authors." The businessman members included Andrew Carnegie, F. W. Woolworth, Walter P. Chrysler, and Solomon R. Guggenheim. The editors of the *New York Tribune*, the *Brooklyn Eagle*, and *Harper's Weekly* represented journalism, as did William Randolph Hearst and Arthur H. Sulzberger. Among the creative artists were Mark Twain and the team of W. S. Gilbert and Arthur Sullivan. National and international leaders, explorers, opera singers, and actors were frequent guests and honorees. The club's revelries were elaborate. When Commander Robert Peary spoke in 1907, having recently returned from an Arctic expedition, "the souvenirs were bonbon boxes in the shape of a snow-covered Eskimo hut." The 1899 "Yule Tyde Feste" featured elaborate decorations, singing, and a wassail bowl of "Brobdingnagian proportions." Although he was a businessman and arguably a writer, Joe was clearly out of his league at the Lotos. Most likely he was sponsored for membership by Henry Rogers, a longtime member whose word would have been respected.[45]

Joe married Phila Calder on April 26, 1893. She was twenty-two, and he was thirty-five. Phila came from Wilmington, North Carolina. She had attended the Mount Vernon Seminary, an elite school for young women in Washington, D.C., graduating in 1891. In 1899 she returned to the seminary as a teacher of art history and in 1905 moved to Princeton, New Jersey, where she studied and then worked at the Princeton University Art Museum as editor of the Index of Christian Art. The couple separated but did not divorce. It is unclear how and when Phila and Joe met, or indeed when they separated. Their life together lasted no more than six years, and possibly much less. Despite Joe's social prominence, Phila's name appeared in the *Fairhaven Star* only at the time of their marriage and in articles about his will.[46]

The Spirit and the Flesh

William did not slow down as he aged. He remained active in the oil business, creating new products, until his death at his Main Street home on August 12, 1910, at the age of eighty-six. He bequeathed the oil business and most of his real estate, stock, and other business interests to Joe, who became the president of Nye Oil.[47] Running the company did not occupy all Joe's time, though. He continued to travel and maintained his interest in porpoises and blackfish. The Hatteras fishery remained productive, and in 1913 some of the porpoises got lucky: they ended up in an aquarium instead of an oil bottle. The *New York Times* reported that "nine porpoises were placed yesterday in the big centre pool of the Aquarium," and that "after their confinement for three days in narrow crates, they took wildly to the water and raised a regular teapot tempest in the big pool rolling and spouting and swimming incessantly." Joe had given the porpoises to the New York Zoological Association, which paid transportation expenses. The following year, a film of the capture and the journey to New York was shown at the society's annual meeting, and Joe was made a life member. Joe also provided the hide of a sperm whale captured off the coast of Cape Hatteras in 1912 that was tanned and used to bind a copy of *Etchings of a Whaling Cruise* by J. Ross Brown, published by Harper & Brothers in 1846, in the collection of the New Bedford Free Public Library.[48]

Joe outlived his father by only thirteen years. By 1920 he was in failing health and spent most of his time in Onset. He was admitted to St. Luke's Hospital in New Bedford early in 1923. On August 30, he checked into Attleboro Springs, a health resort owned by the Methodist Board of Foreign Missions. The sanitarium had a checkered past. It had been founded in 1903 by an herbalist named James M. Solomon, for whom a local businessman, John M. Fisher, built an elegant three-story stone building with turrets and gables on a hundred acres with a lake, lawns, farm buildings, and springs. Despite Solomon's claims of curing cancer, the sanitarium failed and closed in 1906. It reopened under the direction of a husband-and-wife team of Adventist physicians who had previously directed sanitariums in Melrose, Massachusetts, and Hinsdale, Illinois. Drs. Charles Chesterfield Nicola and Mary Byington Nicola, graduates of the University of Michigan Medical School, were adherents of the medical principles of John Harvey Kellogg, emphasizing a healthy diet and hydrotherapy.

The Attleboro Sanitarium closed again after Charles Nicola disappeared overboard while accompanying a patient on a cruise to Bermuda in 1911.[49]

In 1919 John Fisher gave the building to the Methodist Board. When Joe arrived, it was a rest home, offering hydrotherapy, exercise, and a healthy diet. The facility, a Methodist magazine reported, "in no sense suggests a hospital. The parlors, writing rooms and bedrooms might belong in a private home . . . The question, 'How do you feel today?' is definitely barred; patients are not encouraged to talk of their ailments." It was meant to help people "recover from the strain imposed by their work," which was probably not Joe's problem. Attleboro Springs also advertised in the *Journal of Inebriety* as a place to be cured of liquor, tobacco, and drug habits. In fact, no treatment available at the time would have helped Joe. An autopsy revealed that he had died of pancreatic cancer and was suffering from cirrhosis of the liver. Joe died on September 18. His estate was valued at $217,795, including the house on Main Street, property in Onset, the oil company and its real estate, and other investments.[50]

The Houses

The houses that belonged to William and Joe Nye still stand on Main Street, on the harbor, although they no longer belong to members of the family. Some of the harbor frontage was sold, and a house stands between them and the water. William's house is painted a brighter yellow than in his day, and it has been converted to a two-family home. The landscaping of both houses has changed. But they still tell us something about the two men and their relationship.

They were very different. William was, above all, independent. He left home at sixteen to follow a career different from his father's. He was physically brave and adventurous, a hard-driving, hard-working, ferocious competitor. He had traveled across the country and across oceans. He had changed careers several times. Although not much of an innovator, he was extraordinarily good at marketing. Beginning with an existing product, he modified it to fit niches where he anticipated sales. Not satisfied with dominating current markets, he created new ones. Some of his marketing tactics would probably land him in court if used today: making his own labels almost indistinguishable from Kelley's was skating close to the edge. Outside the business world he was an independent thinker, with views on human rights that were decades ahead of his time and religious beliefs that would have been thought outlandish among the Congregationalists and Unitarians of his town. His house—a landmark on the harbor, previously owned by prominent citizens—demonstrated his hard-won financial success and respectability. He was a hard act for an only son to follow.

Joe was creative and innovative, but he lacked his father's independence. His house expressed his flair for the new and visually striking. He rarely strayed far from home, even when he traveled. He worked for his father for a dozen years, inventing and innovating, and then became one of Henry Rogers' protégés—as a Standard Oil representative and then as the engineer in charge of two Rogers projects. He must have been good at these jobs: neither William Nye nor Henry Rogers would have put up with incompetence or even mediocrity. But he wasn't driven the way William was. His interests were focused outside his work: on writing, sailing, and social events. William and Joe would have talked shop together, but it's unlikely that they would have discussed politics, religion, poetry, or interior design.

Their houses, like them, are very different. But they are right next to each other. Their relationship was close enough to tolerate—or perhaps embrace—their differences. Joe remained involved in William's business even when he wasn't working for the company, and he built a cottage in his father's Onset colony as well as the house in Fairhaven. William supported Joe's studies at MIT and his participation in the oil business. He relied on his son to develop new fisheries. When William died, he entrusted his business to Joe, who managed it for the rest of his life.

4

A Home Above

191 MAIN STREET

Let others seek a home below,
We'll be gathered home;
Which flames devour and waves o'erthrow,
We'll be gathered home.

—Adventist hymn

Joseph Bates grew up in one of the oldest houses in Oxford Village. His home at 191 Main Street was built in 1742 on the site of a house dating to the mid-seventeenth century. The ruins of that earlier house still stand among the many ancient trees that shade the house. It is set back from the street, and even now it feels isolated and woodsy. In 1793, when the Bates family moved in, it must have seemed deep in the forest. It is a comfortable two-story house, suitable for the family of a successful businessman like Joseph Bates's father.

We have no reason to think that young Joseph was unhappy at home, but like many boys growing up in busy ports, he dreamed of going to sea. Although his father was not a ship's captain, many of his neighbors were. Joseph could watch ships in the busy harbor from the second floor of his home and from the windows of Fairhaven Academy, the school his father had helped to found and that he attended. He wanted adventure, and adventure meant leaving home. He would spend twenty exciting—often terrifying—years at sea. During those two decades, he visited Fairhaven only occasionally.[1]

In 1807, when Bates was fifteen, he signed on as cabin boy on the *Fanny*, bound for London via New York. On the return voyage, he fell overboard and was rescued before a circling shark could attack him. Two years later, he was sailing from New York to Archangel when the ship struck an iceberg. Soon after that, he was on a ship captured by Danish privateers and ended up in Prussia, where he boarded an American brig to Belfast. From there he went to Liverpool, looking for a berth on a ship returning to the United States.[2] As he recounts in his autobiography, on April 27, 1810,

> a few days after our arrival, a "press-gang" (an officer and twelve men) entered our boarding house in the evening and asked to what country we belonged. We produced our American protections, which proved us to be citizens of the United States. Protections and arguments would not satisfy them. They seized and dragged us to the "rendezvous," a place of close confinement. In the morning we were examined before a naval lieutenant, and ordered to join the British navy. To prevent our escape, four stout men seized us, and the lieutenant, with his drawn sword, going before, we were conducted through the middle of one of the principal streets of Liverpool like condemned criminals ordered to the gallows. When we reached the river side, a boat well manned with men was in readiness, and conveyed us on board the Princess, of the royal navy. After a rigid scrutiny, we were confined in the prison room on the lower deck, with about sixty others who claimed to be Americans, and impressed in like manner as ourselves.[3]

On the *Princess*, sailing to Plymouth, Bates tried unsuccessfully to escape. His captors then assigned him to the gunboat *Rodney*, which was engaged in fighting the French. But Bates saw himself as an American prisoner and refused to fight. He tried repeatedly to escape; he defied orders; he was threatened and punished. His rebellion extended even to church services: " *'O Lord, incline our hearts to keep thy law.'* Poor, wicked, deluded souls! how little their hearts were inclined to keep the holy law of God, when almost every other hour of the week, their tongues were employed in blaspheming his holy name; and at the same time learning and practicing the way and manner of shooting, slaying, and sinking to the bottom of the ocean, all that refused to surrender, and become their prisoners; or who dared to oppose, or array themselves in opposition to a proclamation of war issued from their good old Christian king." He remained an impressed sailor on the *Rodney* and later the *Swiftshore* for three years.[4]

During Bates's impressment, his father—a prominent figure in Fairhaven—sought his release. He wrote to President James Madison, who, along with Massachusetts Adjutant General (and later governor) John Brooks, provided documents necessary for his release. (Bates Sr. had served as a captain under Brooks during the Revolutionary War.) Captain Charles C. Delano volunteered to take the papers to Port Mahon, Minorca, where he gave them to the U.S. consul. It took months for the case to wind its way through the naval bureaucracy, and before Bates could be released, the War of 1812 began. With England at war against the United States, Bates and six of his shipmates—like many others in the same situation—demanded to be considered prisoners of war. They were sent to a crowded prison ship, where they staged a hunger strike. In one escape attempt, fifteen men managed to find their way to London and freedom, but Bates was not among them. In 1814 he was transferred to Dartmoor prison. The conditions were not much better than those on the prison ship, and Bates—along with thousands of prisoners—suffered with inadequate food and clothing, tormented by vermin, disease, and abuse. When the Treaty of Ghent was signed in December 1814, ending the war, the men expected to be released. They were not, and they grew restive; prison officials feared rebellion. On April 6, 1815, guards opened fire on the prisoners, killing seven and wounding sixty. Three weeks later, Bates's captivity finally ended:

> We were liberated from the Dartmoor prison on the morning of the 27th of April, 1815, just five years to a day from the time I was impressed in Liverpool, in England. About two years and a half in actual service in the British navy, and two years and a half their prisoner of war. The western gate of our dreary and bloody place of confinement was at length thrown open, and the soldiers ordered to march out with the prisoners. As we ascended the heights of Dartmoor, we turned to look back on that dark and massive pile of stone buildings where we had suffered so many privations, and then forward to the western horizon which could now for the first time since our confinement be seen stretching away in the distance toward our native country, where were our paternal homes and dear friends.[5]

They were sent home on the *Mary Ann*, a British ship whose captain was also supposed to sail to Virginia and pick up cargo. When the men discovered they were being taken to Virginia instead of the northern ports close to their homes, they mutinied. Having taken over the ship, they docked in New London and then Boston. There they returned the ship to her captain, who was apparently too glad to be rid of them to pursue the matter.[6]

Bates was soon on his way home: "A friend and neighbor of my father (Capt. T. Nye), being in Boston on business, lent me thirty dollars on my father's account, which enabled me to purchase some decent clothing to appear among my friends. The next evening, June 14 or 15, 1815, I had the indescribable pleasure of being at my parental home (Fairhaven, Mass.), surrounded by mother, brothers, sisters, and friends, all overjoyed to see me once more in the family circle; and all of them exceedingly anxious to hear a relation of my sufferings and trial during the six years and three months that I had been absent from them."[7]

Despite his pleasure in returning home, Bates was back at sea in a few weeks, sailing from Annapolis to Bremen. None of his adventures had reduced his love of the sea—or his need to earn a living. He continued to sail wherever he could find a berth until 1820, when he was given the command of the *Talbot*. He later commanded the *Chatsworth* and the *Empress*, of which he was part owner, sailing mostly to South America. His detailed account of this period is colorful, full of adventures and misadventures, novel rituals, and exotic foods. Bates clearly enjoyed his time at sea and in foreign ports. Only his commitment to his evolving religious beliefs exerted a greater pull.[8]

In 1818 Bates had married Prudence M. Nye, the daughter of Captain Obed and Mary Marshall Nye.[9] Prudence was a pious woman, and after his marriage Bates too began to think about religion. There were outward signs. He reformed his behavior, gradually giving up, over the next five years, "ardent spirits," wine, cigars, chewing tobacco, swearing, beer, cider, ale, and porter.[10] He also began to pray. During a storm on a voyage in 1818, the cook—a member of the Close-Communion Baptist Church of New Bedford—led the crew in prayer. "This was the first prayer that I ever heard uttered in a storm upon the ocean," Bates recalled. He began reading the Bible and, in 1824, committed himself to God.[11] He remained unsure of ways to express his religious feelings, though. His prayers had all been solitary:

> I felt such a strong desire for some place of retirement, to free my soul and give utterance to my pent-up feelings, that it seemed to me if I could get into the dense forest I should, in a measure, be relieved. A way soon opened before me. With my Bible for my companion, I passed out of the city and followed the sea shore, until I found an opening into the thick forest, into which I entered. Here I enjoyed freedom in prayer beyond anything I had ever experienced before. It was indeed a heavenly place in

Christ Jesus. When my business would permit, I used to spend the after-noon away somewhere in these forests; and sometimes, for fear of rep-tiles, used to ascend a large tree, and fix myself securely in the branches, where I enjoyed most precious seasons in reading the Scriptures, singing, praying, and praising the Lord.[12]

Yet he "often thought what a privilege it would be to meet with *one* Chris-tian, and how delighted I should be to spend an hour in an assembly of praying Christians, or hear another's voice in prayer besides my own." In 1826 he attended a service at a Dutch Reformed Church in New York. "This was the *first* religious assembly I had met with since I had covenanted to serve God, and enjoyed it much. It seemed good to be there."[13]

When he returned briefly to Fairhaven in 1827, he sought a place to worship. His parents' Congregational church did not suit him, because he did not believe in infant baptism or the trinity. He was baptized by immersion and joined the Christian church.[14] He also joined other men, mostly sea captains, in organizing the Fairhaven Temperance Society. This group formed a "Cold Water Army" of children four and older. Fairhaven's three hundred Cold Water soldiers sang songs like this anthem by the Rev. Mr. Thomas:

> With banner and with badge we come,
> An ARMY true and strong,
> To fight against the hosts of rum,
> And this shall be our song:—
> We love the clear cold water springs,
> Supplied by gentle showers:
> We feel the strength cold water brings—
> "The victory is ours."[15]

Bates's growing family (three children had been born while he was at sea, two of whom survived infancy) and his involvement in church and town affairs made it more difficult for him to leave home, but in 1827 he took a final voyage on the *Empress*. After the ship had left port, he informed the crew that they were to show respect for one another by using Christian names rather than nicknames and to refrain from swearing, that there would be no shore leave on Sundays, and that alcohol would be supplied for medicinal purposes only. (Temperance voyages were on the rise: forty ships sailing from New Bedford in 1830 and seventy-five in 1831 allowed spirits only as medicine.) Bates held morning and evening prayers, as well as Sunday services, and encouraged reading of tracts and the weekly newspaper *Zion's Herald*. Although his autobiography suggests that the crew accepted these measures with little protest, the log book records one desertion and a few cases of drunkenness.[16]

When the *Empress* reached New York in 1828, Bates learned that his father had died. He decided that he had amassed enough money—an amount he had earlier set at $10,000—to retire from the sea, return to his home and family, and devote himself to the causes that mattered to him. To cut the tie definitively, and to add to his assets, he and the other owners sold the *Empress* in 1829.[17]

Bates's mother died that same year, and he inherited the house on Main Street in which he had grown up. He and Prudence lived there until 1831, when he sold the house to his brother Franklin. (Franklin had been living in a house adjacent to the 191 Main Street property.) With the fortune he had at his disposal, Bates could have built or bought a large, impressive house for his still growing family. But Bates's new home was much smaller and less imposing than 191 Main Street, a modest Cape Cod house at what is now the corner of Mulberry and Christian Streets—a ground floor plus a low-ceilinged second floor with two dormers. The house has been remodeled, but it is easy to see which parts have been added. As late as 1949, the room that had been Bates's study—roughly half the front of the house— retained its original dimensions, twelve by fourteen feet. Bates saw the property as more than a home. He planted mulberry orchards and built a barn and a schoolhouse where he hoped to teach children how to cultivate silkworms and process the silk. The silkworm venture was decidedly less successful than his other endeavors.[18]

Now at home on land, Bates continued his temperance work, and he also became active in the abolition movement. He helped to organize the Fairhaven Antislavery Society in opposition to both slavery and the relocation of slaves to Africa, and he remained a staunch abolitionist throughout his life. He expanded the list of things he would not consume, giving up caffeine, dairy products, meat, spices, and sweets—the dietary reforms encouraged by Sylvester Graham. The things of this world—houses, possessions, food and drink—were fading in importance as the rewards of doing God's work took the forefront.[19]

Social reform was closely tied to Bates's developing religious beliefs. Still in search of the right outlet for his convictions, Bates joined Noah Stoddard and Jabez Delano Jr. in building and incorporating the Washington

Street Christian Meeting House, where he worshiped for many years. (The building later became the Unitarian Church and is now part of Northeast Maritime Academy.)[20] Religion for Bates was never a matter of simply finding a compatible church and attending weekly services. He carefully read the Bible and other religious works, including the writings of his contemporaries. He thought about religion, discussed it with his friends, and debated theological issues. In the course of these explorations, he read William Miller's *Evidence from Scripture and History of the Second Coming of Christ, about the Year 1844: Exhibited in a Course of Lectures.* He became convinced of Miller's belief that the Second Coming of Christ would occur very soon, and that it was possible to predict the date. By 1840 Bates had helped to convene a general conference in Boston to discuss the Second Coming. He wrote his own pamphlet on the subject and invited Miller to lecture in Fairhaven in March 1841, at the Washington Street church, and in New Bedford. According to Bates, both lectures filled the halls.[21]

Miller predicted that Christ would appear between March 21, 1843, and March 21, 1844. In preparation, Bates joined his fellow Millerites in holding camp meetings and preaching wherever anyone would listen. Rarely at home, he traveled in New England and then in the South, despite warnings that his abolitionist views put him in danger there. By then, Bates had decided that preparing for the Second Coming was more important than preaching abolition. "I have no less interest in temperance and in freeing of the slave than before: but I am come face to face with a tremendous enveloping cause. When Christ comes, liquor will be forgotten and the slave will be free. The lesser causes are swallowed in the greater." As a historian of the movement observes, Bates went to Maryland "to get slaves and masters ready for Christ's coming, not to change their earthly stations." In Miller's words, "God can and will release the captive. And to him alone we must look for redress."[22]

Bates also settled his earthly affairs. He sold his house and other property to Noah Spooner in February 1844 for $4,500. He never again owned a home, and he used his remaining funds to finance his preaching and religious publications. He and his family moved to a house belonging to John Bunker at 209 Main Street, a bit north of his childhood home.[23]

Bates's conviction that Christ's Second Coming was at hand fit comfortably with his earlier commitments to eradicating the evils of drink and slavery. The rhetoric of abolitionists' appeals has been compared to that of

Joseph Bates. *From the collection of the Millicent Library.*

Christian revivalists; both groups had similar interest in predictions of the end of the world; and both groups were antagonistic toward established churches. Although some who anticipate the end of this world focus on apocalyptic visions and punishment of sinners, the Millerites focused on the blessed, peaceful world that would follow the Second Coming. As one historian puts it, groups like theirs believed that "society had to be Christianized and purged of evils like slavery and alcohol. Men would bring about their own millennium. But the long, slow redemption they envisioned was also a preparation for Christ's return."[24]

Bates's convictions were strengthened by shocks in the political world. Close to home, the Panic of 1837 had shaken faith in the economy, and several American states were forced into bankruptcy between 1841 and

1843. President William Henry Harrison died in 1841, shortly after his inauguration. Technology was moving at what seemed to be an astounding pace, with railroads and steamboats hastening westward expansion and the telegraph allowing rapid communication. The British were forced out of Afghanistan, and the first Opium War between England and China was under way. The Middle East—a region of special concern to religious Christians—was the scene of conflict between Egypt, Syria, and European powers. Bates was especially impressed by the Second Egyptian-Ottoman War, which he referred to as the fall of the Ottoman Empire, in 1840.[25]

The Millerites were probably better convinced of impending change by signs in nature. More than three hundred people died when a tornado struck Natchez in 1840; Mount St. Helens began fifteen years of eruptions in 1842; an earthquake centered in Arkansas in January 1843 was felt as far north as Providence. All these natural portents would have been known to newspaper readers, but the event that Bates cited in his *Autobiography* was the "great comet" of 1843, which he described as "a brilliant stream of light which suddenly made its appearance in the path of the setting sun, a short distance above the horizon, soon after dark, and was very visible every clear night for three weeks in the month of March," adding that "the awfully grand and sublime appearance of this light was the cause of much excitement." Quoting a pamphlet by Henry Jones, Bates concluded: "In regard to the natural cause of this wonder of the world I would be the last man to attempt to assign any other than that Jehovah himself is the cause of it, that he has done it by his own omnipotence to fulfill his word of promise concerning it, and to apprise his oppressed, cast down, and suffering saints, that he is now very soon coming for their deliverance."[26]

The signs, portents, and predictions failed them. In Bates's words, March 21, 1844, "passed, and another twenty-four hours followed, but deliverance did not come. Hope sunk and courage died within them."[27] This "Great Disappointment" subjected the Millerites to ridicule. Years later, Bates told a fellow Adventist that

> he had only a few pennies left and that he had purposely allowed his provisions to run out. As a result, on the morning of October 23 he had to buy some flour and other items for his family. "The boys of the street," he recalled, "followed and hooted after me, and men pointed the finger of scorn at me, saying, 'I thought you were going up yesterday.' . . . You can have no idea of the feeling that seized me. I had been a respected citizen, and had with much confidence exhorted the people to be ready for

the expected change. With these taunts thrown at me, if the earth could but have opened and swallowed me up, it would have been sweetness compared to the distress I felt."[28]

Neither the disappointment nor the ridicule destroyed his faith, although the Millerites disagreed on how to interpret the failure of their leader's prediction. Bates's group, which eventually became the Seventh-day Adventist Church, believed that they had misunderstood the event of October 22. What had been predicted was not the Second Coming but Christ's move to the most holy place in a heavenly sanctuary. From there he would observe humanity's cleansing itself of sin in preparation for the end of the world. Ellen White, an Adventist prophet, "linked the delay of the Advent to the need for morally improving God's people."[29]

Bates and his fellow believers used the years following the Great Disappointment to organize and stabilize their church, to expand its membership, and to create publishing, educational, and medical institutions to support their mission. Bates's main theological contribution came in 1845, when he declared, on the basis of his reading of the Bible, that Saturday rather than Sunday was the true Sabbath. He published this idea in a forty-eight-page pamphlet—one of many he wrote—to spread the word beyond those he could reach in person. As he explained to his wife, when she questioned the cost of publication, "I cannot go everywhere, but a book can." The Saturday Sabbath distinguished church members from both Catholics and other Protestants. Bates's wife, Prudence, did not accept the Saturday Sabbath until 1850 and continued to attend Sunday services. As the story was long told in Fairhaven, "Captain Bates used to take his wife in their carriage to the Christian church on Sunday, but he himself would not enter to worship 'on the pope's Sabbath'; he would return for her after church."[30]

Bates's account of the publication of this pamphlet gives a sense of his financial situation after the Great Disappointment. He had sold his property, paid his debts, and spent his remaining funds on his religious activities. By 1846 he was a poor man. He firmly believed that the Lord would provide, but Prudence was less optimistic. According to the oft-repeated (and perhaps embroidered) account, Prudence told him she needed four pounds of flour, which would ordinarily be bought by the barrel. He returned from the store with exactly four pounds of flour and a few small items and told Prudence that he had spent his last penny:

It was a blow; for while she knew and approved of his free spending for the cause, she had not supposed they were down to nothing. The tears flowed from her eyes. She sobbed, "What are we going to do?" The captain rose to his full height. "I am going to write a book," he said; "I am going to circulate it, and spread this Sabbath truth before the world." "Well, but," said Mrs. Bates, "what are we going to live on?" "The Lord is going to open the way," was the smiling reply. "Yes, the Lord is going to open the way! That's what you always say!" And crying bitterly, she left the room.[31]

The money for printing the pamphlet came from donations, as did the family's livelihood. Bates claimed that "his family never came to want; he never begged; but, living frugally, waiting upon God, he found his wants and his family's needs supplied." Prudence—living in rented rooms in Fairhaven, alone with her children for months on end, dependent on charity, and less committed to the cause—might have told a different story.[32]

The church resumed its evangelical activities in 1849, with membership increasing from 200 in that year to 2,500 in 1851. Bates's true calling was as a preacher. One of his biographers writes that "he presented his message with an utter sincerity and a profound personal conviction that moved his hearers," and he handled hecklers with skill. Nevertheless, he was never able to convince his brother, sister, or children to join the church. After 1850 he spent about three-quarters of his time on the road, preaching in more than thirty towns in 1851; traveling to Canada, western New York, Michigan, and Wisconsin in 1852; and to New Hampshire, Massachusetts, New York, Michigan, Illinois, and Ohio in the six months beginning in December 1853.[33]

Bates still received no funds from the church, and he and his family depended on gifts from supporters for food and clothing. Ellen White wrote in a church magazine: "Let us not forget that they sacrifice their pleasant homes, the society of their families, and travel in the heat and cold for weeks and months together . . . Often they have not means to send to the relief or support of their families . . . Look closely, and see if they are comfortably clothed. Don't wait for them to express their wants . . . Our dear Bro. and Sr. Bates deserve our prayers, sympathy and support. We will remember them in their self-denial and sacrifice, and see that their wants are well supplied." True to her message, White and her husband provided a house for the Bateses in Michigan.[34]

Battle Creek became the headquarters of the church, and the Bateses moved to nearby Monterey in 1858. There Joseph was able to incorporate into church doctrine another of his reforms: healthful eating. Bates had long been an abstemious vegetarian, but he believed that this cause—like abolition—should be subordinate to religious conversion. Michigan, though, was home to several like-minded men, including followers of Sylvester Graham, who had developed the flour used in graham crackers, and the Kellogg brothers, whose early cereals were whole grain and healthful. These practices were incorporated into church teaching in 1863, and the commitment to healthy living led church members to develop medical and educational facilities during the 1860s and 1870s.[35]

Joseph continued to evangelize and administer church affairs in Michigan and beyond. When he and Prudence reached their fiftieth wedding anniversary in 1868, he wrote that he was "trying to get nearer to God by humiliation, fasting, and prayer, mixed with praise for sparing us so long to each other." Prudence lived only two years longer, and Joseph died in March 1872. They were buried side by side in the Poplar Hill Cemetery in Monterey. Their shared tombstone reads: "Blessed are the dead which die in the Lord that they may rest from their labors, and their works do follow them."[36] There Joseph Bates will rest until he travels to his home above.

5

Home Is Not a House

"SPRAY"

In spite of the fact that our natural home is supposed to be on terra firma, there are men born with an absorbing passion for the sea. To them the bosom of the mighty deep is a home of safety.

—*Boston Globe,* November 28, 1891

In 1885 Captain Eben Pierce hauled a derelict oyster boat into a pasture near his house in Oxford Village. As the boat rotted, the neighbors wondered what he was going to do with her. The *Spray* was an eyesore, built—according to local legend—when Adam was a lad. She sat on blocks for seven years, visibly deteriorating, and some of the jokes had undoubtedly turned into grumbling. The neighborhood, home of Fairhaven's oldest houses, was no longer as elegant as it had once been. Sometimes now called Poverty Point, it suffered from the decline of its harbor after a bridge had been built to the south. Nevertheless, its streets were lined with stately Federal and Greek Revival houses, and many of its residents belonged to Fairhaven's oldest families.[1]

Then, in 1892, a stranger arrived, boarding at Captain Pierce's house at 193 Main Street, where he lived above the kitchen. Every morning, he walked a block west to the pasture that had once been a graveyard. Pierce had given him the *Spray*, and he was deciding what to do with her. The neighbors assumed he would break her up; instead, they watched as he spent thirteen months rebuilding her. The bald, bearded man became a familiar figure, and people stopped to chat with him about his project. The *Spray*'s new owner was Joshua Slocum, who would soon circumnavigate the globe singlehanded in his thirty-six-foot oyster boat. His account of that voyage, *Sailing Alone Around the World,* became a classic tale of adventure at sea.[2]

What would lead a middle-aged man to take such huge risks, leaving his wife and children for solitude of a kind that few can even imagine? The voyage probably seemed the logical thing to a man for whom the sea had always been home, and whose answer to the decline of the age of sail was not a lament but a defiant—and victorious—shout.

First Home

Slocum had grown up in a small Nova Scotia town on the Bay of Fundy, the fifth of eleven children. He went to sea in 1860, when he was sixteen. Quickly rising in rank, he sailed to England, China, and the Moluccas. In San Francisco he became an American citizen and, at twenty-one, was given command of a coasting schooner, sailing to Alaska to bring salmon and pelts to the mainland. Five years later he was given command of the *Washington,* sailing to Sydney, Australia.[3]

The residents of Sydney entertained visiting seamen on a grand scale. In 1869 William Walker, a New Yorker who had traveled to San Francisco and then to Sydney in search of gold, had given a grand ball for visiting American Navy men. His daughter Virginia, dressed as Columbia, had dazzled their guests. When Joshua arrived in Sydney in January 1871, he too was dazzled by Virginia's beauty and adventurous spirit. Virginia, the couple's son later wrote, "was heard to remark that as soon as she saw Josh she knew he was just the kind of a man she wanted, not the stuffy sort." They were married after a brief courtship. Virginia was excited about joining Joshua on his next voyage, and—accompanied by her twelve-year-old brother, George—the newlyweds set out for Cook Inlet, Alaska, to catch a shipful of salmon for the mainland market.[4]

As a honeymoon, the voyage was a success. Joshua and Virginia were deeply in love and enjoyed each other's company. Their first child, Victor, was born a year after their marriage. Many years later, George Walker described the voyage as "the greatest experience of his life." Certainly there was no lack of excitement. The scenery and wildlife fascinated them, and they had their first experiences with native Alaskans. There was some genuine drama. Once Joshua had left the fishing camp for what he thought would be an overnight trip to a nearby village. As Victor later told the story,

> My mother was nervous about being left by herself . . . , so instead of turning in she sat up to be on watch until dawn. It was shortly after midnight when she heard footsteps coming directly to her tent and without the customary "haloo" of a friend, and then a hand began to unlatch the flap. With her heart in her mouth she raised her rifle and called, "Sing out or I'll shoot." The intruder distinctly heard the double click of the hammer as it was cocked and returned, and, with an uneasy laugh, "Why, what's the matter, Jinny?" identified himself. On being allowed to enter all he said was, "Well, that was the time you nearly became a widow." But for all his narrow escape he learned to have a new admiration for his wife's self-reliance and for her primal capacity for defending herself.[5]

But as a commercial venture the trip got mixed reviews. In a storm, the *Washington* ran aground and was lost. Slocum persisted, however, and in his son's words, "The fishing was carried out successfully, except for the loss of the vessel." Slocum had already had his crew build a thirty-five-foot whaleboat in case of emergency, and that, plus the ship's two salvaged boats, took them to Kodiak. Virginia, pregnant, sailed on a U.S. government cutter. In Kodiak, Slocum chartered two ships and returned for the catch, which had been under guard in their absence. The salmon were delivered as promised, and the *Washington*'s owners were sufficiently pleased to give Joshua command of the *Constitution,* the ship on which Victor was born. The year the Slocums spent on this ship was a quiet one, sailing between San Francisco and Hawaii, to ports in Mexico, and to Easter Island.[6]

In 1874 the family found themselves in Sydney, visiting the Walkers. Slocum was given the command of a sailing packet, *B. Aymar.* Joshua and Virginia liked the ship well enough to name their second son after her. For two years they carried cargo from port to port in the China Seas, a dangerous route beset by pirates and "blackbirders," slavers who sold their victims to Australian plantation owners. Some of the islands were populated by cannibals, still active and much feared. What Victor remembered, though, was meeting "other little boys like me" for the first time, in the Chinese port of Amoy, and the toys his parents bought him there.[7]

When the *B. Aymar* was sold in 1876, the Slocums had their first experience of living on land. Joshua undertook to build a steamship at Olongapo, in the Philippine jungle. From Victor's account, it is easy to understand why they wanted to get back onto a ship. Joshua built a house on stilts to protect them from hostile local shipbuilders, typhoons, and "venomous creeping things": "Up through the cracks in the split bamboo flooring could crawl centipedes, scorpions, and even a small boa if it took a notion to come in at night and hang down from the rafters, tail first. We found that both centipedes and scorpions had a habit of crawling into our clothes and getting into our shoes while they were not in use . . . Nearby was a swamp filled with crocodiles." Despite the obstacles, Slocum finished the boat and turned it over to its owner. In partial payment, he received the schooner *Pato*. Joshua Slocum had acquired his starter home, a bit smaller than he wanted, but his own.[8]

Homeowner

After a few trips in the China Seas, the Slocums set sail for the North Pacific fishing grounds in the Sea of Okhotsk. In only two weeks, the crew filled the ship with 25,000 salted cod, which Joshua sold profitably in Portland, Oregon. Virginia's share was $60, which she used to buy a Singer sewing machine. While in Portland, they lived for a month on shore. Victor attended school for the first and last time, and they acquired a pet canary named Peter, who sailed with them for many years. They then sailed to Honolulu, where Slocum sold the *Pato*. In San Francisco, he bought the *Amethyst*, which they sailed in the China trade for three years.[9]

While the *Amethyst* was being refitted, Virginia and the children lived in the Clipper Hotel. Slocum took trains to Nova Scotia, visiting family, and launched his career as a journalist, reporting for the *San Francisco Bee*. He returned with his youngest brother and sister, Ingram and Ella, who joined the *Amethyst*'s crew as cook and mother's helper. From 1877 to 1878, they sailed to Manila, Guam, Shanghai, Nagasaki, and Hong Kong, trading in timber. In Hong Kong, Virginia bought English-language books for Victor. At the end of the year, Slocum sold his share in the *Amethyst* and traded up to a share in *Northern Light*, a large, luxurious home for his family, which now included four children—Victor, Ben Aymar, Jessie, and Garfield.[10]

As Slocum's most recent biographer, Geoffrey Wolff, writes: "The Slocums weren't merely investing in a long-haul cargo carrier; they were buying their dream house, and as a dwelling the *Northern Light* was extraordinary. From her figurehead to her rounded stern, she had plenty of the 'wow' factors that real estate agents like to sell. But even more tempting must have been the master's quarters, with room for Virginia's piano and Joshua's library." A reporter for the *New-York Daily Tribune*'s "Local Miscellany" column, who visited the ship while she was docked in the city, might have been writing for the real estate section:

> Descending to the main cabin, one wonders whether or not one is in some comfortable apartment ashore . . . The captain's state room is a commodious apartment, furnished with a double berth which one might mistake for a black walnut bedstead; a transom upholstered like a lounge, a library, chair, carpets, wardrobe and the chronometers. This room is abaft the main cabin which is furnished like a parlour. In this latter apartment are the square piano, centre table, sofa, easy chairs and carpets, while on the walls hang several oil paintings. In front of the parlour is the dining room, which, together with the other rooms, exhibit a neatness of which only a woman's hand is capable.[11]

The life lived in these luxurious quarters was domestic. Victor wrote that Virginia "reflected the culture of her home in Sydney. She was both artist and musician." She took charge of the children's education: "Every day from 9 to 12, school was conducted in a consistent manner. Spelling, reading and arithmetic, suited to our different ages . . . Discipline was maintained by a switch stuck over a picture in the cabin and the culprit had to fetch it himself when it was needed, but that, I must say, was not often . . . Saturday was field day, devoted to the cleaning and tidying of our rooms and mending of our clothes. On the Sabbath we had Sunday School. We memorized the Anglican catechism and learned collects."[12]

Joshua's library gives a sense of how a man who had left school at the age of ten could become a gifted writer. The five hundred volumes on the shelves included essays by Lamb, Addison, Irving, and Macaulay; poetry by Tennyson and Coleridge; scientific writings by Darwin, Huxley, and Spencer; and novels by Dickens and Cervantes. Victor remembered his father "reading Irving's *Life of Columbus,* and the table discussions of the great navigator's triumphs and misfortunes as well as the shameful treatment of the Indians by the gang of cruel adventurers at his heels."[13]

A ship on the open seas in the late nineteenth century, no matter how luxurious, was not floating suburbia. During the Slocums' voyages on *Northern Light* they rescued five stranded Gilbert Islanders and raised money to send them home from Yokohama. Sailing in the Sunda Strait in 1883 when Krakatoa erupted, they were enveloped in ash and could see the ocean boiling.[14] Slocum also found himself dealing with incompetent and sometimes mutinous crews. The *New York Sun* summarized the difficulties:

> The Northern Light was in trouble during her whole trip. She left Hunter's Point in August, 1882, for South Africa, broke her rudder, and put into New London. Her crew refused to work one night, insisting that they had been overworked. They were put in irons for several days. Marvel Knowles, the first mate, assaulted a sailor named Murphy, and Murphy killed him with a knife. After the vessel got to sea two sailors were put in irons for stealing from the larder, and another sailor ran away at a South African port. On the trip the ship had three different first mates and four different second mates. She was compelled to put into Port Elizabeth with nine feet of water in her hold, and in a storm off Hatteras her foremast came down.[15]

This account, though, omits the attempted mutinies, one of which led to Slocum's being tried in New York for imprisoning a crew member, assault, and cruelty.

At Port Elizabeth, South Africa, Slocum had taken on a new third mate, Henry Arthur Slater. Slater proved to be incompetent and violent. Slocum had him put in irons, and when he escaped he was restrained more heavily, eventually being confined for fifty-three days in a space too small to move around in. When the ship arrived in New York, Slocum asked for a revenue cutter to put the ship under guard, and he charged Slater with mutiny. Slater accused Slocum of abuse, and both men stood trial. Slater also filed a civil suit against Slocum. The *Sun* reported these events under the headline "Boarding Up a Mutineer." The more sensational *Tribune*—the same paper that had offered a glowing description of the Slocums' quarters eighteen months earlier—provided more lurid coverage, headlined "Fifty-three Days in a Box: Horrible Treatment of a Ship's Mate." On November 27, Slater's civil suit was filed and Slocum, unable to post $2,000 bail, was sent to the Ludlow Street Jail, where Slater was also being held. A grand jury handed down a criminal indictment against Slocum on December 11, and the trial began two days later. Ten days later, Slocum was convicted of "imprisonment without justifiable cause and from malice" but acquitted of assault and cruelty.[16]

Then, on January 12, Slater arrived in the office of B. S. Osbon, editor of the *Nautical Gazette,* and withdrew his civil suit against Slocum:

> Since I have been at liberty I have found out that Capt. Slocum ordered me to be brought up on deck every day, and that I should have sufficient food and water every day. Mate Mitchell told Capt. Slocum that if I was brought up on deck I would create a mutiny and murder all the after guards. I do not blame Capt. Slocum for the treatment I have received . . . I fully believe that the suits instigated against Capt. Slocum have been made for the purpose of blackmailing him and getting money out of him by making me the tool of designing persons . . . I know very well while we were on board the Northern Light, if I had said the word, that the crew would have mutinied at once.[17]

Despite Slater's retraction (which the *Tribune* did not report), the guilty verdict against Slocum stood. It may have influenced the judge, however, who was clearly sympathetic to Slocum in pronouncing sentence:

> The law imposes a penalty of not more than five years' imprisonment or a fine not exceeding $1,000. I have received from several gentlemen, shipping merchants of this city, a petition in your behalf . . . I have also received a report from the Shipping Commissioner who . . . gives an excellent report of your character. I also take notice of the fact that you, by your skill and attention, saved the lives of several of your sailors from death by cholera . . . I am satisfied that your act was not prompted by hatred or malice, but for the good of your ship. Considering all these matters I shall temper justice with mercy, and shall not imprison you. The law gives me great discretionary powers. The extreme fine is $1,000, but I learn that you are a poor man and could not pay that amount.

The fine was $500, which Slocum's friends assured the court would be paid. The *Tribune* asserted that the fine "can hardly fail to have a wholesome influence upon other sea-captains of brutal tendencies."[18]

Slocum may have been a poor man. He sold his share in *Northern Light* at a loss. Homeless—that is, without a ship—the family split up. Virginia and the children went to live with Joshua's married sisters while he sought a command. Virginia enjoyed the respite from the sea. Victor wrote that his mother "found the change from the mutinous turmoil of the last year and a half a very welcome one. Voyaging with cutthroats was to her like voyaging with a volcano under the hatches, and the nervous strain caused by the constant alarms at sea had undermined her health." Slocum was not, perhaps, quite as poor as the judge believed, because he was able to buy the bark *Aquidneck* in Baltimore with what was left of his savings from selling the *Pato*.[19]

Virginia's Last Home

Garfield, the youngest Slocum, remembered his new home clearly though he was only a toddler when the family set sail for Brazil in 1884:

> The saloon on board the *Aquidneck* was a beautiful room, parquetry floor, doors, paneling, and ceiling painted flat white, open scrollwork over the stateroom doors painted light blue and gold. The captain's room had a full size bed, porthole, etc., and the rooms a single bunk, a bracket lamp (oil) held by a metal bracket, two metal rings to allow the lamp to remain upright when the ship rolled or pitched. There was a long table and in rough weather racks were put on the table. The table was built around the mizzenmast. Swivel chairs were bolted to the deck around the table. There were also some loose chairs, a skylight with colored glass, a canary that sang all day—a beautiful singer. Also a square grand piano was bolted to the deck. A large lamp was bolted onto the mizzenmast. There were wall bracket lamps, and double doors in the companionways, forward and aft. There was a cabinet with glass doors for carbines, guns and revolvers and ammunition. The pantry was off the saloon. Plates and saucers were kept in boxes on a shelf built the right size, with slots: cups, mugs, soup tureens hung on hooks. There was a store room for groceries, canned goods, etc. for all hands . . . On the roof were pens for sheep, pigs, and fowl . . .
>
> Father had a large library on board the *Aquidneck*. He also bought a lot of books and toys for me.[20]

Between Pernambuco in Brazil and Buenos Aires, Virginia became ill. She died on July 25, 1885, and was buried in the English Cemetery at Buenos Aires. She was thirty-four years old. Their middle son, Benjamin, recognizing how much his father loved and relied on his mother, later wrote, "Father's days were done with the passing of mother. They were pals." A few days later, Slocum ran the ship aground on a sandbar.[21]

A New Mate

Slocum repaired the *Aquidneck*, and the family sailed to Boston, where, on February 22, 1886, he married his first cousin, Henrietta Elliott. She

Joshua, Hettie, Garfield, and Victor Slocum on the *Liberdade*.
Courtesy of the New Bedford Whaling Museum.

was twenty-four, a seamstress who had never been to sea. Six days after the wedding, they set sail for Montevideo, with Victor—now a seasoned sailor—and Garfield. Henrietta's first experience at sea was not encouraging. They encountered hurricanes and, when threatened with mutiny, Slocum shot two of the crew members. He was charged with murder, acquitted, and released. He hired a new crew, and it soon became clear that several had smallpox. He buried nine men at sea, and the ship had to be disinfected. Finally, the ship was stranded and lost. Rather than accept the U.S. consul's offer of passage home for himself and his family, Slocum decided to build a thirty-five-foot sailing canoe from the wreckage. It took six months, and on May 13, 1888, the *Liberdade* was launched, named in honor of the law freeing Brazil's slaves, which passed that day. Slocum told the captain of a ship that provided supplies that "we have had a very pleasant voyage, and to ourselves a very interesting one." The *Boston Daily Globe*, though, described the Slocums' time on the *Aquidneck* and *Liberdade* as "a tale which Rider Haggard would grasp with pleasure." Against all odds, the *Liberdade* made it to Washington, D.C. At the end of his account of the voyage, Slocum wrote, "With all its vicissitudes I still love a life on the broad, free ocean"—an attitude born of what the *Globe* called his "stoical indifference . . . to his hardship, his independent spirit and determination to bring his family home at his own expense."[22]

The *Globe* described Hettie as "every inch a sailor" and reported that when the *Liberdade* sailed alongside a passenger ship, "a gentleman passenger looking over the rail at Mrs. Slocum, a comely woman of 40, who stood by the cabin door, remarked fervently: 'If that captain ever dies I'd like to marry that woman. She's the pluckiest woman I ever saw.'" (Hettie was not forty, but twenty-six.) By the time they reached New York, however, it was clear that the reporter had mistaken Hettie's feelings. When asked whether she was going on another voyage, she answered: "Oh, I hope not. I haven't been home in over three years, and this was my wedding journey." She added that to go to Boston, "I shall travel by rail. I have had enough sailing to last me for a long time." Her cousin later remembered that Hettie "was not wholly for that life. It was bad all around taking Virginia's place as a wife and trying to do right by the children."[23]

According to a report by a New York journalist, written in 1898 and "which has never been related," Slocum wrote his first account of the journey for a newspaper. He offered the story to its editor:

> The offer was accepted, and after several hours of elaborate collaboration between a writer and the captain a "story" was laid before the editor which he valued at $20, paying that sum at once to Slocum. With this money Captain Slocum refurnished his wardrobe and tidied up his boat a bit. Then, at the editor's suggestion, he invited the public to call and see the Liberdade at 10 cents a head. The published account of the voyage had advertised the captain so well that he was speedily and for several days in receipt of a substantial stream of little silver coins, and when he set sail for Boston he had nearly a peck measure of dimes for a cargo.[24]

Without a ship, Slocum traveled to Boston and wrote the full-length story of the adventure, *Voyage of the Liberdade*. The family did not live together. Slocum stayed with an aunt; the two older boys shared lodgings; Hettie and the two youngest children lived with her sister. Garfield later wrote, "Father did not come to the house." Slocum sought work in the Boston shipyards, where his skills would have been useful. His temperament, though, was not suited to the job, and he found himself unemployable. And then he met Captain Eben Pierce, who offered him the *Spray*.[25]

Bachelor Pad

Slocum must have seen rebuilding the boat as a sensible thing to do. Hettie, living with relatives, could earn enough as a seamstress to support herself and the younger children. Victor and Ben were independent. Boarding with Captain Pierce, Slocum would have no living costs. He was able to earn enough working occasionally in the Fairhaven boatyards to pay for materials for his project, which cost $553.62. Next to sailing, building ships was his favorite occupation. He spent thirteen months rebuilding the *Spray*, which gave him plenty of time to think about what he would do with her when he finished.[26]

Obviously, he would sail the *Spray*. He had rebuilt her to suit himself, and it is unlikely that he ever thought of selling her. He tried fishing for a while, and even invented a new sort of net for mackerel, but that had never been something he enjoyed, nor was it particularly profitable. If he was going to sail, he would sail to distant ports, as he had always done. Before he started work on the *Spray*, he had a plan to use the boat for what we would now call ecotourism. He told a reporter, " 'The Spray's first voyage will be to the West Indies. She will be fitted entirely into cabin room and can easily accommodate eight or ten persons.' These will be chosen from among Capt. Slocum's friends and will be those who have a genuine love for ocean travel or are scientifically inclined. On her deck will be fitted a large aquarium, and a collection of foreign fish, shells, and sea vegetation will be made."[27]

That plan seems to have been abandoned early on. So why not sail around the world? And he would sail alone. After all, who else would go with him? If Virginia were still alive, she would have, of course, but Hettie would never willingly go to sea again, and it isn't clear that he would have wanted her company. Victor had become a sailor, but he had other commitments and needed to earn a living. Ben had no desire to go to sea, and Jessie and Franklin were too young. As for hiring a crew, that was probably the last thing he would have considered after the mutinies and legal consequences he had suffered. It would be a great adventure—probably his last—and perhaps he could make some money by writing about it. Although *The Voyage of the Liberdade* wasn't a bestseller, it may have given him the confidence to write what he hoped would be a more exciting and popular book. Before setting sail, he had made arrangements to write articles for several newspapers, including the *Boston Globe*, the *Louisville Courier-Journal*, and the *New York World*, so writing about his voyage was clearly part of his plans early on.[28]

There is no reason for anyone else to write about his voyage, for no one could do it better than he did. *Sailing Alone Around the World*, in the words of Guy Bernardin, a French writer who re-created the voyage for the centennial, "still reads like a philosophy manual for life at sea. A sailor's book, written by one of the purest sailors the ocean has borne, translated into every language, marked with reserve and subtle humor, this tale remains the Bible of all who sail the sea."[29] If you have never read it, you should, even if you have never sailed. For now, I will simply say that his voyage was a great success. The *Spray* performed as he had hoped, he experienced enough danger and adventure to enjoy himself and write a good book, and he was received with enthusiasm in nearly every port.

Slocum returned to the United States a famous man. He traveled to Washington and was taken to the White House to meet President Theodore Roosevelt. His safe return was reported in newspapers across the country, from San Francisco to Boston, with short articles in newspapers like the *St. Tammany Farmer* in Covington, Louisiana, and the *Bourbon News* in Paris, Kentucky. The *New York Sun* noted that "the Spray is laden with curios, and Capt. Slocum says that the American flag has made him welcome wherever he has been."[30]

A long article in the *Omaha World Herald* included dramatic quotes from Slocum: "More than once I was in danger of assassination"; "I was determined to do it, and I have done it." It also included one of the few references he made to loneliness: "For a little while after being out from Boston I found an exhilaration in the novelty of the situation, but that soon wore off and I must admit I was a little lonesome. It was a great relief to see a sail, and a joy to be able to speak to a human being."[31]

In August, when he visited the city, the *New York Times* described him as "a perfect type of the weather-beaten, knockabout sailor" and claimed that "his wife and four children . . . tried to dissuade him, but he would not be deterred." Referring indirectly to the *Spray*'s extraordinary self-steering ability, the reporter wrote, "When he desired to sleep he lashed his wheel fast and trusted to Providence."[32]

Slocum wasted little time in cashing in on his celebrity. Docked in Erie

Basin, in the Red Hook section of Brooklyn, he began writing a series of seven articles for *Century Illustrated Monthly Magazine,* the first of which was published in September 1899. New York society welcomed him at the Players, Aldine, and Twentieth Century clubs. In Boston, using the articles he had sent to newspapers while sailing, as well as his logs and port documents, he began work on a book manuscript. *Sailing Alone Around the World* was published, with illustrations, by Century (New York) and Sampson Low, Marston (London) in March 1900, just as the magazine series ended. The book was favorably reviewed and sold very well. Slocum also went on the lecture circuit, illustrating his talks with three hundred stereopticon slides. In 1901 he exhibited the *Spray* at the Pan-American Exposition in Buffalo. Along with copies of *Sailing Alone* and *The Voyage of the Liberdade,* Slocum offered for 25 cents a "Sloop Spray Souvenir Booklet," which contained lengthy reviews of his book as well as a small piece of *Spray*'s first mainsail. Hettie arranged the reviews and added notes.[33]

The Farm

In March 1902 Slocum bought land in West Tisbury, on Martha's Vineyard. The farm, which he called Fag End, included a house, described by a contemporary as "one of the most ancient on the island—an oak-ribbed ark of a dwelling with warped floors and tiny window panes and open fireplaces." Garfield said that his father "had liked the house because of the large timbers and because the knees put him in mind of a ship's hold." Slocum rebuilt the house in a way that reflected his voyages, adding overhanging eaves like the ones he had seen in the South Pacific, and a Japanese-style roof. According to one of Slocum's biographers, a "neighbor recalled the house as having a 'marine flavor.' Beside the front door the captain arranged shells and coral." Further "evidence of a seafaring man's touch" included "starfish, sea fans, brain coral and some old scallop shells."[34] Just as he had made his ships into houses, he tried to make his house into a ship.

Despite his efforts, though, he never felt at home. After less than two years, he was spending most of his time on the *Spray,* sailing in New England in the summer and in the Caribbean in winter. The farm was Hettie's home, not his. He was in West Tisbury so rarely that the *Vineyard*

Gazette reported on July 30, 1908, that "Captain Joshua Slocum of the sloop *Spray* is on the Island and has been a recent guest of Mrs. Slocum at West Tisbury."[35]

Lost

After the celebration of his voyage and the success of his book, Slocum seemed for the first time in his life to have no destination. He sailed to ports not too distant from home, and he began to neglect both his appearance and his boat. When Slocum visited the Roosevelt family in 1906, Archie Roosevelt said, "the boat was the most incredibly dirty craft I have ever seen."[36] In the same year, Slocum and the *Spray* were in Riverton, New Jersey, and he invited a group of children on board. Slocum had always welcomed young people to visit his boat, hoping to encourage their interest in sailing. This time, though, something went very wrong, and on May 26, Slocum was charged with assaulting twelve-year-old Elsie Wright. The charge has elsewhere been described as rape. We don't know what happened. Slocum's general slovenliness may have led to his accidentally exposing himself, or something more serious may have taken place. Elsie may not have known what the word meant. In any case, Slocum was arrested, and bail was set at $1,000. He spent forty-two days in jail. Elsie's parents and doctor confirmed that no rape had taken place, and Slocum pleaded no contest to a lesser charge. According to the report in a Philadelphia newspaper, "It is generally thought in Riverton that the hardships through which he has passed have unbalanced the Captain's mind."[37] Soon after his release, though, Slocum was in Oyster Bay taking Archie Roosevelt on a five-day sail to Newport.[38]

Slocum continued sailing around New England and the Caribbean, and on November 14, 1909, he left the Vineyard, headed for South America. He was never heard from again and was presumed lost at sea. He was declared legally dead in 1924.[39]

6

A House for Friends

6 CHERRY STREET

Today soon becomes yesterday.
—ALICE OMEY, member of the Colonial Club Board

In 1914 sixty-five-year-old Mattie Coggeshall wrote her will. She had a great deal to bequeath—the spacious home that she had built on the harbor at 6 Cherry Street, its furniture, investments, silver and china, her books, furs, jewelry, and family photographs and mementos. But she had no obvious heirs. Her husband, children, grandchildren, nieces, nephews, sisters, and all but one of her husband's siblings had already died. Except for a few small bequests, she decided to leave everything to a group of friends who shared her love of Fairhaven history.[1]

A Fairhaven Girlhood

Martha Gould Jenney was born on May 7, 1849, in her parents' small Greek Revival home on Pleasant Street. Her father, Josiah, had died of "brain fever" (probably meningitis or encephalitis) a few months before she was born, leaving his pregnant wife, Clarissa Bennett Alden, and Mattie's older sisters, ten-year-old Kate and five-year-old Elizabeth. The Jenneys, Bennetts, and Aldens were large Fairhaven families, and many of them lived nearby and helped the bereaved widow and her daughters. Clarissa managed by taking in boarders. In 1869, when Mattie—like her sisters before her—graduated from Fairhaven High School, she went to work as a clerk for Mrs. Bartlett Allen, a New Bedford milliner.[2]

In 1873 a local newspaper reported that "Fairhaven is destined to have a sensation one day next week. Cards of invitation have been circulated for the wedding of one of its fairest belles, at the Congregational church. We hear that a young New York merchant is to be the happy man." Mattie and John East Coggeshall were married on October 23. John had been raised in New Bedford, the son of Bradford Hammond Coggeshall, a cooper, and Sarah Shaw Coggeshall. The Coggeshall family lived at 460 Acushnet Avenue, at the foot of Mill Street, in one of the city's oldest houses. When John's ancestor George East built it in 1780, it had served both as a tavern and—thanks to his religious wife, Elizabeth—as a church for visiting preachers. It had long rooms, low ceilings, and a large center chimney. The pulpit used by those early itinerant preachers remained in the house.[3]

John began his career as a bookkeeper in his father's cooperage, but by the time of his marriage, both he and his brother, George, had moved to New York City. Describing him as a merchant was a bit of an exaggeration. In various censuses, he was listed as clerk, bookkeeper, auditor, and eventually assistant treasurer, usually for the Sawyer-Martin Electric Company.[4]

Marriage and Family

After their marriage, John and Mattie moved to Brooklyn. They lived in a brownstone on Fulton Avenue and later in a brick house on Carlton Avenue in the Fort Greene neighborhood. The Carlton Avenue house, recently built, had four stories, including a basement partly above street level, with a service entrance a few stairs down from the sidewalk. It was a typical New York row house—narrow, but extending two large rooms back from the street. Theirs was a comfortable middle-class home in a pleasant neighborhood of similar houses and tree-lined streets. The Coggeshalls lived within walking distance of Fort Greene Park, a gracious public space designed by Frederick Law Olmsted and Calvert Vaux, and several theaters.[5]

We know little of Mattie's life in Brooklyn. John's brother George lived in Brooklyn Heights with his wife, Jennett, and their daughter, Janet; the two families probably socialized. John and Mattie usually had one live-in servant. From her will, we know that Mattie had Brooklyn friends close enough that she wished to remember them with bequests of money or jewelry. Although she had been raised in the Congregational church, she was confirmed in the Episcopal church on April 6, 1900, by Abram N. Littlejohn, bishop of Long Island, at the Church of the Messiah at Greene and Clermont Avenues in Brooklyn. The event was commemorated by the gift of a small book, *The Narrow Way: A Complete Manual of Devotion,* which rested on the bedside table in her bedroom on Cherry Street.[6]

John and Mattie had two children: Edward Bradford, born in 1875 in Brooklyn, and Catherine, known as Kate, born there two years later. Both attended Brooklyn schools. Edward was one of the first students to enter the Brooklyn Boys' High School when it opened in 1892, and he graduated in 1894. Kate graduated from the Brooklyn Girls' High School in 1895. After graduation, Kate taught in the primary department at Miss Upton's School for Girls.[7] In 1903 she married James S. Hubbard, and the young couple lived with her parents at 359 Carlton Avenue until 1907. Their only child, Bradford Coggeshall Hubbard, died on July 6, 1905, two days before his first birthday.[8]

Edward moved to Denver, where in 1903 he married Mary F. Lowerre of New York, who was nine years older than he. Edward's career was probably in agriculture: he was an officer of the Colorado State Board of Horticulture. He was also an artist, and two of his paintings of ships, as well as a ship model that he built, were in the Coggeshall house. Edward and Mary had a daughter, Kathryn, who was born in 1907 and died of convulsions the next year.[9]

By 1908 death had become a frequent visitor to the Coggeshall family. In addition to the grandchildren, John's brother, George, had died in January 1907; his wife had died a year earlier. George's daughter and her husband had died in 1898, suffocated in a natural gas accident in their home. Both Mattie's children died of tuberculosis in 1907. Mattie's sister Kate had died in 1874; her sister Elizabeth died of peritonitis in 1904. Both Elizabeth's children had died in the 1870s.[10] The cumulative grief from all these losses must have been overwhelming. John and Mattie now had no family but his unmarried sister, Mary E. Coggeshall, who had epilepsy and lived with a caregiver in New Bedford, and their son-in-law (James Hubbard) and daughter-in-law, Mary L. Coggeshall. John and Mattie's generation would be the last in their families. In his early sixties, John retired, and the couple decided to return to Fairhaven.

Building a New Home

Mattie's bachelor uncles, Dexter and Benjamin Jenney, had lived in a small house near the corner of Lafayette and Cherry Streets on land owned by the Jenney family. Mattie had inherited part of the site in 1862, when her grandparents died, and more of it in 1898, as one of her uncles' heirs. She acquired the balance in 1908, when her sister Elizabeth's share was conveyed to her by Elizabeth's widower. John and Mattie hired Frank A. Sistare, who had built several houses in the area, to build a three-story house. The existing buildings were razed. Planning and construction took a year, and the final bill, presented in May 1909, was for $10,269.70.[11]

Mattie was building a home that would be comfortable for a middle-aged couple and suitable for entertaining. The house was placed on the corner, with a large yard from its south side down to the harbor. It is finished with clapboard and has a curved front porch with a balcony above it. The front door opens into a vestibule leading to an entrance hall, two parlors, a dining room, sunporch, breakfast room, kitchen, and butler's pantry. The second floor has a large central hall, five bedrooms, and one and a half bathrooms. Four of the rooms are arranged so that they could have been used as suites. The gabled third floor has one finished room and storage space. Dentil moldings decorate the parlors and dining room, and Corinthian columns mark the hallway and the parlor fireplace. The ceilings are high, with chandeliers of the locally manufactured Pairpoint glass.

Mattie Coggeshall left no letters or diaries that would allow us to reconstruct her life after she returned to Fairhaven, but there is evidence of her social activities. She attended Episcopal services at the Church of the Good Shepherd, then housed in the old Stone School House on North Street. She probably spent time with the Alden, Bennett, and Jenney relatives whom she had known as a child and young woman. She socialized with her high school friends and "presided over" a reunion clambake for them in 1913. It was held at Fort Phoenix, and of the sixteen surviving members of the class that graduated in 1869, eleven attended with their spouses and guests. Although it was mid-August, the men wore three-piece suits and the women, long dresses and elaborate hats. Later that year, she hosted a "victrola concert" at her home for the benefit of the King's Daughters, a Christian service organization that she remembered in her will.[12]

An important part of her social life was the Colonial Club. She and John

The 1913 Fairhaven High School reunion and clambake. John and Martha Coggeshall are in the first row, second and third from the right.
Courtesy of the Fairhaven Colonial Club.

became charter members when it was founded in 1912, suggesting that she had been active in its predecessor organization, the Colonial Dames. The town's centennial year, according to the club's by-laws, was "the opportune time . . . to form a historical society." In hopes of "being custodians of many of their family relics, with the assurance that they will be well cared for," the members solicited donations or loans of items of historical interest to be housed in the Academy building, once a private school, then (and now) owned by the town and "generously loaned" for the club's collections. The club's main objects were "the proper care and preservation of such articles of historic interest as shall be given or loaned" and "to foster an interest in local history." But also important, the club hoped "to promote among its members good fellowship and the highest form of social life." These objectives were combined in the goal of establishing "a home furnished, so far as possible, with the beautiful household furnishings of the past." The club organized an antique show at which many donations of furniture, china, linens, and other household goods were displayed.[13]

The Academy building was not designed to be a museum. When it was built in 1798, it had had two classrooms on the first floor and a single large meeting room on the second. In the 1870s, the upstairs had been divided into a music hall (complete with organ) and a billiard parlor. By 1883 it had fallen into disrepair and was used for storage. In 1907 the building was threatened with destruction, lying nearly in the path of the new bridge across the Acushnet River. Henry Huttleston Rogers, who had redesigned the town entrance, had it moved to its present location. In 1912 the town entrusted the building to the Colonial Club, which raised $1,600 for improvements. The club had gas lines installed, added a bathroom, installed a fireplace and a donated furnace, repaired the roof, and had the walls painted. They were sufficiently forward-thinking that they installed electric lights, though gas would have been cheaper. Even with these improvements, the building wasn't suitable for the club's collections. It was poorly insulated, and items kept there were subject to extremes of temperature and humidity. Fabrics, furniture, and art were not protected from damaging sunlight. Once divided, the upstairs room wasn't really large enough for lectures or other programs. It certainly wasn't conducive to socializing. The Colonial Club had a home, but not a comfortable one.[14]

Despite the shortcomings of the Academy building, the club began a busy schedule of activities. Meeting at the home of their president, the board adopted by-laws and elected officers. They solicited donations and loans of antiques. Less than a month after receiving permission to use the Academy, they organized a Fourth of July gathering there, and in August they held a lawn party. New Year's Day in 1913 was the occasion for a tea party, and on Washington's Birthday they held another tea party, for which some of the members dressed in colonial costumes—a tradition that continued into the twenty-first century. They also arranged to have an operetta presented, with an admission charge of 50 cents, and in April organized a whist party "to replenish our treasury."[15]

Both men and women joined the Colonial Club, but the women took the lead. They held all the major offices and set the agenda. They negotiated with town officials about the use of the Academy and dealt with the contractors who did the repairs. Most of the contributions, whether of antiques or of cash, came from women. It would be nearly a decade before these women won the right to vote, but they had developed the skills they needed to act effectively in the public sphere, largely through participation in women's organizations that encouraged public speaking, mastery of parliamentary procedure, minute-taking, financial record keeping, and other activities.[16] Mattie was not an officer of the club, but she remained committed to it.

In February 1914 Mattie Coggeshall was diagnosed with uterine cancer. Four months later, John Coggeshall suffered an embolism. He had not recovered when, on July 2, he developed meningitis. He died on July 7 and was buried in Riverside Cemetery. In October 1915 the club's secretary reported that Mattie had "offered the gift of a very valuable collection of stamps, autographs and coins to the club. The stamps as a memorial to her son Edward Bradford Coggeshall and the coins and autographs as a memorial to her husband John East Coggeshall." The club accepted the gift, which was housed in the vault of the Mechanics Bank of New Bedford.[17]

Planning for the Future

Along with the devotional volume given to her when she was confirmed, two books rested on Mattie's bedside table: Tennyson's *Locksley Hall* and Frederick Trevor Hill's 1901 handbook, *The Care of Estates.* With John dead, and her own illness advancing, Mattie was deeply concerned about what would become of her house and belongings. Four months after John's death, she had made her decisions. In her will, dated November 24, 1914, she made some small bequests: $100 to friends and former servants, and to the Church of the Good Shepherd and the King's Daughters; jewelry and furs to friends in New York and Fairhaven. To her son-in-law, James S. Hubbard, she left $4,000, a diamond ring, and anything that had belonged to his late wife, Kate. To her daughter-in-law, Mary L. Coggeshall, who was living with her at the time of her death, she left furs, an opal ring, clothing, and everything that belonged to Mary's late husband, Edward. She also arranged for a monthly stipend of $60 (later reduced to $40) to be paid to Mary as long as she did not remarry. To her sister-in-law, Mary E. Coggeshall, she left an opal ring that had belonged to Kate. In anticipation of money that would come to her or her estate when her sister-in-law died, she made a bequest to St. Luke's Hospital.

Then she set up a trust, with her house and land to be given to the Colonial Club "as a museum for the preservation and exhibition of documents, writings, books and all kinds of furniture and personal property of historic value and interest, particularly in relation to said Fairhaven and the inhabitants thereof, and for the preservation and exhibition of articles of interest because of their having been used by old families of Fairhaven." Clearly aware of the dual objectives of the Colonial Club, she added, "My said residence may be used by said Club, while it is a Museum, as a meeting-place for said Club and such social functions may be carried on there as said Club may elect." She added that "no money shall be supplied by my Trustee for any lunches or repasts of any kind."[18] All the assets of the estate not otherwise assigned went into the trust for the maintenance of the house and its contents. If the Colonial Club did not accept the gift, the house was to be used as a home for elderly women in need. When Mattie died, on April 16, 1916, the will took effect.

A New Home for the Colonial Club

Apparently, no one in the club had known of Mattie's plans. The gift was announced to the executive committee on May 1, 1916, at the same meeting where her death was noted "with deep feeling." At the annual meeting in June, the chair of the Gifts and Loans Committee, Elizabeth Tripp, reported the various artifacts that had been donated during the year. She continued:

> And now I come to the wonderful gift of Mrs. Coggeshall—so unexpected and unusual that no one at the present time can realize or foretell its possibilities.
> As we have a clearer perspective at our journeys end, so our friend could see the opportunities of this club to help and to uplift our town, and this committee have only one suggestion to make in regard to the use of this splendid gift, and that is if possible this beautiful home on the river may from the beginning be the fulfillment of Mrs. Coggeshall's wishes in *whole* not in part. That it should be a place of memorials for all that is worthy of a place there and that also it should be a home for the homeless. The house is large and the income no doubt sufficient to maintain a home at once even if the number taken in would have to be limited to a few. Not to wait for this end until the house has lost its meaning as a home and is only a place of relics but to start at once to give help and shelter to the homeless while Mrs. Coggeshall['s] name

will mean the name of a friend, and not simply the name and gift of a stranger.

Miss Tripp's wish to house the homeless came from the provision in the will to be followed if the club was unable or unwilling to accept the house. It was never used to house the elderly, but as the home of the Colonial Club the house became a place for friendship and a different sort of community service. So that Mattie would be remembered as a friend, the club celebrates her birthday every year.[19]

In July, the executive committee called a special meeting of all the members at the Academy building, and the group voted "to accept the Coggeshall Estate to be known as the Coggeshall Memorial. And that the club would endeavor in every way to carry out Mrs. Coggeshall's wishes in regard to the use of her gift." At a special meeting of the club's executive committee on August 21, held at the Coggeshall Memorial, the lawyer for the estate gave the club president the keys to the house. The executive committee looked over the house and adjourned until September, when they began tending to practical details and planning how to use their new home.[20]

The first question to be decided was which of the furniture and fittings in the house the club should keep. The executive committee met at the house on September 11, 1916. They voted to give many pieces of furniture as well as Mattie's "toilet articles" to her daughter-in-law, Mary L. Coggeshall. Everything else—including the dining room furniture and other pieces, china, books, and family photographs—remained in the house. Mary L. Coggeshall gave the club the paintings and model ship created by Edward.[21] Next, the board had to decide what to do with its new home. The club remained responsible for the Academy building. Coordinating the use of the two buildings, and finding time and funds to maintain both, would occupy the club's officers for decades to come. Although the Coggeshall Memorial had an endowment for maintenance, the Academy building did not.

Before receiving Mattie's gift, the club had created a schedule of activities designed to provide opportunities for socializing and fundraising. An annual lawn party, tea parties, and whist parties met both goals. The Academy was open to members and guests two afternoons a week in the summer at no charge; tea was available for 25 cents. The club promoted knowledge of history by offering lectures at its meetings: a local historian, Henry B. Worth, spoke on the town's two first settlements, Fairhaven and Oxford villages; longtime residents Job Tripp and Daniel Deane offered their reminiscences; the town's librarian developed a list of books about colonial history, and Flora Leighton gave a talk about them; Walter Sherman lectured about the Salem witch trials. They organized exhibits of antique coverlets, shawls, needlework, dolls, and china. The monthly and annual meetings often included musical performances or group singing. The members also had work days when they sewed rag rugs for the Academy building.[22]

These activities continued after 1916, and the acquisition of the Coggeshall Memorial made it possible to add events that flourished in a more domestic setting. The house changed the nature of the club. Beginning in 1917 it was open from 2 to 6 every day except Wednesday, and on Sunday and Tuesday evenings. Twice a month, the club offered teas that included a lecture or musical performance. These smaller gatherings, in a real *home*, enhanced the possibilities for friendship. A large membership (the club had a waiting list beyond its 250 members) meeting in a formal auditorium setting was unlikely to achieve intimacy. Tea in a comfortably furnished parlor was quite different. The club began using the Academy for its original purpose—offering classes, including Miss Randall's course in basketry, taught every other Tuesday.[23]

Mattie's gift also altered the club's collections. Most of the documents, furniture, and artifacts donated to the club had been from the eighteenth and early nineteenth centuries: colonial-era deeds and military documents, early American furniture and household implements, family Bibles, and the like. There were also relics of the whaling era: marine artifacts, Asian porcelain, and scrimshaw. Some of the furniture and books that Mattie had inherited from her family and the Coggeshalls were of that time, but most of the furniture, decorative objects, and china were typical of a turn-of-the-century middle-class home. Over time, those too have become antiques, but when the club acquired the house, its furnishings would have been contemporary—much like the blend of family heirlooms and new furniture in the members' homes—and not at all like a museum.[24]

Another impetus for change in the club's activities was World War I. The money raised at the December 1914 whist party was sent to Cara Rogers Broughton (the daughter of Henry Huttleston Rogers, who was living in England); she reported that with it she bought "225 pairs of nice warm stockings . . . for the soldiers." Beginning in 1917 David M. Cheney taught current events, focusing on the war, one evening a month. In May 1917 the club sponsored a talk on Red Cross work and voted to form a Red Cross auxiliary. Dr. Thompson gave first aid lessons to anyone interested, whether or not they were members. By autumn of that year, the Red Cross was using the Academy building so extensively that the club removed many of its artifacts and held almost all events at the house. The Red Cross continued to work from the Academy until January 1920. When a Naval Reserve station was established on Fort Street in 1917, the club opened the Coggeshall house on Sunday afternoons and evenings throughout the winter to entertain the sailors living in the barracks. The club's 1918 annual report estimated that five hundred reservists had attended the Sunday entertainments.[25]

The executive committee voted in April 1917 that "the Coggeshall house be offered to the Government to be used as a hospital in case of war in our vicinity." Fairhaven never came under military attack, but in 1918, like much of the country, the town fell victim to the Spanish influenza, and emergency hospital space was needed. Because the will and trust did not provide for such a use, the house had to be requisitioned by the government. On October 2, the town's board of health voted "to commandeer the building designated as the Coggeshall Memorial . . . to be used as an Emergency Hospital during the present epidemic." The Boy Scouts helped club members move "everything except the Victrola and two tables" from the first floor, and "articles of historic interest" were locked in a room on the third floor. At the suggestion of the selectmen, a member of the club volunteered to join the staff at the house. When the first volunteer contracted the flu, a second stepped in. During the month of October, twenty-nine patients were admitted, and seven died.[26]

The board of health discontinued use of the building at the end of the month, and the town paid the club $37.51 for the use of coal, electric lights, and telephone. The club had the house cleaned and painted, installed new electrical fixtures, and bought new window shades and draperies at a cost of $500. The annual report that recording secretary Elizabeth B. Tripp submitted to the members on June 2, 1919, reflects the views of at least some of the members: "The year 1918–'19 has in some ways been an unusual one. We have had the gratification of knowing that both the Academy Building and the Coggeshall Memorial have been used for the benefit of Humanity. This knowledge, particularly in regard to this beautiful building, has been peculiarly satisfying, for deep down in our hearts many of us have long wished that the Coggeshall Memorial might stand for more than it does at the present time."[27]

In the 1920s, the club became an active collector of local history material and launched research projects. They began buying works by local artists, usually (though not exclusively) of local subjects. They purchased manuscripts and maps created by Henry B. Worth and bought a safe to house them. They also recognized the importance of recording important present events. In the June 1922 report of the Historical Committee, Alice Omey noted: "While the main object of the club is the collection of things typical of the long ago, we must not lose sight of the fact that today soon becomes yesterday, and this present of ours will be the dim and distant past of future generations. It is in our time that the World War has taken place, and it should be in our time that such records and souvenirs as can be obtained should find a home in Fairhaven's museum. Our small town played an honorable part in this conflict for the right, and it must not be forgotten by those that come after us." The club therefore compiled a detailed record of members of the Fairhaven community who had served in World War I and gave a copy to the town archives.[28]

The club also commissioned a photographer to take pictures of historic doorways in Fairhaven. A club committee identified the doorways and, in 1926, hired a Mr. Packard to do the work at $2 per doorway. His photos were placed in an album and duplicated as postcards that the club sold. The day after the devastating 1938 hurricane destroyed many homes, club member Mary Taber Williams documented the damage with photographs that she donated to the club. The board also held an essay contest inviting townspeople to write about their personal experience of the storm. The cost of publishing the essays was prohibitive, but prizes were given and the essays were transcribed and archived. In 2014 several of them were excerpted in the *New Bedford Standard-Times* and others were read at the club's annual dinner.[29]

The club's activism did not always sit well with the trustees. They balked at buying the more expensive works of art and declared that the doorways project did not fall within the guidelines of Mrs. Coggeshall's will. The club, through their lawyer, pushed back. Alice Omey, a member of the board, "advised the Executive board to use their own judgment in regard to a proper use of the Coggeshall funds under the terms of the will; demanding their right as a club rather than asking for them as favors." In almost every case, the trustees backed down and paid the bills.[30]

The club also expanded its social activities. The house remained open for tea and socializing, and card parties, musicales, exhibits, and lectures became more frequent. The club offered a class on parliamentary law and began organizing annual automobile outings to historic sites. Public offerings suffered a temporary setback, though, in December 1928, when the Massachusetts Department of Public Safety banned the use of the Academy for "assemblage purposes" until a second exit was added. The club turned the matter over to the town's selectmen for resolution, and a fire escape was added.[31]

As maintaining the Academy became more expensive and the Great Depression took its toll on the club's finances, members began negotiating with the town. The town agreed to take responsibility for maintaining the exterior of the building, while the club took care of the interior and paid for heating and insurance. The club remained responsible for the interior of the building until 1975, when the town took it back. Even then, many of the artifacts that the club owned remained at the Academy. When the Fairhaven Historical Society opened the building as a museum in 1992, most of its holdings were gifts or loans from the Colonial Club.[32]

Changing Times

World War II dominated the club's business during the 1940s. The board ordered blackout curtains, turned the basement into an air-raid shelter, debated moving paintings to a safer location, and created emergency exits. They also had to deal with reductions in income from the trust fund as bonds with high interest rates were called in. But, as they had done in World War I, they raised money for relief efforts and opened the house to soldiers stationed at Fort Rodman, across the harbor, and Camp Edwards (near Sandwich). As the war continued, they were forced to stop heating both the house and the Academy and to hold meetings at the town hall. Because of its greater seating capacity, the club opened these events to as many guests as members wished to bring.[33]

In the 1950s, the Coggeshall house was used less frequently. Television began to occupy the leisure time of the members, who no longer spent afternoons at the club. In the 1960s and '70s, more of the members began to work outside the home, and membership declined. The club eventually met only one evening a month and became less active in collecting and entertaining. Nevertheless, the Washington's Birthday tea continued to draw a large audience, with the house opened free to the public. Beginning in 2013 the club collaborated with the Whitfield-Manjiro Friendship Society to hold a springtime Cherry Blossom Festival. Finally, in January 2017, the assets that Mrs. Coggeshall had placed in trust were no longer adequate to maintain the house, and the trustees decided to sell it. Without a home for its artifacts, the club decided to arrange for their sale as well. The house for friends that Mattie Coggeshall envisioned and made possible for more than a hundred years will soon be empty, its furniture and paintings scattered.

7

You Can't Go Home Again

11 CHERRY STREET

If you save a life, you are responsible for that life.

—Chinese proverb

On June 27, 1841, five fishermen from a small Japanese village were starving on a desert island. They had survived for more than five months after their small boat was wrecked, living in a cave with only rainwater to drink and very little food. Three were brothers, and one of those had broken his leg while getting to shore. They had little hope of surviving much longer. On that day, though, they saw a ship. They removed what clothing they had and waved it from a high point on the island. Soon a boat from the *John Howland,* a whaling ship from New Bedford, came ashore and took the men back to the ship. The ship's log said simply that they "found 5 poor distressed people on the Isle. Took them off. Could not understand anything from them more than that they was hungry."[1] One of the starving men, Manjiro, later wrote: "The Japanese could not believe they had been saved. They were afraid that it was just a dream. When they approached the main boat, they saw it was about 180 feet wide, with three masts and eight auxiliary boats. Rope hung like cobwebs in all directions. The scores of white sails, fully unfurled and waving in the ocean breeze, were a truly magnificent sight." His description was accompanied by a detailed watercolor painting of the ship.[2]

The Japanese sailors—Captain Fudenjo and his two brothers (Juruke and Goemon), Toraemon, and Manjiro—were surely thinking of nothing more than survival. The *Howland*'s captain, William H. Whitfield of Fairhaven, was simply doing the right thing by saving men whose lives were in danger. None of them would have given a moment's thought to the fact that rescuing Japanese sailors was fraught with political problems and threats to their lives and futures. Even if they had, it would not have changed their life-or-death decisions. It was a reflexive act of survival for some, and mercy for the others.

Long-lived Fears

As early as the sixteenth century, the rulers of Japan had feared the influence of Christian missionaries, whose efforts at conversion subverted the nature of their state. They also knew that even the most sincere religious men could be used as wedges to open doors to unwanted economic and political influence. In 1587 the Japanese military government, the shogunate, banned Christian missionaries. The order was enforced but apparently was not adequate: Japanese people who came into contact with foreigners elsewhere could be contaminated. In 1633 a new ban was added: Japanese people could not travel outside the country. Still, those converted to Christianity before the decrees were strictly enforced were viewed as unreliable. In the early seventeenth century Christians were persecuted, and lower-echelon leaders believed that the shogun would view their zeal in doing so as a sign of loyalty. By the middle of the seventeenth century, as many as 300,000 Christians had renounced their faith or been executed. Between 1633 and 1639, a series of decrees made it illegal to send Japanese ships overseas without proper certification. Within ten years, even the possibility of certification was removed, with death as the penalty. More important for our castaways, the shogunate "decreed death for Japanese who, having been overseas, returned," and forbade Japanese sailors to serve on foreign ships.[3]

A few loopholes allowed for necessary trade. The Portuguese (a Catholic nation with missionaries) were banned, but the Dutch (Protestants) were permitted to trade at certain ports. When a Dutch ship arrived, one historian writes, "the captain would then order his crew to unload the guns and lock all Bibles and other Christian literature into barrels. In at least the early years the crew was obliged to tread on images of the Madonna and child (*fumie*), a test that had been found particularly effective for interrogation of *kirishitan*."[4]

In the nineteenth century, some British and American captains hoped that rescuing and returning Japanese castaways might gain them access to Japanese ports, but this was not the case. Their ships were fired upon and turned back. The practice was codified in 1825, with an order issued by the *bakufu*, or shogunate: "All Southern Barbarians and Westerners, not only the English, worship Christianity, that wicked cult prohibited in our land. Henceforth, whenever a foreign ship is sighted approaching any point on our coast, all persons on hand should fire on and drive it off . . . If the foreigners force their way ashore, you may capture and incarcerate them, and if their mother ship approaches, you may destroy it."[5]

These orders, prohibitions, and punishments were in place when Captain Whitfield rescued the five castaways, and both he and the Japanese would have been aware of them. Yet they became considerations only after they were safely on land and had to decide where to spend the rest of their lives. In the meantime, the castaways recovered their strength and worked alongside the crew. Young Manjiro proved especially useful, quickly learning English words and working hard, often as a lookout to watch for whales from the mast. Six months later, in December 1841, the *John Howland* reached the harbor of Honolulu, in the Sandwich Islands.[6]

A Cosmopolitan Port

In the first half of the nineteenth century, Honolulu became the most important port for Pacific whaling vessels, which stopped there to be repaired and to purchase water, food, and supplies. The permanent residents of the port were native Hawaiians and European missionaries and merchants, but visiting crews brought a great variety of nationalities and ethnicities to the streets. Herman Melville's portrayal of the streets of New Bedford—filled with free blacks, fugitive slaves, Yankees, and Pacific Islanders—was equally accurate for Honolulu. But because of Japan's laws, Japanese sailors were rarely seen.[7]

Captain Whitfield took the castaways to the office of Dr. Gerrit P. Judd, a physician serving with the American missionaries in Hawaii, who had been in Honolulu since 1828. Lacking a common language, the men communicated with gestures. Judd mimed praying and bowing with his hands together; the Japanese recognized the gestures. Then he showed them coins and a pipe that had been left with him by shipwrecked Japanese sailors eight or nine years earlier; they recognized the items.[8]

With their nationality established, the men were registered as residents of the island and given a place to live. Captain Whitfield gave them each a jacket and trousers and a half-dollar; the ship's crew gave them each an overcoat. Then Captain Whitfield asked Captain Fudenjo's permission to take Manjiro back to his home in Fairhaven. Fudenjo was reluctant, because he wanted his crew to stay together and attempt a return to Japan. But Manjiro wanted to go with Whitfield, and Fudenjo consented. The *John Howland* continued her whaling voyage, with New Bedford as the final destination. On the way, Whitfield and his crew taught the young man English, geography, American history, and the history of exploration. When they arrived in Fairhaven on May 7, 1843, Whitfield introduced the fourteen-year-old boy as "My son, John."[9]

Stranger in a Strange Land

It was not immediately clear where Manjiro would live. Whitfield and his first wife, Ruth, had lived at 11 Cherry Street, in Oxford Village, but Ruth had died in 1837 and Whitfield's aunt Amelia was living there. Whitfield was about to travel to New York to visit his brother and then to Bridgewater, Massachusetts, to marry Albertina Keith. He had met her when she was visiting her uncle Alexis at 13 Cherry Street, and they had become engaged in 1839. Whitfield arranged for Manjiro to live with the Eben Akin family on Oxford Street in his absence. Jane Allen, an Oxford Street neighbor, tutored him in English, and he was soon ready to attend the one-room school on North Street. There he learned reading, writing, spelling, and some patriotic American history. He long remembered that George Washington, whose picture hung in the schoolroom, could not tell a lie, even when he had chopped down a cherry tree. Jane's sister Charity mended his socks and baked molasses cookies for him. After Whitfield returned with his new bride, they moved to a farm in the Sconticut Neck area of Fairhaven, and Manjiro lived with them. He "helped with the farming," he later reported, "but when he had time, he practiced penmanship."[10]

Manjiro quickly became part of the Whitfield family. In his 1851 testimony on life in the United States, he said that in 1844, "Captain Whit-field and his new wife had a baby boy and named him William Henry. His face was as lovely as a polished jewel. Whitfield's sister, who married a man who had secretly stolen another man's wife and eloped, now lived with the Whitfields. She also took care of the newborn baby, for whom her affection increasingly grew." Whitfield took his paternal role seriously and planned Manjiro's education. After only a year in elementary school, Manjiro enrolled in the Louis L. Bartlett School of Mathematics, Survey-ing, and Navigation at 42 Spring Street, where his friend and classmate Job Tripp found him "the brightest member of his class": "he fairly soaked up learning, shy and quiet in his demeanor [and] always gentle and polite." Manjiro described Bartlett as "a versatile and well-educated man, about thirty years old." He also served an apprenticeship with a cooper.[11]

Whitfield had always attended the Congregational Church, but when he brought Manjiro to services, he was told that the boy would have to sit in the area set aside for those of African descent. Rather than be separated from his adopted son, or accede to prejudice, Whitfield began attending the Unitarian Church, where no such prohibition applied. When Whit-field was at sea, Manjiro often attended church with Warren Delano. Pres-ident Franklin Delano Roosevelt remembered his grandfather "telling me all about the little Japanese boy who went to school in Fairhaven and who went to church from time to time with the Delano family."[12]

It is impossible to know how the people of Fairhaven responded to Manjiro's presence. He would have been an oddity, for although sailors from foreign ports were frequently seen on the streets, Asians rarely came to the East Coast. And foreign sailors did not live in town or attend school. The Whitfields, their neighbors, and Manjiro's teachers and schoolmates all seem to have been fond of him; those who saw him only at a distance may have been less friendly. Certainly the Congregationalists were not cordial. But there is nothing in Manjiro's later writing to suggest that he felt unwelcome. In 1848 he wrote to his adoptive father: "O Captain, how can I forget your kindness, when can I pay you for your fatherly treatment? Thank God ten thousand times and never will forget your name . . . Give my best respects to all your friends and your kind neighbors and my affec-tionate regards to your wife, Aunt Amelia, and Mr. Bonney family. Tell them what quarter of the world I am in. I can never forget kindness they have done to me."[13] At the same time, it was clear that Fairhaven was not

Manjiro's home. By 1846—three years after arriving—he was working on a plan to return to Japan. He wanted to see his mother and his homeland.

Reunited

In 1846 Captain Ira Davis offered Manjiro a berth on the whaling ship *Franklin*. Captain Whitfield was at sea, but Mrs. Whitfield gave permission. She also gave Manjiro a letter of introduction to Father Samuel Chenery Damon, the chaplain of the Seaman's Chapel in Honolulu and editor of *The Friend*, a quarterly magazine. Father Damon, not yet thirty years old, had graduated from the Andover Theological Seminary in 1841 and settled in Honolulu in 1842. He might know what had become of Manjiro's shipmates and, in any case, could be helpful to a young, inexperienced sailor.[14]

The voyage on the *Franklin* would have discouraged someone less determined than Manjiro. The first port they visited was Guam, where Manjiro learned that the Japanese government treated foreign sailors badly. In a letter to Captain Whitfield, he "expressed a desire to help Japan open a port so that whaling crews would be treated well." While at sea, they encountered Japanese boats, but their sailors either spoke unfamiliar dialects or were afraid to talk to foreigners. Then, in Honolulu, he received the worst news of all: one of his companions, Juruke, had died. Toraemon had decided to stay in Honolulu, but Fudenjo (who now used the name Denzo) and Goemon had tried to return to Japan. The coastal guard stations had made it impossible for their ship, the *Florida*, to take them ashore, and they were now back in Honolulu.[15]

Manjiro returned to the *Franklin*, but it soon became clear that Captain Davis had become deranged. The crew put him in irons and turned him over to officials when they reached Manila. Davis's condition was obvious, and the crew members were not charged with mutiny. The *Franklin* continued its voyage, returning to Honolulu in October 1848. Manjiro used the opportunity to write to Captain Whitfield and to Charity Allen, who had helped care for him in Fairhaven. They finally reached New Bedford in August 1849. As a whaling voyage it was successful, and Manjiro's share of the profits was $350.[16]

The next step in Manjiro's plan was to go to California, where he could quickly earn enough money to fund a voyage to Japan for himself and his fellow castaways. With Captain Whitfield's agreement, he got a berth on a lumber ship headed to San Francisco, joining the hordes of young men flocking to the gold fields. California would not have been a comfortable place for him. Anglo miners would have assumed he was Chinese, so he would have suffered from anti-Chinese prejudice. The Chinese would not have accepted him, either. But he didn't need to stay long. By his own account, after earning $600 in little over two months, he thought he had enough money for the voyage. He returned to Honolulu to begin the journey home.[17]

Manjiro remembered the experience of the castaways on the *Florida*, who had been unable to reach the shore because of the Japanese coastal guard stations. His solution was to find a ship that would take them near the coast and then offload a smaller boat that they could sail to an accessible island. He arranged for them to be employed by Captain Whitmore on the *Sarah Boyd* and bought a sailboat, the *Adventure*, for $25. Father Damon and other residents of Honolulu provided encouragement and material assistance. Father Damon solicited help for their voyage: "To complete the outfit is wanted—a compass, a good fowling piece, a few articles of clothing, shoes, and a nautical almanac for 1850. Will not some benevolent person aid forward the enterprise."[18]

The U.S. consul, Elisha H. Allen, provided an account of their lives since leaving Japan, explained their plan, and added, "I trust they will be kindly treated by all persons whom they may meet. I am informed by the Chaplain of the Seamen's Friend Society, that John Manjiro has sustained a good character and has improved in knowledge. He will tell his countrymen of Japan how happy the Americans would be to make their acquaintance, and visit them with their ships, and give them gold and silver for their goods."[19]

This letter would in all likelihood have done more harm than good, offering evidence that the men had violated the Japanese bans on living abroad and working on foreign ships and asserting the commercial goals of the United States. Manjiro makes no mention of using it. However, his statement to the consul illustrates how carefully he had planned the voyage:

> On learning that Captain Whitmore would land them at Loochoo Islands, Manjiro, with the assistance of a few friends, purchased a good whaleboat, oars and sails. Having learned the science of navigation sufficient for all practical purposes, he supplied himself with a quadrant, compass, charts, &c. It is not expected that the Sarah Boyd will come to

an anchor at the Loochoo, but launch the whaleboat off the islands, and leave the three Japanese to make the best of their way to land. Although when at the Loochoo, they may be far from their native shores, yet Manjiro (whom we shall now call Captain Manjiro) thinks he knows enough of the relative situation of the Loochoo and Japanese Islands to find his way across. He says that annually a large Japanese Junk visits the Loochoo Islands for the purpose of receiving tribute money, and that the junk leaves Japan in February and returns in June. He supposed they might get passage in her—at any rate they would make the trial!

Damon added his endorsement: Manjiro "is a smart and intelligent young man, and has made good use of his opportunities."[20]

Before leaving, Manjiro wrote to Captain Whitfield: "I never forgot your benevolence of bringing me up from a small boy to manhood. I have done nothing for your kindness till now. Now I am going to return with Denzo and Goemon to my country. My wrong doing is not to be excused but I believe good will come out of this changing world, and that we will meet again. The gold and silver I left and also my clothing please use for useful purposes. My books and stationery please divide among my friends."[21] It is an oddly mixed message: He had left valued possessions behind, in case he returned. Now those possessions were to be given away. But he also thought he and Whitfield would meet again, even though he now knew how vast the world is and how difficult it would be ever to leave Japan.

Going Home

The *Sarah Boyd* sailed in October 1850, and by New Year's Day they were approaching Loochoo, now known as the Ryukyu Islands. Manjiro wrote a letter encouraging Toraemon, who had stayed behind: "It will not be long now before we return to the home province. Because our journey has been easily accomplished, you should also obtain a passage and return home by all means." They lowered their boat and headed for shore.[22]

Despite high seas and strong winds, they managed to land their boat in the Ryukyus. They told the villagers about their shipwreck and long absence and were met with kindness. One of the young men, Manjiro later testified, "said he would take care of them and not to trouble themselves." The villagers gave them food and water but also reported the event to government officials, who decided that the returnees should be sent on to Naha, the capital of the Ryukyus, and then to Kagoshima, the capital of Satsuma, where they arrived on August 1. During this time, they were well cared for, but they were under constant guard. Each group of officials interrogated them about their shipwreck and activities abroad, and they submitted their findings to the shogunate. The returnees were then ordered to travel to Nagasaki, where they arrived on October 1, a year after leaving the Sandwich Islands.[23]

The interrogations in Nagasaki lasted nine months. They began by determining whether Manjiro and his companions had become Christians. "A brass plate about 11 inches square, engraved with human figures, was brought out, and the three were ordered to tread on it."[24] This was the *fumie*, the image of the Madonna and child, which had been used as a test of faith for centuries. The questioning covered the shipwreck and their lives abroad, but Manjiro was a unique source of information about the West. He had brought a map of the world and used it to show them the places he had visited and to tell them about what he had seen in America.

He explained the political system: "People elected a man of wisdom and learning for president who held office for four years. However, if the man were highly virtuous and enlightened . . . they allowed him to remain in office . . . The current president is called Taylor. He was said to be just in administering punishment, justice, and law. Because the country was governed in such a way, the people would say the United States was better than any country in the world." He noted that American "officials are hard to distinguish as they never display the authority of the office. They do not demand courtesies from citizens along the road." In fact, he said, "there is no distinction between classes. Even a man of low rank may become an official."[25] He described technology: weather vanes, drawbridges, telegraphy, steamboats, trains, and whaling ships that could travel across oceans and process oil while at sea.[26] He even commented on mathematics: "The principle of counting is much the same but their *abacus* is different. It is a piece of thick purple stone a foot square with a wooden frame. They count by inscribing numerals with what looks like a nail. When it is wiped with the fingers, numerals all disappear."[27]

Manjiro also told his interrogators about American agriculture, food, holidays, and customs. He said that Americans ate meat, which Buddhists would not do, and praised a food he had not previously encountered: "Eggs, oil and salt mixed with flour is good food. They call it bread." The Fourth of July was celebrated much as it is in Fairhaven today: "Men with fixed bayonets parade the streets accompanied by musical bands playing such instruments as drums, pipes and gongs. Blank shots are fired. The people go out to see the spectacle and every house entertains guests at dinner." Even the bathroom did not escape comment: "Toilets are placed over holes in the ground. It is customary to read books in them."[28]

Manjiro had visited Boston and San Francisco. He had worked on western whalers, a New England farm, and the California gold fields. He knew the instruments and formulas of Western navigation. He could read, write, and speak English. After the interrogation—and especially as Japanese officials realized that a confrontation with the West was imminent—his knowledge was valued. For now, though, he was on trial.

Finally, on June 23, 1852, the three castaways received their sentences. They were to be sent to Tosa, their home province, which they could leave only with permission. Their boat (of interest to officials because of its construction, fittings, and instruments) became the property of the government, but they kept their books, guns, and other possessions. They were given Japanese silver in exchange for the coins and gold they had brought with them, and they were sent to Kochi, the capital of Tosa. They were interrogated yet again, for seventy days. This time the interrogation was recorded by a prominent artist and scholar, Kawada Shoryo. His account, illustrated with his paintings and Manjiro's drawings, was presented to the ruler of Tosa on October 25, 1852. At the end of the interrogation, the three men "were forbidden to have any occupation related to the sea," but they were given pensions and permission to return to their village.[29]

On October 1, 1852, Manjiro arrived at his home. "After thirteen years' absence," he reported in a letter to *The Friend*, "I was joyfully welcomed by my mother. My father died before I left home. My mother had mourned me as dead; under that impression, she had built for me a tomb." According to Kawada, after he had greeted the rest of his family, "they all drank in celebration and shed tears on hearing his story of hardships."[30]

Now Manjiro had to begin a new life. His first assignment, started on October 19, was to work with Kawada to redraw the world map that he had shown his interrogators and to help Kawada transcribe and illustrate his testimony. Manjiro had not learned to read and write Japanese, and Kawada knew no English. Their work together educated both of them. Manjiro also returned to Kochi to teach English and foreign affairs to young samurai.[31]

Manjiro Nakahama. *From the collection of the Millicent Library.*

Two Worlds

While Manjiro was celebrating his return to Japan, the United States was planning an expedition to open the nation's ports to American ships. Commodore Matthew Perry's four-battleship flotilla—known in Japan as the "Black Ships"—arrived in Tokyo Bay on July 8, 1853. Perry's mission lasted only ten days, but he said he would return in a year for a response to President Millard Fillmore's letter demanding the opening of the ports. Eight days after Perry's departure, the shogun ordered Manjiro to come to Tokyo (then called Edo). The officials had read a report of the young man's interrogation in Nagasaki, and they thought he might be valuable to them. They questioned him, and he told them what he knew about the United States. He also kept his promise to Captain Whitfield and urged the leaders to open ports where American seamen could seek help in emergencies. Manjiro's knowledge and articulateness impressed the officials of the shogunate, and he was made a samurai—a court official in service to the nation. His rank was symbolized by wearing two swords and by taking a surname, Nakahama.[32]

With Perry's return imminent, officials were divided over how Manjiro should participate in the negotiations. Some advocated using him as an interpreter (the earlier negotiations had been conducted in Dutch and Chinese because no one present knew both English and Japanese). Higher officials were wary. The Lord of Mito wrote: "It will be imprudent, in view of the times, to leave that man loose at pasture, but to make him too confined and ill at ease would reduce his usefulness. Treat generously, while guarding carefully. There was once a dragon tamed and domesticated that one day drove through wind and cloud in the midst of a hurricane and took flight. Once that man changed his mind and was taken away on an American ship it would be to repent too late." Another official cautioned: "I do not think that Manjiro has any thoughts of treason, but upon getting on board that ship, there is no telling what might happen. Considering the fact that Manjiro was taken to America by that foreigner, we do not know what method he might use in talking to the men on the ships." The Kanagawa Treaty, or Treaty of Peace and Amity, signed on March 31, 1854, opened two ports to U.S. trade and guaranteed the safety of shipwrecked seamen. Manjiro's only role in the negotiations was to translate documents. He met none of the American officials. He was, however, given the job of caring for the gifts that Perry left for the Japanese. These included a "quarter-sized locomotive, car, and tender, several miles of track and electric telegraph instruments with connecting wires"—all objects that Manjiro had described in his interrogations.[33]

Still in his twenties, Manjiro began to serve Japan outside politics and diplomacy. He translated one of the books he had used at Bartlett's school: Nathaniel Bowditch's *New American Practical Navigator*, an essential reference first published in 1802 and still consulted. He later said that the work "tried his patience, and made him grow old by about three years faster than he should." He completed it in 1857 and became a professor of navigation at the Naval Training School. Two years later, he wrote the first textbook for Japanese students of English.[34]

In 1858 the United States and Japan signed a commercial treaty, and Japanese officials traveled to Washington. Manjiro served as the official translator for the mission, returning to the United States aboard the *Kanrin-maru*, the first Japanese ship to cross the Pacific. He reveled in being at sea again. One of the U.S. Navy officers on board wrote in his journal: "Old Manjiro was up nearly all night. He enjoys the life, it reminds him of old times. I was amused last night, heard him telling a story . . . which he followed with a song."[35] In San Francisco, Manjiro acquired a sewing machine for his mother and the equipment needed to produce daguerreotypes "for the purpose of taking the likeness of his mother; 'and when that is done,' he said, 'it will be useless!'" In fact, the first likeness he took was that of his wife. And far from being useless, the equipment aroused so much interest that he developed a photography business that he eventually turned over to a friend.[36]

The *Kanrin-maru* stopped in Honolulu on the return voyage, and Manjiro spent some time with Father Damon and told him about his interrogation, his career, and his family, noting that he had "been very often consulted respecting questions relating to Americans and foreigners." He invited Damon to visit the *Kanrin-maru*, where he introduced him to the Japanese officers. Damon's "surprise and astonishment were great when Captain Manjiro presented us a translation of Bowditch's great American work upon Navigation"—a book that then existed only in twenty hand-written copies. Damon gave Manjiro a bound volume of *The Friend* for 1852–1859. Manjiro also left a letter and gift for Damon to send to Captain Whitfield. He told his old friend, "Capt. you must not send your boys

to the whaling business"—excellent advice in 1860. "You must send them
to Japan, I will take care of him or them if you will . . . I wish for you to
come to Japan. I will now lead my Dear Friend to my house, now the port
open to all nations . . . I will send to you suit of my clothes. It is not new,
but only for remember me."[37] In an accompanying letter, Damon told
Whitfield more about his conversations with Manjiro: "He is placed in a
position where he is constantly watched, in other words, there are 'many
eyes in Japan,' so he says. The reason why he had not written us is that he
could not get his letters out of the country."[38]

In 1868 the Meiji Restoration brought the Japanese emperor back to
the throne, and Manjiro lost his government position. Instead, he was
appointed to a professorship at Kaisei School (which became Tokyo University in 1877). Nevertheless, he still played a role in foreign policy. In
1870 he was attached to a mission to Europe that sailed to San Francisco
and then traveled to New York by train. Before leaving for the transatlantic
voyage, Manjiro took a detour to Fairhaven. He walked across the draw-
bridge that he had drawn in the record of his interrogation (recently rebuilt
after a destructive hurricane) and found Captain Whitfield still living on
the Sconticut Neck farm. He visited with his teacher, Jane Allen, and his
classmate Job Tripp. He spent the night in his second home.[39]

Manjiro became ill in Europe and returned early to Japan. He had a
mild stroke and retired. In 1884 Father Damon visited him: "We found
our friend the father of a most promising family . . . He is now about sixty
years of age, but not possessed of a great amount of this world's goods,
being dependent upon his sons for his support. We most sincerely wish the
Japanese government might honor itself, by honoring its old and faithful
servant with a liberal pension." Manjiro was living with his oldest son, Dr.
Toichiro Nakahama, in 1898 when he had a brain hemorrhage. He died
at the age of seventy-one. After his death, the Japanese acknowledged his
contributions more openly, beginning with a children's book about him
published in 1900.[40]

Home Is Where . . .

Though Manjiro was grateful to his Fairhaven friends, the town was not his
home. He had lived there only briefly, and his energies were soon focused
on returning to Japan, no matter how risky an undertaking that might

be. Like most castaways, he did manage to return. But he had changed, and Japan was changing. He was no longer a poor, illiterate fisherman in a small village. He was an English-speaking world traveler, with a knowledge of the United States and western technology shared by none of his countrymen, elevated to the rank of samurai. And Japan was connecting more closely to the western world, albeit reluctantly. The home he found there was not the one he had left, and—beyond his family circle—it was not completely welcoming.

During the debate over Manjiro's role in the negotiations with Perry, a Mito clan official expressed the government's ambivalence: "As for Manjiro, I guess you trust him. I cannot help but admire someone who loved his homeland so much that he came back. I wonder, however, if that American barbarian educated Manjiro as part of a scheme. After all, he must have realized that Manjiro was young and impressionable . . . I wonder if his goodness was sincere or if he was patronizing and calculating. Manjiro's life was saved by him, so Manjiro will not do anything harmful for America. Even though you trust him, his meeting with the Americans on the ship should be reconsidered." Manjiro was a loyal subject, but he was too worldly to accept the government's views unquestioningly, and he sometimes spoke his mind. He was never trusted: "constantly watched" and placed in positions where he had little influence. Samurai who did not want ports opened to American ships regarded Manjiro as a traitor and threatened him. One historian notes that "the shogunate regularly provided body guards for Manjiro, who carried a six-shot revolver, and he barely escaped several assassination attempts and attacks on his house." In Japan, as in Fairhaven, he was in many ways an outsider.[41]

After his death, Manjiro's two families and two homes connected. Manjiro's and Whitfield's sons, Toichiro and Marcellus, corresponded, and in 1898 the Whitfields were invited to Philadelphia to attend a reception on the newly built Japanese cruiser *Kosagi,* whose paymaster was another of Manjiro's sons, Keizaburo Nakahama.[42] The United States and Japan, too, became more closely connected. Japan had joined Great Britain, France, and Russia in the war against Germany in 1914; the United States joined the effort in 1917.

Soldiers from both nations were still at war on July 4, 1918, when ten thousand people gathered at the Fairhaven High School stadium for a remarkable ceremony. According to a local account:

The whole town, in fact, was in gala attire. American and Japanese flags and bunting were to be seen on every hand. The town hall, the library, the churches, as well as the stores and blocks in the business section were liberally adorned with bunting, and for the whole length of Washington Street from the Mattapoisett line and continuing across the Fairhaven–New Bedford bridge, banners were displayed from wires stretched across the street at intervals. At the Rogers' Memorial Monument at the end of the bridge, Japanese and American flags were placed at each corner of the shaft. Many homes displayed flags of both nations.[43]

The occasion was the presentation of a samurai sword, the gift of Manjiro's oldest son, Dr. Toichiro Nakahama, to the people of Fairhaven. Viscount Ishii, Japan's ambassador to the United States, presented the sword, and Captain Whitfield's grandson Thomas—now a Fairhaven selectman—accepted it on behalf of the town. Two of Manjiro's schoolmates joined the dignitaries on the platform, and one recalled that Manjiro had hung a May basket for her and written her a poem. The speakers retold the story of the rescue and of Manjiro's life in Fairhaven and in Japan, and the sword was placed in the library on permanent display.[44] In February 1920 the library received another gift from Japan: a copy of Manjiro's four-volume manuscript account of his adventures, bound in silk.[45] More recently, a Japanese theater company presented "John Manjiro's Dream," a musical.[46] Whatever doubts the Japanese government may have had about Manjiro during his lifetime, his posthumous reputation was secure.

Five generations of the Whitfield and Nakahama families have corresponded and exchanged visits. Manjiro's grandson Kiyoshi, who had visited Fairhaven on a tour of New England colleges, attended Brown University. In 1924 his father—the donor of the samurai sword—visited his son and stayed with the Whitfields at 11 Cherry Street.[47] Their communication was interrupted in December 1941, with the declaration of war between the United States and Japan. The families of some Fairhaven servicemen in the Pacific theater objected to the display of the samurai sword and Manjiro's portrait, and the Select Board asked the trustees of the library to remove them. The portrait was put into storage, but the trustees felt that "the removal of the sword was a foolish idea, as it had nothing to do with the present war lords of Japan." The next day the trustees wrote to the Select Board: "Since Pearl Harbor the public criticism . . . has been too meager to merit notion. In the opinion of the Trustees the removal of the sword is uncalled for." It remained in place.[48]

After the war, Japanese officials began again to travel to Fairhaven, visiting Captain Whitfield's grave and former home. Eventually the town became a destination for Japanese tourists. In 1987 officials from Tosashimizu, in southern Japan, came to Fairhaven to arrange for the towns to become sister cities. The relationship was celebrated that October by a visit from Crown Prince Akihito and Princess Michiko, who began their tour at the Whitfield home and viewed the one-room school, the stadium where the sword ceremony had taken place, the library, and the town hall. The crown prince gave the town a collection of prints, and the library presented the visitors with a painting of Manjiro, Captain Whitfield, and the *John Howland*. Finally, a delegation from Fairhaven visited Japan to sign the sister city agreement.[49]

Manjiro Nakahama is celebrated in both Fairhaven and Japan, with visitors from each country traveling to the other, and with an annual fall festival alternating between Tosashimizu and Fairhaven. In 2008 Dr. Shigeaki Hinohara, a Japanese physician and philanthropist, raised money to buy and restore Captain Whitfield's home at 11 Cherry Street. A year later, one hundred donors came from Japan to dedicate the Whitfield-Manjiro Friendship House. The house was Dr. Hinohara's gift to the town of Fairhaven, with the sole condition that it be operated as a museum and cultural center. Cherry trees from Japan have been planted in a nearby park, and when they bloom in May a Cherry Blossom Festival held by the Whitfield-Manjiro Friendship Society includes exhibitions of kimonos and Japanese drumming.[50]

The house at 11 Cherry Street is a symbol, rather than a home. Manjiro and Captain Whitfield spent far less time there than they did at sea or at the Sconticut Neck farm. Later generations of Whitfield's family did live there, and later generations of Manjiro's family visited. It is a physical manifestation of the connection between two families and two communities. Manjiro, never truly at home in Fairhaven or Japan, is now revered in a house shared by both.

8

The Biggest House in Town

109 GREEN STREET

The greatest glory of a building is not in its stones, nor in its gold. Its glory is in its age, and in that deep sense of voicefulness, of stern watching, of mysterious sympathy, . . . which we feel in walls that have long been washed by the passing waves of humanity.

—JOHN RUSKIN

The brick house at the corner of Green and Center Streets was built by Nathan Church, said to be the wealthiest man in Fairhaven, in 1840, at a cost of $22,000. He had accumulated his fortune as the owner and agent for a number of whaleships. Building in brick was ostentatious in a town of clapboard and shingles, and Nathan and his son were said to have "examined every brick which went into the construction." It is a large, imposing building, set high above the street, but the exterior is not showy. It retains the symmetry of Federal architecture ornamented with columns of the Greek Revival style. The three-story house sat on a large lot, some of which has since been sold, in the very center of town. With high ceilings and large rooms—six bedrooms, two parlors, a formal dining room, and servants' quarters—it was designed to impress. Both back and front staircases are graceful. Carved columns decorate the parlor, and the cornices are elaborate. Anterooms and alcoves make the house especially charming. Church died in 1859, and six years later the building was sold to David M. Hammond for only $10,000. Hammond died a year later, and in 1867

George F. Tripp, president of the National Bank of Fairhaven, bought it for $6,500.[1]

The house seems to have exerted an unusual attraction on bankers. In 1879 Walter Pellington Winsor bought 109 Green Street—a bargain at $4,000. Winsor was not the wealthiest man in Fairhaven (Henry Rogers had no competition for that title), but he probably ranked second. The son of Captain Alexander Winsor, he had grown up in the other brick house in the town center. He began his banking career in 1864 at the First National Bank of New Bedford and spent the years from 1866 to 1874 advancing to secretary and treasurer of the Union Mutual Marine Insurance Company. In June 1874 he became cashier of the First National Bank of New Bedford and in 1891 became its president. Additional wealth came from his association with his boyhood friend, Rogers. Winsor was a director of Rogers' Virginia Railway Company, vice president of the Atlas Tack Company, and treasurer of both the Fairhaven Water Company and the Millicent Library. He was also a director of the Union Street Railway Company and Wamsutta Mills. Winsor's wife, Mary, often carried out Rogers' charitable activities in town, and Rogers chose Winsor to be an executor of his estate. According to town tradition, Rogers used to sit in the wing added to the Center Street side in 1890 to watch the construction of the Memorial Church diagonally across the intersection.[2]

Winsor altered the house dramatically. The entrance had been on the south side, on Center Street, with a porte-cochère. He reoriented the building so that the entrance was on Green Street, requiring changes to the interior. "By a partition through the formerly large parlor two smaller rooms are obtained in the east side and the former will be used as a dining room," the *Fairhaven Star* reported. "Nearly throughout the lower story partitions have been taken down and re-erected, new doors put in, etc. the fireplaces rebuilt in modern style and the general interior rearranged. A bathroom and a watercloset will be fitted up in the second story." He had parquet floors installed over the heart-of-pine boards.[3]

Reorienting the house had made it possible to remove the entryway stairs and porte-cochère, leaving room to build a conservatory. Here Winsor could enjoy his avocation of horticulture, which had interested him since he was a boy. He later built detached greenhouses as well. In 1892 he hired Peter Murray as his gardener. Murray had emigrated from Scotland to Boston in 1888 and had held positions in Dedham, Massachusetts, and

Portsmouth, New Hampshire. Under Murray, Winsor's greenhouses won numerous prizes. When the greenhouses opened to the public for a week each year, they received hundreds of visitors. They were best known for dahlias and orchids until Murray developed a carnation called the Winsor Pink in the early 1900s. In 1905 Winsor gave up his greenhouses, and Murray turned them into a commercial venture. Six years later, the Winsor Pink became internationally famous when Princess Mary of England chose it as her coronation flower.[4]

The house itself, the wealth of its owners, and the added touch of a royal connection must have made it irresistible to Barney Zeitz, an immigrant entrepreneur from across the harbor seeking to showcase his success.

Coming to America

The Zeitz family was part of the first great wave of Jewish migration to the United States from Russia and Poland. Anti-Jewish government policies had long made life in Russia extremely difficult. Jews were restricted to living in the "Pale of Settlement" and could not own land. Boys as young as eight or nine were subject to conscription into the tsarist army for twenty-five years. Anti-Semitism was rampant among Russians, and violence took the form of pogroms, organized massacres. Tsar Alexander II, who succeeded to the throne in 1855, eased the plight of Russian Jews somewhat, reducing the period of conscription to five years, loosening travel restrictions, and allowing Jews to attend universities. But when he was assassinated in 1881, popular sentiment against Jews rose almost immediately, and Alexander III restored earlier harsh policies. A mass migration began. Between 1881 and the beginning of World War I, fully a third of the Jews living in the Pale of Settlement had left. It took desperation, courage, and money to leave. Russia provided the desperation, but the emigrants had to find the courage and funds to get to western Europe—usually Germany—and onto a transatlantic ship. Then, as now, human traffickers and con men preyed on those seeking passage to a new home. Those who were able to board the ships traveled in steerage, in appalling conditions. Their goal was economic and religious freedom, and a remarkable number of people were willing to risk the dangers.[5]

Exactly when and how Barney, his brother Phillip, and his parents, Kopel and Fanny, came to the United States remains a mystery. They traveled between 1883 and 1885, soon after Barney's birth. (Indeed, one account says that he was born at sea.) Fanny and Kopel were in their early twenties. Most European immigrants entered the United States at the port of New York, but the Zeitz family arrived in Galveston, Texas. Galveston had a small Jewish community dating back to the Civil War; by 1900, 3.5 percent of Galveston's white population was Jewish. According to family lore, Kopel became a peddler. A third son, Meyer (later known as Charles), was born in Galveston in 1886. Soon after his birth, the family moved to New Bedford, where five more children were born: Harry (1887), Jacob Frank (1888), Isaac Morton (1895), Annie (1898), and Fisher (1900). One historian's generalization about the immigrant families of this era probably held true for the Zeitzes: "The young age at marriage for both spouses, the disruptive migration to America, and the steady stream of American-born children that usually followed, meant that financial insecurity would persist."[6]

We can't be sure why the Zeitzes chose New Bedford, but it was likely because of family ties. Two of Fannie's relatives—Philip and Samuel Genensky—had established themselves there by 1888 and were active in the growing Jewish community.[7] In New Bedford, Kopel worked hard to support his family. He began in a new field: the manufacture and bottling of soda and mineral water. The recent invention of metal bottle caps with crimped edges and the development of inexpensive bottles strong enough to withstand the pressure of carbonated water had created the industry. Kopel worked for the New Bedford Bottling Company, located at 32 Morton Court. The sons went to work as soon as they could, Barney as a clerk and Philip as a machinist. But in 1904 Kopel could no longer face his difficulties. He ended his life by shooting himself in the head. His oldest sons were in their teens or early twenties; the youngest was four.[8] The brothers launched a string of enterprises to support the family.

In 1905 Jacob and Philip started the Zeitz Brothers Bottling Company at 50 Howland Street, where they lived with their widowed mother. Barney had gone into the junk business a few doors up the street. By 1907 the brothers owned both their own bottling company and the New Bedford Bottling Company, where they and their father had been employed. Charles was working in the junk business on Front Street. In 1909 Philip added a pawn brokerage on Union Street to the bottling business, and Barney, Harry, and Jacob joined him the next year. In 1911 they expanded the pawn brokerage to another storefront, at 121 Union, with Harry and Isaac

Morton listed as salesmen. By then the family was living at 225 Acushnet Avenue in a building they owned.[9]

In 1912 Barney started another business—one that was to generate the family's fortune. At 90 Union Street, where one of the pawnshops operated, he opened a hardware store that he later moved to 132–34 Union Street, adding a branch at 767 Purchase Street in 1916. Part of Barney's hardware business involved buying used equipment from bottling companies, manufacturing plants, and other businesses, and either selling it for scrap or repairing and reselling it. He began advertising in the *American Bottler* magazine in 1915: "Wanted: Second-hand soda water machinery, all makes and styles; please write description, stating lowest cash price." He also bought and sold used and wrecked cars and salvaged boats. In 1917 he added the name "Mercantile Wrecking Company" to the hardware business. City directories sometimes listed him as being in the junk business; he preferred to describe it as "metal." It could also have been listed as "salvage." The most accurate description of his business was his own: "My business is to take an enterprise and make a success of it that 99 out of 100 would classify it as a failure . . . I buy and sell; yes, sir; practically anything that there is a dollar to be made in it."[10]

The Wreck of the *Port Hunter*

On November 2, 1918, the *Port Hunter*, a freighter carrying supplies to American forces in France, was nearing the western entrance to Nantucket Sound. A tugboat was entering the sound from the opposite direction, towing two coal barges. At about quarter to two in the morning, the two ships collided, opening a huge hole in the freighter. Water flooded the forward compartment, and the *Port Hunter* began to sink. The tugboat's skipper pushed the freighter onto a shoal so that it would not sink in deep water, and boats rescued the crew. In two hours the *Port Hunter* had sunk to the bottom, leaving only a small part of the ship above water.[11]

The cargo—clothing, railroad parts, steel, lead, ammunition, motorcycles, machine guns, phosphorus bombs, and trucks—was worth $5 million. It was government property and should have been recovered immediately, but for some reason the U.S. Navy took no action. As a Vineyard Haven resident recalled, the ship became instead "quite a source of revenue for a lot of families in town":

One of the hatch covers apparently came loose and the cargo began to float around. That's when we got the word that the cargo boxes were coming ashore on the north side of the Island. So a bunch of us boys headed down toward the Herring Creek . . . and sure enough, there were all sorts of things coming ashore in boxes . . . For a time there was "finders keepers," and fishermen were bringing leather jerkins into the town wharf, and selling them right off the boats for a dollar apiece . . . And they were bringing those things in by the hundreds . . . That brought all the merchants from New Bedford here.[12]

Of course, Barney Zeitz was one of those merchants. During a congressional investigation of the incident, however, he testified that he did not buy anything. "I read some of the notices—that is the main thing that interested me—posted, not to touch any of the merchandise . . . they said an ensign or lieutenant situated right in the island at Vineyard Haven put them up there . . . I came down with the intention of buying merchandise from the islanders, and when I read that notice I didn't buy any." Instead, Barney sent a telegram to Brigadier General Frank T. Hines of the Quartermaster Corps urging that a guard be set on the *Port Hunter,* a measure that was taken belatedly at the beginning of January. This wasn't selfless patriotism: he was hoping to salvage the cargo legally, with exclusive rights. Those hopes were dashed by the news that the contract had been awarded to someone else. But weeks passed, and no salvage operations were visible.[13]

Barney learned that the job was being rebid on an emergency basis, so he got in touch with Colonel A. W. Yates, the Quartermaster Corps officer in charge of the project. When Yates asked him how soon he could start, he said "in five minutes' time." There was one small problem: the navy required a $200,000 bond, and Barney had only $50,000. But he convinced Yates to let him do the job: "I told him I could raise an equipment ten times better than the competing concern that was lying there with Noah's ark . . . I exaggerated with him. I tell you frankly I was trying hard to get it. I lost all hopes when the other concern got it. I had spoken to people who are well versed in this business and who could aid me in a hundred different ways in working this thing. They were all ready to go at a moment's notice. I exaggerated considerably. I will admit that."[14]

Col. Yates gave him the benefit of the doubt. Barney asked if he "could put up this $50,000 and let me work a few days to see if I could really accomplish as good as any other concern could," and Yates agreed. Barney always said the contract was "awarded . . . I wouldn't say given, because I worked very hard for this."[15] The Mercantile Wrecking Company started the project almost immediately. Barney was in over his head. He had never taken on a job so big—or a ship so big. He was used to salvaging pleasure boats and fishing boats, not freighters. And he had always been interested only in the vessels themselves, not in their cargo. This was a huge project. A Vineyard Haven resident recalled:

> This Barney Zeitz, he hired the sanitary laundry in Oak Bluffs, run by Mr. Nichols, and he employed quite a few people there, all fifty or so people, to launder these things. They'd been in salt water of course and they were washed, and they were pressed and packaged and sold to mainland buyers. They would hang these out to dry in the yard by the laundry. There's a fence around the area, almost like a chain link fence. In the evening, why, men on the outside of the fence would come equipped with fish lines and poles and throw the line over the fence and hook out a few leather vests.[16]

Despite bad weather and thieving locals, Barney pulled a team together, got the job done, and collected the money. His contract with the navy provided for him to get 50 percent of the appraised value or sale price of the salvaged goods.[17]

It is difficult to determine how much profit Barney netted from this project. The cargo was worth $5 million, but much of it—including the railroad parts and other heavy equipment—was not part of the contract. And a lot of the clothing that was Barney's main object had vanished during the three months that passed before he was contracted to do the job. At the congressional hearing investigating the navy's poor performance in salvaging the cargo, he said he had gotten $639,000, but a large percentage of that would have gone to the investors who had put up money to cover expenses. He refused to discuss his costs at the hearing because he had not yet settled with those investors. It is generally believed that he walked away from the project with between $200,000 and $300,000—enough to start him and his brothers on a new, profitable, and glamorous path to prosperity.[18]

Crossing the Harbor

Until the *Port Hunter* salvage operation, most of the Zeitz family lived in New Bedford. (Meyer did not live with them. He had joined the army under the name Charles Coleman and was stationed in New Jersey at the time of his death in 1926.) Philip lived above his clothing store on South Water Street until his death in 1910, but Fannie and the other six children lived together. In 1911 they had moved to 225 Acushnet Avenue, which remained the family headquarters for a decade.[19] But as soon as they could afford to do so, the family moved across the harbor to Fairhaven. They bought two large bungalows on Huttleston Avenue, one for Fannie and the other for Harry, who had married Cecile Bornstein, the daughter of a wealthy Boston shoe manufacturer. Harry, Cecile, and their three children lived there until 1932.[20] And in 1924 Barney bought 109 Green Street, which became the family home. Fannie stayed on Huttleston Avenue until the late 1920s, when she moved in with Barney. The unmarried brothers—Jacob Frank, Fisher, and Isaac Morton—were already living there, along with Annie and her husband, George Helford, and their daughter Ruby. They made some changes to the house, including a dumbwaiter that ran from the butler's pantry to Annie's second-floor sitting room. Ruby recalled riding up and down in it. Either the Winsors or the Zeitzes added a bathroom to the first floor, three more to the second (one with a china tub), and one to the third. They undoubtedly undertook a great deal of redecorating.[21]

In some ways, the move was puzzling. The Zeitzes were (to varying degrees) observant Jews, and although New Bedford had synagogues and a vibrant Jewish community in which they participated, Fairhaven did not. Their many business interests were centered in New Bedford. But the towns are only a bridge apart, and there may have been some cachet in being on the east side of the harbor. Certainly living at 109 Green Street sent a clear message that the Zeitzes had arrived. Just in case that message wasn't clear enough, in 1926 the brothers bought another property two blocks from the house: the Tabitha Inn, the luxurious small hotel built by Henry Huttleston Rogers. Some people in town disliked having the property fall into the hands of an outsider, and there may have been a touch of anti-Semitism in the frequent descriptions of the property being "commercialized" by its new owners.[22] In fact, there is little to suggest that the inn changed very much when the Zeitzes bought it. But the Tabitha Inn was a minor investment compared to the empire the brothers were building in New Bedford.

Alfred Hitchcock Plays a Cameo Role

In 1922 the brothers created the Zeiterion Realty Corporation. Throughout the 1920s and '30s, they acquired rental properties and added new businesses, including a "private bank" that made numerous loans. The profits from the *Port Hunter* enabled them to borrow additional money for these enterprises, and their habit of prompt repayment pleased the banks. Even during the Great Depression, they prospered. With cash in hand and good credit, they were able to buy property at bargain prices. Their most visible efforts were focused on theaters. The Zeiterion Realty Corporation bought a site at Purchase and Spring Streets that had been a factory but most recently had been used as an automobile dealership. They razed the building and broke ground on March 14, 1922, for their flagship property, the Zeiterion Theater, which was to showcase vaudeville and other live shows. Built at a cost of $800,000, it was large (seating more than twelve hundred people) and elaborate.[23]

This was the era of movie palaces. Even before "talking pictures" were made, entrepreneurs in cities across the country—many of them European immigrants—were building theaters on a grand scale. In New York, Samuel Lionel Rothapfel (known by the nickname Roxy) built the Rialto, Strand, Regent, Rivoli, and the grandest of them all, the Roxy—a name that became synonymous with splendid showplaces. In Los Angeles, Sidney Patrick Grauman built his Egyptian and Chinese theaters—exotic fantasy buildings. Architects specializing in theaters became well known and much sought after. Many of these theaters were enormous, seating more than five thousand people, with balconies, orchestra pits, lavish washrooms, and wide corridors lined with original art. The Zeiterion was on a smaller scale, but otherwise it fit right into the theatrical spirit of its times.[24]

Theaters of the era can be divided architecturally into two types: the classical, modeled on European palaces and opera houses, and the "open air," designed to give theatergoers the illusion that they were under an open sky. The Zeiterion is a classical theater. The outside of the building is tapestry brick with white terra-cotta trim, two stories tall. When built, it had a large, impressive marquee sheltering its well-dressed patrons from the elements and separating it from the streetscape with bright lights and colorful posters.

But the interior is what impresses. As one theater historian observes, "Anyone with a little loose change might dwell in marble halls for a couple of hours. And the keener the competition among owners and builders, as more theatres arose, the more *marble* the halls became."[25] Obeying this rule, the Zeiterion lobby—an "antechamber designed to keep our minds off the fact that we are waiting"—is supported by marble columns. Thomas Lamb, the leading architect of the classical school, argued that "to make our audience receptive and interested, we must cut them off from the rest of city life and take them into a rich and self-contained auditorium, where their minds are freed from their usual occupations and freed from their customary thoughts."[26] Accordingly, the walls of the theater's auditorium are covered in silk tapestry ornamented with a frieze of dancing figures in classical style, in gold leaf. The original seats were leather. The ceiling is paneled and painted, including an oval scene of a sunset, and it is lit by an enormous cut-glass chandelier imported from Czechoslovakia at a cost of $7,000. The colors are ivory and rose. Like other theaters of its time, it has a Wurlitzer organ—used, along with a pit orchestra, for showing silent films. And both inside and outside, an ornate giant Z painted in gold on dark red announces its ownership, just as Roxy's R did in his New York theaters. The design accomplished its purpose; according to a recent chronicler, "The uncommon elegance and beauty of the theater knocked New Bedford on its ear."[27]

The philosophy behind these palaces must have appealed to Barney Zeitz and the other successful immigrants in the movie business, from the owners of small-town theaters to the emerging Hollywood moguls. These were palaces that replicated the homes of the wealthy but were open to all, "a shrine to democracy where the wealthy rub elbows with the poor," in the words of the architect George Rapp, who designed hundreds of movie theaters; a place where "the public can partake of the same luxuries as the rich," as Harold Rambusch, a decorator best known for his work on the Roxy, put it.[28]

Many movie theaters began life as venues for live theater and vaudeville. The first show at the Zeiterion was a musical revue, *Troubles of 1922*, starring George Jessel and featuring a monologue that became his trademark: phone conversations with his invisible mother. In his history of New Bedford's downtown, Carmen Maiocco writes: "Every seat, over a thousand of them, was filled on opening night. The theater was packed again shortly thereafter, when the film star Rudolph Valentino and his wife Natasha came to town to dance the tango. The women of New Bedford came in droves, ignoring warnings from their priests and pastors to avoid such sinful spectacles." But vaudeville's popularity declined, and the theater closed briefly in the summer of 1923. It reopened in September as the State Theater, showing silent movies, beginning with the New England premiere of D. W. Griffith's *The White Rose*, a melodrama starring Mae Marsh and Ivor Novello. In 1927 it showed *Down to the Sea in Ships*, which had been filmed in New Bedford, Dartmouth, and Fairhaven. (The film had premiered at the nearby Olympia.) In 1949 the State Theater premiered the talking version.[29]

In 1926 the brothers bought the New Bedford Theater on Union Street, which had been showing silent films since 1914. The theater was built in 1896, and Maiocco notes that "around the turn of the century on Union Street, evening gowns and tuxedoes were the order of the day, as the city's gentry packed the house to see the likes of Lionel Barrymore and other theatrical stars of the era." Barney and his brothers would have seen the "gentry" parading on the same street as their hardware store, perhaps lending some extra pleasure to buying a potential moneymaker. The New Bedford Theater was three stories high, with two balconies, a grand marquee, and an adjoining ice cream parlor. In 1926 this theater was the first in the city to show talking pictures. "When Al Jolson belted out 'Mammy' in *The Jazz Singer*, it was standing room only." Within a year, "talkies" had taken over the market.[30]

It was expensive to convert a theater to sound: one historian estimates that "it cost upward of $10,000 to equip a modest-size theatre with the Western Electric system, plus Vitaphone and Movietone modifications to projectors, running another $3,000." (Vitaphone and Movietone were two of the technologies for film with sound. Warner Brothers used Vitaphone, and RCA used another system, Photophone.) It was also somewhat risky because of these competing technologies and unsettled business models. But the Zeitz brothers invested in the soundproofing, acoustical alterations, and equipment for both their theaters, and in 1932 they added the Empire Theater, at Pleasant and Elm, to their chain. Eventually the family owned five theaters in the city plus the Academy Theater in Fall River, the Paramount in Newport, Rhode Island, and the Civic Theater in Portland, Maine.[31]

The Zeitz brothers. *Courtesy of Jeff Dawson / Spinner Publications.*

The movie business was highly competitive, among both the studios and the local theaters. Eventually, the big Hollywood studios organized their own chains of theaters through exclusive contracts, but now they needed to promote their films and court theater owners. Harry, the president of the family's theaters, was invited to world premieres, visited Hollywood, and selected the films to be shown. In November 1925 Harry attended the Stage and Screen Ball at the Hotel Astor in New York, an event sponsored by Metro-Goldwyn-Mayer. Three years later, the *Fairhaven Star* reported that he again traveled to New York "to be present Wednesday night at the world premiere of the new Warner Bros. talking picture, *Glorious Betsy*, with Dolores Costello and Conrad Nagel, at the Warner Bros. Theatre."[32] The movie was based on the romance of Elizabeth Patterson (the daughter of an American shipping magnate) and Jérôme Bonaparte (the brother of Napoleon I), and included some talking sections within a silent film. Movie stars and directors visited local theaters, too, and a 1951 photograph shows three of the Zeitz brothers with Alfred Hitchcock, who was publicizing *Strangers on a Train*.[33] Harry's daughter, Elaine, was an aspiring dancer, and he introduced her to Hollywood visitors who could advance her career.[34] By far the showiest event was the 1956 world premiere of *Moby Dick*, held at the Zeitzes' State, Empire, and New Bedford Theaters. Gregory Peck and Friedrich von Ledebur, who played Queequeg, led a grand parade, waving from a Cadillac convertible owned by one of the brothers. Peck stayed at Harry and Cecile's house, and their grandson Barney remembers that the women in the family were thrilled.[35]

On his visit to New York in 1928, the *Star* reported, Harry also arranged "for the opening attraction of the Movietone [sound system], which is scheduled for Saturday, May 5, at the State." In 1931 Harry arranged for the State and New Bedford theaters to have "exclusive first-run showing of all the Radio and RKO-Pathe product" for ten years. He had already made a similar deal with Fox, Warner Brothers, and First National. Theaters competed not only for films but also for technology. The Zeitz theaters had an exclusive contract for Vitaphone in New Bedford, and when the owners of the Olympia Theater, then part of the Publix chain, used the term in advertising for the debut of their sound equipment, Harry asked Vitaphone to intervene.[36]

Living Large

The brothers worked hard, and they enjoyed their wealth. In 1932 Harry bought his own mansion, at 37 Taber Street in New Bedford. According to the *Star,*

> This house which was built about 10 years ago at a cost reported to have been about $70,000, including the land, is considered one of the finest homes in New Bedford . . . A two-car garage, sunken garden and a wide variety of trees and shrubbery . . . add to its attractiveness as a home, as well as three large tiled bathrooms and a half dozen fireplaces. The house measures about 80 feet in length, including the breakfast porch at the east and the sun porch at the west end. Both within and without, the colonial type of architecture was followed in its construction and its well kept grounds have helped to make it one of the city's show places.

The unmarried brothers often joined Harry's family for dinner, and Harry's grandson remembers frequent Sunday dinners there.[37]

The family papers include receipts for many purchases of new cars, mostly Cadillacs. There are receipted bills from New Bedford's Wamsutta Club and for clothing bought at expensive New York shops (DePinna, Saks Fifth Avenue, Brooks Brothers). Winters were sometimes spent in Miami Beach, at the Vanderbilt Hotel or the Fontainebleau, and they visited the Moulin Rouge in Hollywood. A man who grew up across the street from 109 Green Street remembered hanging out of his bedroom window when he was a teenager to watch glamorous guests arriving for weekend house parties. Celebrities sailed up in large, fancy cars, the men dressed elegantly and the women scantily.[38]

But the next decades brought some sad changes to the family. Fannie died in 1930, and Annie died four years later after being ill only a few days. Her daughter, Ruby, was raised by her paternal grandmother. George Helford died in 1945, and Barney followed a year later, after a six-month illness. Jacob Frank died in 1953, and Fisher died in 1959, both after long illnesses. During World War II, the Tabitha Inn was taken over by the U.S. Navy, and Coast Guard cadets were billeted there. In 1944 it was sold to the Fall River Diocese and converted to a nursing home, Our Lady's Haven.[39]

After the Zeitzes

In 1960 the Zeitz family sold 109 Green Street to investors who turned it into the Center Green Rest Home. The new owners rendered the interior of the house unrecognizable. The dining room was turned into a waiting and smoking room. Six toilets and a utility sink were installed near the kitchen, which was redesigned for institutional cooking, with yellow Formica throughout and cabinets obscuring all but a small middle section of the windows. The parlors were divided by a corridor. The front parlor, painted pink, contained seven beds, each with a small chest of drawers and the sort of bell that used to be found on the front desks of hotels. The back parlor and the conservatory each had five more beds. Annie's sitting room became the hospital room for acutely ill residents; the rest of the second floor accommodated seventeen beds. Plywood partitions ran from floor to ceiling. The third floor provided quarters for the caretaker and his son. The butler's pantry became the area for drug storage. An enormous internal telephone system connected the rooms to a central nursing station. Holes were drilled through floors and ceilings to install a sprinkler system, and fire escapes were added to the outside. The original outer doors were replaced with steel.[40]

The convalescent home was run poorly and dishonestly. In 1992, according to the state's attorney general, the owner, Leonard Alfonso, was "indicted on two counts of larceny, 13 counts of filing false Medicaid claims, and 13 counts of perjury." He was convicted in 1993. The "Center Green Rest Home, Inc." was also indicted, and the state closed it down. Residents were hurriedly moved to other facilities—so hurriedly that clothing, personal possessions, photographs, bed linens, and even drugs were left behind. The house stood vacant for two years, and the pipes froze and burst, flooding everywhere.[41]

Salvation came in the form of Sharon Challingsworth and her husband, Daniel Georgianna, who were living with two of their sons in a small house on Sconticut Neck. They bought the building in 1996, when it had been vacant for several years. The house was a mess—a maze of plywood partitions and linoleum floors. They had to begin by undoing everything that the rest home owners had done. They did much of the tearing out themselves. One evening Dan had gone back to Sconticut Neck, and Sharon was looking at the damaged floor under a radiator. They had torn out layers of linoleum, so she was looking at Mr. Winsor's parquet, ruined by leaks of various fluids. She picked up a few loose strips of parquet and saw wood underneath. She picked up a few more and saw what looked like fine old wood flooring. She found she couldn't stop. The next morning, when Dan realized she hadn't come home, he returned to Green Street to find her surrounded by mountains of old parquet, sitting on a beautiful heart-of-pine floor. Removing partitions disclosed intact cornices and other details that had survived the institutional conversion. "For six months," Sharon said, "there were no fewer than seventeen people working on that house every day." When they moved in on August 1, there was no running water in the kitchen. The plumber said he'd have it up and running by Thanksgiving, and he barely made it. Sharon scouted out antique windows, appropriate doors to replace the institutional steel, and countless other architectural artifacts.[42]

After years of work, the house was its elegant self—architectural detail intact, floors refinished, plaster repaired and painted, plumbing, wiring, and heating all in working order. It was not the Church house, the Winsor house, or the Zeitz house, but the next stage in its evolution. And Sharon and Dan decided it was too big for them. In 2004 they sold the house to John and Vanessa Gralton, the present owners. The Graltons have furnished much of the house in antiques of the Victorian era. In a tribute to the first owner, they have hung reproductions of portraits of Nathan Church and his second wife, Sarah, in the hall.[43]

9

Homeward Bound

10 WILLIAM STREET

Then for America we will steer,
To see our wives and families dear,
When every man can take his glass
And drink success to his favorite lass
For we know we're homeward bound
Hurrah, we're homeward bound

—Traditional sea chanty

Most sailors love the sea, but they also love their homes and families. Alexander Winsor was a clipper ship captain, and he loved the sea—especially when he could cross it at great speed. But he also loved the home he owned at 10 William Street, a house that embodies the sharp line he drew between sea and land, career and home. Those two worlds came together only at the end of his career, when his second wife, Emily, sailed with him.

Born to Sail

Alexander, the oldest son of Captain Zenas and Lucinda Wadsworth Winsor of Duxbury, Massachusetts, grew up with six brothers and sisters in a large house that is now an inn. In 1824, when he was fourteen, he took his first voyage, sailing on a ship under his father's command.[1] Twelve years later he took command of the *Molo,* owned by Thatcher Magoun, a prominent builder and owner of ships whose business operated from Medford and Boston. As the *Molo* approached the port of Stockholm, Winsor turned the ship over to a local pilot, who ran her aground on Gotland Island. Although the pilot was legally responsible, Winsor feared that the loss of both ship and cargo on his first command would put an end to his career.[2] He reported the loss to Magoun and described the actions he had taken:

> Having since my misfortune been favoured with good weather we have succeeded in getting all the Iron out from betweendeck . . . and have commenced getting up the lower deck in order to get the Iron out of the lower hold . . .
>
> Mr. Ames the 1st officer of the unfortunate Ship Molo will on his arrival at Boston will visit you and render you all information possible respecting my misfortune and will also inform you correctly the courses and distances from the time of leaving Port Baltic up to the moment the Ship struck and after referring to the chart I think you will be satisfied that the Ship was steered on a proper course and that nothing but the error in the compasses can account for the dreadfull misfortune. The Pilot I had on board has been imployed as pilot in the Baltic fourteen years without ever meeting with any misfortune and has at all times steered the same courses . . . I hope and pray you will not think that the Ship could have been managed in any better manner.[3]

The "error in the compasses" was caused by the large cargo of iron the ship was carrying—a cargo that Winsor managed to salvage and sell. Magoun was sufficiently impressed that he continued to employ Winsor, giving him command of the *Timoleon*, a smaller vessel, in 1838.[4]

Before sailing on the *Timoleon*, Winsor established himself in Fairhaven. He was an eligible bachelor—successful in his career, handsome, and charming. In 1838 he married Sarah Pellington Allen, the daughter of Captain Silas Allen of Main Street, Fairhaven, and his English-born wife, Sarah Pellington. Soon after their marriage, the couple moved into the house at 10 William Street. In a village of shingle and clapboard, where many houses were designed and constructed by shipbuilders, it stands out dramatically. Its thick walls, built of irregular stone, are faced with brick on the street side. No designs of shells, fish, or anchors decorate it. It is three blocks from the harbor, and the wind that Winsor treasured when sailing is noticeable only if you see the trees blowing outside. You cannot see the harbor, even from the third-floor windows. The house would fit comfortably into a city neighborhood far from the ocean, and it evokes no thoughts of the sea.[5]

Although he began his sailing career at an early age, Winsor was well educated. His correspondence with Magoun demonstrates an understanding of international markets and canny business sense. At some point, he must have done a great deal of reading. Several of his journals and many of his letters survive, and they show a mastery of literary style and penmanship with only occasional grammatical and spelling errors. Winsor was also talented at drawing, and his journals are unusually beautiful. They are journals, rather than logs, and provide information about far more than latitude, longitude, weather, and passing ships. Winsor wrote about his passengers, his crews, and his pleasures and frustrations. Reading them tells us what he loved about the sea.

"We soon leave all the others astern"

More than anything else about sailing, Winsor loved speed. He was a skillful captain, and—rarely sleeping—he was always alert to opportunities to take advantage of wind and currents. He took great pride in outpacing other vessels, and he complained about ships too poorly designed to allow a rapid passage. His favorite ship seems to have been the *Flying Cloud,* whose command he assumed in 1859. When launched in 1851, the ship was lauded in newspapers: "The bow cuts the billows like a knife, and from the stern they glide away in smooth, graceful, and quiet ripples, so that the keel seems scarcely to have cloven the sea . . . She looks anxious to fly off, and as if she would go, if they would only untie her from the wharf." She had set records under other captains, including an 1854 voyage from New York to San Francisco in 89 days, 8 hours. In 1859 Winsor sailed her from New York to London in 18 days, setting a record that lasted well into the twentieth century. Traveling from London to Hong Kong in 1860, he wrote: "Beat the Robin Hood seven days on the passing—the smartest English ship in the China trade. She was laid on in London to run against the Flying Cloud & £400 bet that she would beat her. Other bets of £200 and 300 in her favor, but the Flying Cloud came in ahead." On the return voyage to London, on August 8, "we got the Typhoon in good earnest. I have been going to sea thirty-five years & never saw such a gale as this before. It has made the Flying Cloud look like a wreck. Still no ship could behave better."[6]

Winsor also took great pride in the *Herald of the Morning,* another record-setting ship, which he commanded on his last voyages. When the *Herald* was in San Francisco in 1868, Winsor wrote to the owner, Thatcher Magoun, "People say the Herald is in good order & a great many have been on board to look around & among others editors & reporters & this morning I saw they had mentioned the Ship in the papers. I inclose the *puff* although it may look like vanity in me to do so but thought it would be a satisfaction to you to know how others speak of your ships abroad."[7] When Winsor and the *Herald* returned to the city in November 1870, another "puff" appeared in the *San Francisco Bulletin*. It alludes to Winsor's explanation of the extended length of the voyage and to his wife's presence:

> Moored at Cowell's wharf, on the northern boundary of the city front, is the *Herald of the Morning*, by universal consent acknowledged to be the belle of the merchant marine. In every port which she has visited, this beautiful craft has called forth the encomiums of the patrons of marine architecture. It is not because of gaudy trimmings or recent construction that the vessel attracts notice; she is simply judged on her merits and remarkable state of preservation. The ship is now 16 years old, has been in constant use, and yet, under the command of Captain Windsor, she is lovelier to-day, in the estimation of both land-men and marine, than bran new ships. When lying in the stream she reminds one of the saucy, piratical crafts so essential to marine romances, and could readily be picked from a fleet of vessels by her jaunty, coquettish air. Her interior arrangements are admirable. Every bit of brass or copper is highly polished, and neatness and order characterize every department from stem to stern. The cabins are spacious, convenient, and tastefully furnished. The scrupulous cleanliness and brightness noticeable is only found where woman's refining influence is felt, hence the condition of the vessel may, to some extent, be accounted for. The comforts of Jack in the forecastle have not been neglected, and it is seldom that sailors find themselves in a more favorable vessel than the *Herald of the Morning*. The ship is owned in Boston by Messrs. Magoun & Son; she came from New York with an assorted cargo, consigned to George Howes & Co., making the passage in 147 days. During the passage she experienced a succession of heavy gales, and adverse winds, otherwise she would have made the trip with customary dispatch.[8]

No matter what ship he commanded, Winsor's competitive instincts came to the fore. He kept track of speed records and compared his ships' performance to them. In 1851 he was sailing the *Audubon* from New York to San Francisco and keeping a sharp eye out for other ships on the same route: "Came up with and passed Ship Robert Hooper of Portsmouth from

New York for San Francisco sailed about twelve days before us"; "A Bark in company bound South fared up in sight in the calm but whether she will out sail us or not remains to be proved. We have out sailed every vessel we have seen this passage so far"; "Spoke Ship Courier of New York from Richmond for San Francisco 53 days out & out sails the Audubon." When the *Gertrude* sprung multiple leaks, forcing the crew to heave the cargo overboard to lighten the ship, he noted that they were "making dreadful slow progress. Still we seem to get along a little better than some of our neighbors . . . She's a rum one to look at but a good one to go."[9]

Even when a voyage took so long that he felt compelled to apologize for the ship's performance, he compared himself to others: "It is an old saying that misery likes company so it makes me feel a little more comfortable to find that some other Ships have, & are still making longer passages than we did." On another slow crossing, he pointed out that "I never could make a Ship go in a calm . . . but when she *could* go I have kept her up to her work . . . she run from 50o S to the equator (in the Pacific) in sixteen days. It has never been done in less time & only twice in the same time."[10]

His harshest words were reserved for ships that couldn't keep up the pace. Winsor wrote that he was "never was more disappointed in a ship in regard to her sailing qualities than I am in this one," the *Hussar,* which "cannot go fast loaded." "A ship came up & passed us & it does not require an extra smart one to do so." The *Sea Nymph,* which he commanded in 1857 on a voyage from New York to Melbourne, was "anything but a fast sailer." She was also uncomfortable: "Ship is continually rolling both rails under & the water rolling athwart the deck. She is the worst ship I ever had my foot in & I wish I was out of her. I would not make another voyage in her for the price of her."[11]

Of course, speed depends on weather as well, and bad weather was a constant source of complaint. Heavy rain was "trying weather to sails & ropes as well as to my feelings." In 1851, sailing from Valparaiso to San Francisco, Winsor wondered, "How I am ever going to get this Ship eight degrees to the north against such a wind as we have had the last three or four days I know not. I shall die with old age before I accomplish it. We have got some small children on board. They may live long enough to S. Francisco." From San Francisco to Manila, constant rains made it "impossible for me to gain a mile," and without sun for several days he was not sure of his location. Heavy rain also hampered visibility and "causes me much anxiety while running the ship without an observation among these rocks & shoals but such are the comforts of a sea life." A few days later, a single line in the journal reads: "Calms ~ Calms ~ Calms."[12]

Bad weather and slow sailing affected Winsor's mood. His second wife, Emily, sailing with him to San Francisco in 1868, wrote: "The North East Trade wind left us and we are in what is called the Doldrums (that come between the NE & SE Trades). They last about five days and are sudden rains showers not much wind. Capt got the Doldrums because we were not getting ahead any." Winsor often took bad weather personally. About halfway between Calcutta and New Bedford, he remarked, "I suppose this is the first & only time that ever calms & NW winds was known here. I dare say this is for my special benefit."[13] On a later voyage, he became defensive in explaining delays to the ship's owner:

> It is generally considered by those that reside on the land, & have a good warm home to go to, where it comes on cold, & stormy that a long or short passage is always optional with the poor D—l in command, and wholly depends on the amount of ambition, energy, or activity he may be blessed with, without ever taking into consideration that it is possible for him to meet with any obstacles too great for him to overcome by a proper amount or display of the above mentioned qualities. Hence, it is useless for me to try to exonerate myself, or offer any excuse for this remarkably long passage, but will endeavor to give you a brief account of the winds, weather, & other troubles I have had to contend with then you can judge for yourself . . .
>
> I feel very like letting go the anchor & giving it up for it seems to me there never was such a time as we are having since the children of Isriel passed through the Red Sea.[14]

Yet when his own judgment caused problems, he quickly took responsibility: "Strong squalls from WNW. During one of them the fore topsail split & went all to pieces. Fair play, I was a little to anxious to get what distance I could out of it. I kept the sail on to long. However mistakes sometimes happen in the best regulated families. We soon got up another and went on again."[15]

Sailing near both the equator and the South Pole meant suffering extremes of heat and cold. En route to Canton, Winsor found the November heat "enough to kill aligaters": "The decks are so hot that it makes my feet very uncomfortable walking about with stockings & shoes on." He soon had to reduce the allowance of water to three and then two quarts a day. "On deck in the shade thermometer stands at 100 most part of the day. Rather warm for two quarts of water. I could drink that quantity this moment." Between Singapore and Calcutta, "Sun is pouring down & the perspiration rolling down my face & my heart beating like a pendulum to an eight day wooden clock. These is times that tries mens souls." Near Cape Horn, though, he and his passengers had the opposite problem: "I am obliged to go into my bed to warm my feet. All the passengers sitting around the cabin with their Scarfs & shawls on & cannot even then keep comfortable . . . Saw the Sun for a rarity!" A week later he "ventured to shed my jacket, one pair of stockings & mittens & have with some exercise managed to keep quite comfortable."[16]

Weather and other natural phenomena could also be a source of pleasure. Winsor often commented on the presence of the sun, and he enjoyed warm breezes not only because they moved the ship along. He observed wildlife closely: "a shoal of Porpoises came playing under the bow being a different kind from those seen in the North Atlantic Ocean having white noses & no fin on the back. I tried to catch one of them but did not succeed. Also saw a large Shoal of Sperm whales very near the ship." As he sailed toward Indonesia, "Saw six sperm whales lying on the surface of the water intirely still & spouting occasionally. We passed them at the rate of four knots within three hundred yards but they took no apparent notice of us. They were about twelve miles from the land but not on soundings. They probably knew that we was no whaleman consequently did not deign to pay us much attention. Our 3d officer & cook are whalemen. They rated them at eighty barrels each. Perhaps their eyes magnified some but they were large fish & I had the best view of them that I ever had of a sperm whale."[17]

Sailing in unfamiliar waters, he came across species he did not recognize. "Imployed myself fishing & caught eight nice ones. I know of no name for them, but I found them to eat well . . . I caught a noble red fish. Weighed about ten pounds. Made us a good breakfast." Six weeks out of New York, en route to San Francisco, "Saw the first Albatross which seemed to be rather out of his Latitude and appeared somewhat wilder." He spotted the first albatross on his *Hussar* voyage on the same day that a "noble turtle . . . drifted past . . . asleep on the water. To much trouble to get a boat out to catch him so I concluded to let him have his nap out quietly."[18]

Winsor rarely commented on the appearance of the night sky, though he undoubtedly observed the stars to navigate. But on board the *Hussar,* "we had a total eclipse of the moon. The sky was cloudless & moon full, & I don't know as I ever saw a more magnificent sight. I sat & looked at it till 10 o'clock or after when the moon was perfectly covered. The shape of her was to be seen, of a dark reddish cast. This is the first total eclipse I ever saw."[19]

Winsor carefully noted the appearance of land masses that were new to him, sometimes speculating on what they might be and nearly always drawing them in his journal. His drawings are carefully executed and not ornamented with imaginary detail. His other drawings are of the ships that he encountered, often in color and always elegant.

"Most all passengers seasick"

People were Winsor's most troublesome cargo. He worried about their health, safety, and comfort—often with good cause. Every journal that mentions passengers notes that they are seasick at least some of the time. But seasickness was less troubling than accidents and more serious illness. Early in the *Sea Nymph*'s voyage to Melbourne, "at 9 A.M. we buried a child about six years old, one of the second cabin passengers, its death caused by falling down the hatchway." The next day, the ship rolled so badly that "she hove one of the passengers across the deck & broke his leg above the knee very badly. The Doctor thinks he will be obliged to amputate." A month later one of the crew fell overboard.[20]

On only four of his voyages did Winsor find his passengers worthy of comment. Sailing to Canton in 1852, the *Gertrude* leaked badly, and storms caused the ship to roll, bringing "great quantities of water on deck." His passengers were missionaries, and this is the only voyage in which Winsor mentions religious services. On the first Sunday after the storm he noted, "Religious services performed by the passengers." During the following weeks, the leaks continued and the crew dumped much of the cargo of coal overboard to lighten the ship. After three weeks, "All the Ships company attended religious service performed by the passengers." The situation must have been dire to lead the entire crew to prayer. Later in the voyage, noting that "it has been calm three fourths of the time," slowing their passage, he added that "the mates impute it to the Missionaries." Except for the mates' suspicions, the missionaries apparently caused little trouble, and their prayers may have comforted the crew.[21]

Winsor's 1857 voyage to Melbourne on the *Sea Nymph* carried eighty-six passengers, including a baby born five weeks after they set sail. Winsor at first described the passengers as "troublesome," but it soon became clear they were worse than that. Some of them got into a knife fight, and one of the passengers robbed the cook. After six weeks at sea, he described them as "a regular set of pirates & I ought to have carried them all to Botany Bay," the Australian penal colony. Only the doctor on board and his wife could be considered respectable. All in all, "it has been the most unpleasant passage I ever made & no man can imagine the trouble, anxiety & perplexities that I have had unless he has carried such a lot of passengers."[22]

In the winter of 1861–1862, sailing from Hong Kong to South Africa, Winsor noted that he was carrying 253 British troops, plus 10 officers, a lady, a servant, and 4 children in the cabin. "No piece or comfort for me on this passage," he added. And indeed, it was a difficult trip for the passengers. Eight of them died, and by the time they arrived all but one were "invalids." Winsor was also troubled by the punishment of one of the soldiers: "twenty six lashes, with a cat, on his bare back."[23]

Winsor's attitude toward the passengers on the *Audubon* in 1850 had been far different. They were a single man, G. Hussey Jr.; Mr. and Mrs. A. T. Harris; and the Webb family: husband and wife, four children, and two related women. The captain socialized with them, and about two months into the journey he made some sort of faux pas:

> All the passengers in good health. Some of them on *unspeakable* terms with the *Capt.* I suppose think he is a queer fellow but I hope they will think better of him before they arrive at San Francisco. In this case of difference with the passengers I must acknowledge myself wrong, but cannot bring my Indian disposition low enough to confess it to them. I hope it will wear off soon for I find it very unpleasant to be tied up with a man that I cannot associate with. If this wears off & I am imposed upon by every one in the Cabin I will not resent it again for it is a complete folly to be at variance with Passengers. I would gladly leave the Ship today if I could, although I have as fine people for passengers as there is in world. We have all been on good terms, nothing has occurred to mar our comfort and happiness till this foolish act of mine and I find it affects them all for I can notice a kind of stillness & coolness toward me that I have not discovered before. Consequently I have kept myself as reserved & still as possible for fear getting the ill will of the other passengers for God knows I do not wish it.[24]

Captain Alexander Winsor. *From the collection of the Millicent Library.*

This is the longest entry about passengers in any of the journals, and the only one suggesting that Winsor tried to develop any sort of relationship with them. The coolness soon thawed, and the captain once again enjoyed the passengers' company. He worried about their comfort in the extreme cold and was happy to note at the end of February that "all the passengers have got on deck again & commenced their exercises & passtimes again. All getting anxious to see the Sun." He even mentioned one of the ladies by name: "Mrs. Harris was taken sick yesterday & today is not as well. Hope she will recover again in a day or two."[25]

As they approached their first port, the passengers tended to their wardrobes: "This day there has been a general overhaul of baggage among the passengers. Ladies getting out their Bonnets & trimming them anew; removing all the spots of mildew on their dresses; asking one another if they think it will ever come out again in the world, etc. & making all other necessary preparations for going on shore in Valparaiso." Two days later, "the Ladies have imployed themselves washing, & I must say they are the most amiable set I ever was acquainted with for they are not the least ill tempered even on a washing day."[26] The ladies provided a welcome distraction from the difficulties of a prolonged voyage (18,000 miles in five months—more than double the record time for the trip). Usually, though, passengers were a nuisance at best and a danger at worst. And the crews often were not much better.

"A great set of pirates"

By the 1850s, it had become difficult to find capable crews. The young men who had once sought adventure at sea now preferred to try their luck in California's gold fields. Shipowners complained in their letters, and captains reported difficulties in their logs. Those seeking berths sometimes falsified their records, claiming experience they did not have and omitting criminal convictions; and the agents who provided crews were not always diligent or honest. Desertions were common. Crews on American Navy ships in the 1850s, one historian writes, "included deserters from other ships, violent felons, aimless drifters, earnest immigrants, luckless runaways, and sober, steady men, all crowded willy-nilly, eating, sleeping and working together . . . They ranged from highly skilled seamen to landsmen who provided unskilled brawn."[27] The inability to recruit sailors led unscrupulous agents to shanghai men in the major ports, including San Francisco.[28] Winsor suffered from the shortage of qualified sailors. He described the problem in a letter to Thatcher Magoun sent from San Francisco in 1868: "It will cost me about four hundred dollars *blood money* to get a crew. The landlords are now selling Sailors at $20 a head over & above $60 advance. This piratical practice has now been in operation about two weeks & there is no alternative but submit to their infernal robbing."[29]

Part of Winsor's difficulties in sailing the *Audubon* to San Francisco came from "having a very poor crew," three of whom became sick. "We have not enough to handle the sails when the wind blows strong therefore I am obliged to go along cautiously," he recorded in his journal. The ship went on to Manila, where Winsor hired a Philippine crew, whom he found inadequate: "To much wind for Studdingsails with our crew of Phillipines to steer. They don't know how to work with anything that's not made of Bamboo."[30] He stopped in St. Helena, where he took on two "Consul men"—sailors who had left their ships in foreign ports for whom the American consul would find berths. Winsor wrote that the "two men put on board by the Consul at St. Helena yesterday refused to work & yet remain of the same mind, but I hope they will think better of it soon, & give me no further trouble." The next day, "the two Consul men still refusing to do any duty put them both in irons where I mean they shall continue unless they consent to do duty & conduct themselves properly." The men continued "mulish" until February 17, when Winsor removed the irons "as they promised to go to work & conduct themselves properly the remainder of the passage. They have been in irons twenty two days."[31]

On the *Sea Nymph* voyage to Melbourne, with the piratical passengers, Winsor also had trouble with the crew. Early on, he reported that both the cook and the steward were drunk. A few days later, a sailor fell overboard but was rescued, while another was lost in the same way. On the return voyage he "sent a man away from the wheel for bad steering. He became impertinent & I took hold of him to correct him. He drew his knife & stabbed me slightly in my face. I stilled him with a belaying pin & now have him in irons, where I intend to keep him a while."[32]

These problems paled in comparison to those created by the crews of *Herald of the Morning*, despite the much-admired quarters the ship provided for them. Winsor sailed the *Herald* from New York to San Francisco and back in 1868 and again in 1870 on the same route. In 1868 he told Magoun that "the 2nd officer (the one that fell overboard) proved (after the whiskey evaporated) to be a very good man." Alcohol was the source of many of the disagreements and fights among the crew members. Two years later he reported: "I discharged Mr. Gunner. I cant get along with him any longer. He keeps full of rum in port and is not good for much at sea."[33]

On both voyages, mysterious problems arose around Mr. Judge, the first mate, whom Winsor had evidently sailed with often before. In May 1868, on board ship, Winsor said that Judge was "the best mate he ever had," and both captain and mate thought that on the westward voyage they had "a remarkable peaceable crew." In a letter to Magoun on September 2 of the same year, Winsor wrote that "Mr. Judge is an A1. officer in every respect"; but a month later, as they prepared to leave San Francisco, Judge

> was knocking the cook down & about till he was bleeding all about the deck. The cook was so drunk he could not stand up without holding on to something. I remonstrated with Mr. Judge as gently as I could under the circumstances, but he got very wrathy & very saucy, in fact I have never had a mate use such language to me before. He has packed up his things this evening & says he is going to leave the ship tomorrow morning . . . This is the first time I have had any trouble with Mr. Judge, & he is wholly in fault now & if he had ever been in the habit of drinking I should have thought that was the trouble now for I don't think any sane man would use such language as he did. As have said before he is a first rate officer but don't think he was ever accused of being a gentleman.[34]

Perhaps Judge was wise to leave the ship in San Francisco, because the crew on the next voyage of the *Herald* was a "great set of pirates":

> I buried one of them yesterday, murdered by the others. They put two sheath knives into him chock to the handle. They have threatened to kill me and take the ship into the nearest port [and] have threatened to set her on fire. They are all armed with knives and pistols and ready to blow anyone's brains out at any time. The second mate is a miserable good-for-nothing, thin but as big a villain as any of the crew, and joins them in all their rascality. I have no doubt but this lot of pirates shipped in New York for the purpose of killing Mr. Judge, thinking he was coming in the ship again, and they would have surely killed him before we had been ten days out.[35]

In 1871 Judge applied to Thatcher Magoun for a position, and Magoun asked Winsor's opinion. Winsor provided a measured response: "I have a good deal of feeling for him & am willing to wink at a great many of his faults, & if you feel disposed to have him given the ship again I have no objection for I think you may go farther & do a great deal worse, & if you decide to try him again (which I should advise) please drop me a line as I wish to write him before he joins the ship." Winsor's doubts came from Judge's propensities for "fighting" and "romancing," but he nevertheless recommended that Magoun "try Mr. Judge once more." Magoun asked about another mate, who Winsor said "is about as good as the average . . . He is a very good man at sea, but not to be depended on in port."[36]

"A good warm home to go to"

When he was at sea, Winsor rarely mentioned his family in his journals. His first wife, Sarah, stayed at home in Fairhaven with their children. He noted only once that he wrote to her, though he surely sent other letters. On June 1, 1858, he recorded, "This day my daughter is seven years old," though other birthdays and anniversaries went unremarked.[37] Alexander and Sarah were married in 1838, when he was twenty-eight and she was twenty-three. They had three children: Alexander Jr. (1845), Walter Pellington (1846), and Sarah Frances (1851).[38] When his wife Sarah died, in 1865, Winsor was at sea. It is likely that he learned of her death only at the end of his voyage. He had left San Francisco in February on the *Sea Serpent,* sailing to Hong Kong, where he spent the summer, and then on to Wampoa in September, arriving in New York in November. On the rear flyleaf of his copy of Nathaniel Bowditch's *American Practical Navigator,* a book that he would always have with him, he wrote: "My beloved wife departed this life Nov. 23d 1865 aged forty-nine years, eleven months & five days. Virtuously & happily she lived & as a faithful servant of the Lord. She fell asleep in the Lord & now lives & reigns in Heaven."[39]

Winsor did not rush into a second marriage, although his daughter was young enough that her care would have been a concern. But in 1868, when he was fifty-eight, he married Emily Pope, twenty-one years his junior. She sailed with him on *Herald of the Morning* until he retired in 1872. Winsor never explained, or even mentioned, the decision to allow his two worlds to meet. Possibly being absent for his wife's final illness and death influenced him. Perhaps Emily persuaded him: she may have thought of sailing to San Francisco as a honeymoon, or an adventure. In any case, they left Fairhaven for New York, where the *Herald* was docked. In New York, the captain met a host of Emily's relations, who visited the ship in such numbers that Winsor, Emily recorded, "said the 'Herald' looked like a passenger ship just in from sea." Emily noted with pleasure that her husband had given her the largest cabin: "The accommodations are fine for a lady passenger, a handsome dining room, large after cabin, with double staterooms on each side, with French bedsteads, lounge &c &c.," and "the bathroom joins my room and the tub can be filled from the deck with rain or salt water." She later discovered the pleasures of "a little house over the gangway to the Cabin that has windows on three sides and a nice seat. I can look out from there in all weathers day or night." In storms, "my room is decidedly the best place, has a side light and two deck lights, and is very dry. The Kittens found it out and would not stay any where else."[40]

Emily was "a lady passenger." She had little interaction with the crew and no shipboard duties. She spent her time sewing, reading, and eating. She got a great deal of sewing done, both utilitarian hemming of sheets and pillowcases and decorative needlework. When they had been at sea for four months, "Capt was tired seeing me wear the grey striped dress, and asked me not to wear it again . . . I riped up the grey one, for the pattern as it fitted so nicely, to make an English calico (that the Capt brought for me)." Two days later, she wrote: "Finished my dress and put it on. It is made full waist with a little ruffle up the front fits beautifully. Capt compliments me highly on it, did not know I had such an accomplishment." Her reading was varied, including a biography of Marie Antoinette and Trollope's *Last Chronicle of Barset.*[41] Emily was never seasick, and she developed a healthy appreciation of shipboard food. "When I came on board had not much appetite, but A. W. bought some ale for my benefit entirely, which has been a great help to me, he insists upon my taking a glass every day, but will not take any himself, as he is fleshy enough, is anxious I should increase in weight, had me weighed when I came on board. I then turned the scale at 121 lbs."[42]

She did venture on deck during good weather and discovered a liking for "signalizing"—using a system of flags to identify one's ship, indicate latitude and longitude, and notify other ships of nearby dangers or one's own need for assistance. "I enjoy signalizing vessels so much that the Capt allows me to have it done many times when he does not care for it. I stand by with the book to look out the numbers, Capt looks with the glass and calls the signals, mate with two sailors run the flags up & down, we have to work quick, if we are going in opposite directions, as we pass so soon." She joined Winsor on deck in the evening, and he pointed out constellations visible only in the Southern Hemisphere. Winsor slept little, especially during bad weather, but Emily would "go up for an hour if I wake, and we have a social chat, it shortens the night." Once, when the sailors were catching birds, she joined them. "Capt thought I would not succeed but I soon caught one of the largest, it was an Albatros. The hook takes them in the upper part of the bill and does not injure them at all. At one time we had three of them walking about the deck they are very handsome and did not seem at all afraid."[43]

Emily Pope Winsor. *Courtesy of the New Bedford Whaling Museum.*

One Sunday, "the Captain asked if I would like to go to Church. I agreed. We then walked deck which was as near as we could come to it, and sung together Old Hundred. Afterward we went below and opened a bundle [of tracts] the Bible Society had sent on board for the sailors."[44]

As they approached San Francisco, she wrote: "I have enjoyed the passage very much, more than I ever should another, as everything is so new to me. Going in the capacity that I do I have every privilege, and am at liberty the Capt says to go *where* I please and do *as* I please, but I never go forward of the main mast without his being with me." Throughout her journal, she expressed concern and affection for her new husband, and confidence in him. "I never feel any fear as the Capt is on the alert all the time."[45]

Clearly, the experiment was a success for Emily, but what about Alexander? His journal contains no mention of Emily's presence on board, but she passed along some of his comments. He was impressed with her sewing and "thinks I have been very industrious." He clearly enjoyed her company when the weather and his responsibilities allowed them to spend time together. As they arrived in San Francisco, she described the beauty of her cabin, decorated with baskets of fruit and flowers sent by Winsor's business associates and with furniture and silver newly polished by the steward. "This traveling and having your house with you is delightful . . . He is delighted to have me here, thinks it is next to going home."[46]

Yet "next" was not quite good enough, and both of them had begun to look forward to living on land.

Homeward Bound

The Winsors spent three weeks in San Francisco. The captain unloaded his cargo and found a new cargo to take to Boston. They dined out and entertained on board but declined invitations to the opera: "A.W. does not like Opera." Emily admired the city, with its broad streets, elegant houses, and thriving gardens. But she became ill. Winsor feared she might have smallpox, because there was an epidemic in San Francisco, but fortunately she did not. Diagnosed with typhoid fever, Emily worried that she would not be well enough to sail when the *Herald* was ready and that she would have to stay behind. She did sail with the ship, but the illness had taken its toll. On the voyage home, she wrote, "I have kept no regular journal this passage but have taken life easy. I think I did too much on the last passage sewing & writing. We both did a great deal of writing in Port many nights sitting up very late."[47]

Winsor commanded the *Herald* for one final voyage, from New York to San Francisco and back in 1870. Emily accompanied him, but if she kept a journal it has not been found. The voyage was unpleasant, with bad weather, slow progress, and "the greatest set of pirates for a crew that ever was afloat before."[48] Both Winsors were ready to retire from the sea. When they were in San Francisco in 1868, the captain had said that going home was desirable but it "would be poor policy for him to do at present." Emily envied "Capt. F.", whom she met there: "I wish AW could have a situation like his. He is supervisor of all the ships that leave Port, at a salary of $10,000 per year."[49]

The misery of the 1870–1872 voyage did the trick, and the Winsors settled in their William Street home. Winsor joined other retired sailors in town, where, according to one of his grandsons, "his sea going experiences were heard with great interest by the group of old residents who gathered in the apothecary shop in Phoenix Block and who decorated the corner with a Revolutionary war cannon."[50]

Emily died in 1880, and three years later Alexander married Emma Alan Richmond, a forty-two-year-old widow. When he died in 1890, Winsor left a sizable estate. The house, furniture, and $10,000 were left to Emma, who lived at 10 William Street until her death in 1918. Another $10,000 was left to his daughter, Sarah Fuller, with the balance divided between his two sons. In Fairhaven's Riverside Cemetery, a four-sided obelisk marks the resting place of the captain and his three wives. Another memorial is an orchard in nearby Acushnet. Founded by Alexander's grandson Bancroft Winsor and his wife, Beatrice, the orchard was named after his favorite ship, the *Flying Cloud*.[51]

The captain's obituary in the *Fairhaven Star* noted, "It is nearly twenty years since Capt. Winsor retired from active life, and most of that time has been passed in this town in quiet, happy home life, such as a sailor knows so well how to appreciate."[52]

10

"Perfectly Safe"

PALMER ISLAND LIGHT

There are times when the ocean is not the ocean—not blue, not even water, but some violent explosion of energy and danger: ferocity on a scale only gods can summon. It hurls itself at the island, sending spray right over the top of the lighthouse, biting pieces off the cliff. And the sound is a roaring of a beast whose anger knows no limits. Those are the nights the light is needed most.

—M. L. STEDMAN, *The Light between Oceans*

We often think of lighthouses as "symbols of noble solitude" and of their keepers as lovers of seclusion. This was the reality for some men and women who lived alone on offshore stations that could be reached only by long boat journeys. As one keeper of Rhode Island's Sakonnet Light said, "You could drop dead in winter and no one would find you till spring."[1] Many lighthouses, though, were located near towns or in busy harbors, where the keepers and their families were part of their communities and had easy access to social events. From 1922 to 1938 Arthur and Mabel Small kept the Palmer Island Light, in the harbor between Fairhaven and New Bedford, and were very much part of the local social scene. They were at home in their lighthouse much as their friends were at home in their more conventional dwellings. In fact, Arthur Small felt more secure in his lighthouse than he would have in town: "Here I am on this island," he told an interviewer, "perfectly safe, working and painting pictures, while you wander around in New Bedford, crossing streets with automobiles and trolley cars whizzing by, just missing you by a few feet."[2] In their generation, before lighthouses were automated, being a lighthouse keeper was a desirable career for a small group of men who had served in the armed forces. That had not always been true.

Getting It Right

The colonies had lighthouses before the Revolution, and establishing them was an early order of business for the new republic. A nation with a long coastline and an economy dependent on shipping needed to ensure the safety of its military and commercial fleets. In 1789, two years before moving on to freedom of speech and other basic rights, Congress enacted legislation making lighthouses the financial responsibility of the federal government.[3] Unfortunately, more than financial assurance was needed. No adequate system for siting, building, maintaining, and staffing lighthouses was put in place, and decades of mismanagement and corruption followed. Lighthouses were placed where they were not needed; they were equipped with inefficient lamps; and they were staffed by untrained and sometimes incompetent keepers. It took more than half a century for the government to deal with these problems. In 1852 the Light House Board, established a year earlier to investigate the failing system, made its report. Sweeping changes resulted, especially in the way that lighthouse keepers were hired. Instead of being a patronage job handed out according to political allegiances and connections rather than qualifications, the position of keeper was professionalized. The newly established board "tightened requirements for keepers, provided training, and instituted inspections . . . Nominations still were made by the customs collectors but were endorsed by the Light House Board before being forwarded to the secretary of the Treasury. Candidates had to be between eighteen and fifty, be able to read, write, and keep accounts and do the requisite manual labor, pull and sail a boat, and have enough mechanical ability to make minor repairs." They served three-month apprenticeships and then took a certification test.[4]

Throughout the late nineteenth and early twentieth centuries, living conditions for keepers gradually improved. Lighthouses were repaired, and living facilities were updated. Where there was arable land, farming was encouraged, and barns were constructed for keepers' livestock. For stations distant from markets, fuel and rations were provided. If distance made it impractical for keepers' children to attend school, the state and federal governments paid for books and traveling teachers. By 1918 the Lighthouse Service (the official name beginning in 1912) was trying to reduce the isolation of the most distant keepers by providing telegraph, telephone, or radio service.[5] Some lighthouse stations were said to be so "tastefully planned, well-built, and located in picturesque sites" that people sought to rent rooms in the summer, and in 1889 an official reported that "the Board has been compelled to prohibit them from taking boarders under any circumstances."[6] A system of traveling libraries was established: lighthouse inspectors delivered a carefully built wooden crate with two shelves of books and magazines; these were circulated among the lighthouses and included fiction and nonfiction provided free or at large discounts by publishing houses. Congress agreed to fund these after learning that "lightkeepers were made more contented and better satisfied with their lot by having reading matter supplied them."[7]

The Lighthouse Service ran on something of a military model. Many of the keepers had served in the army or navy, and there was an unofficial system of ranks. By 1889 keepers were required to wear uniforms, and the board "found that it adds much to the appearance of the *personnel*, and does much to raise the *esprit de corps*, and to preserve its discipline." Discipline was strict, enforced by unannounced inspections. Intoxication or allowing the light to go out meant immediate dismissal, and keepers were expected to stay at their posts in times of danger, like captains of ships.[8]

Lighthouses varied greatly in design and staffing. The white or striped conical towers most often pictured on postcards were but one kind of structure. If the best place for a light was a small rocky island—or just a large rock—a minimal structure atop metal legs might house both light and keeper. In some cases, the light was simply placed atop the keeper's house. Some lights were designed for a single keeper, with or without family. Others required a keeper and assistants—again, with or without families. The great variety of design and staffing meant that keepers had a wide range of domestic experience.

The only detailed account of life in American lighthouses in the early twentieth century was written by Connie Scovill Small (not related to Arthur and Mabel), who described living in several kinds of Maine lighthouses in the 1920s and 1930s in her autobiography, *The Lighthouse Keeper's Wife*. Her husband's first assignment was the Channel Light. She lived ashore and only visited him there. The lighthouse was cylindrical, so "all the rooms were round," she noted. "The kitchen and living room were combined into the one room at this landing level . . . The second deck was a bedroom . . . It was difficult to sleep in this room; the wind whistled around the tower and pieces of driftwood hit the tower, sounding like avalanches. Above the bedroom was the lantern deck." The cellar had a feature common to nearly every lighthouse: a cistern to collect rain that was the station's only source of water for drinking and washing.[9]

In 1922 Connie and her husband moved to Avery Rock, "a one-keeper family light." Located on a "bare pile of rock," the light was inaccessible during cold weather. In the first winter, the couple didn't leave between October and May. Although the island was tiny, the house was relatively spacious, with six large rooms, including a kitchen with a pantry large enough to hold provisions for several months: home-canned vegetables, meat, and fish as well as "slab bacon, salt pork, sugar, cereal, lard, dry beans, canned milk, and soda crackers" delivered by boat. The light was directly above the living quarters.[10]

After four years, the couple moved to Seguin Light, a three-keeper station with quarters for families. The main house was brick, with two stories of living space. The first floor had a kitchen, dining room, living room, and a hall; the second had two large bedrooms and a small alcove. The light was above the keeper's house, reached by an iron spiral staircase. The first assistant, his wife, and their children lived in another wing, and the second assistant and his family lived in a separate building next to the foghorn. The residents shared childcare and sometimes met in the evening to play cards.[11]

In 1930 Connie and her husband moved to the St. Croix River Light Station—a posting similar to the Palmer Island Light. Connie described it as "a little paradise." The five-acre island had a house with a light tower and several outbuildings: a bell tower, boat house, barn, oil house, utility building, and a windmill to supply power. Family, friends, and tourists visited the island in summer. The mainland was close enough for them to develop close friendships and for her husband to attend meetings of the Masonic lodge.[12]

This range of experience was common in the Lighthouse Service and was shared by Arthur and Mabel Small, as well as two other Smalls: Tom and Judson.

Band of Brothers

Arthur Small came from a family of lighthouse keepers. His brother Tom was the keeper of two lighthouses in Boston Bay: the Narrows Light in the 1920s and Deer Island Light in the 1930s. As well known as Tom was his cat, who "would climb down the ladder, hind feet first, leap into the bay, and dive for fish. When she caught one, she'd return to the ladder with the catch in her mouth." Their brother Judson was an assistant keeper on Deer Island in the 1920s. Arthur had served at the Narrows Light from 1919 to 1922, when he moved to Palmer Island. Like many keepers, the Small brothers all had had maritime and military experience.[13]

Arthur Small was born in landlocked Brockton, Massachusetts, in 1885, but at fourteen he began fishing from Gloucester and from ports in Maine. He served in the Merchant Marine as well, delivering cargoes up and down the coast and eventually in both oceans. He had rounded the Horn of Africa and navigated the Straits of Magellan several times. He was not fond of either place, commenting once that "there's very little romance about Cape Horn, or anywhere below fifty-two south latitude, for that matter. It's cold and ugly down there." In 1906 he joined the U.S. Navy's Great White Fleet, circumnavigating the globe from 1907 to 1909. He then sailed with the Coast Guard and in the Coast and Geodetic Service. Sometime before World War I, he married, and he and Mabel had two sons: Wesley V., born in 1913, and Allan A., born in 1919. After World War I, he joined the Lighthouse Service, beginning at Boston Light on Little Brewster Island. The family went to live in a very old house on the island, and, as he later told the *Fairhaven Star*, "their principal entertainment was taking trips to Boston, an excursion that required three or four hours."[14]

From about 1919 to 1922 Arthur served at Narrows Light in Boston Harbor, sometimes known as "Bug Light" because its hexagonal frame, resting on iron stilts, resembled a spider. It had four rooms, with the light on the iron roof. It was not a comfortable place to live, and Mabel and Wesley joined Arthur only in the summer. In warm weather, though, they had lots of visitors, and they enjoyed watching the old sailing ships that were fast disappearing. Mabel recalled that "at meal time, someone was always jumping up from the table to see what was going on outside; perhaps it was a bark or brigantine or even a transport carrying troops to France during the war."[15]

Arthur saved more than one life while serving at the Narrows. During one winter storm he rescued two Italian fishermen, but the most dramatic rescue was of his brother Tom. One very cold winter day, Tom was headed for Bug Light from Boston Light when his sailboat capsized. Men came out from Hull to rescue him, but they couldn't see him and gave up. According to one account, as they headed back, "they passed Arthur Small, rowing out in search of his brother . . . 'He's gone, Small, it's no use,' they shouted at Arthur. But Keeper Small kept rowing out to where he believed the tide would take his brother's sailboat." Arthur shouted, and Tom heard him and called back. Arthur picked him up, rowed him back to Boston Light, and returned to his station.[16] In 1922 Tom became the keeper of Bug Light, remaining there until 1929, when a spark from his blowtorch set the station on fire. His wife and son were visiting friends on shore at the time, and he was able to escape. "Near the end of June, a party of engineers dredging near the site recovered Jimmy Small's little bank containing two dollars in pennies" and returned it to the boy.[17]

When Tom became keeper at Bug Light, Arthur moved to the Palmer Island Light, which was much better suited to family life. The six-acre island is nearly in the middle of the New Bedford–Fairhaven harbor, with the towns on either side easy to reach by rowboat. The island was so accessible that in the 1870s and '80s it boasted a hotel and popular dance hall. These were long gone by the time Arthur, Mabel, their two sons, and several tabby cats moved into their two-story white house at one end of the island, with the lighthouse and oil house at the other. The boys attended school in Fairhaven, commuting by boat when the weather was fair and boarding with a mainland family in winter.[18]

Arthur's duties were those of any lighthouse keeper, and these were more extensive than most people realize. In an interview with Edward Rowe Snow, the preeminent historian of New England lighthouses, Small emphasized the dramatic parts of his job:

> It is a popular idea that there is very little to do except for striking a match once a day to light the lamp . . . Few of these landlubbers realize that if a fog comes in during the middle of the night the keeper must be ready to turn on the fog signal at once, for if the fog bell is silent for a moment, even then a great vessel may be feeling her way up into the harbor depending on the ringing of the fog signal bell for her safety. The channel in New Bedford Harbor is so narrow . . . that if a large vessel went down, all shipping in or out of the harbor would be at a standstill.

The coal for the electric light company could not reach the pier, and the cotton steamers likewise would find it impossible to dock. In a short time all the city would be seriously crippled.[19]

He didn't mention the dangerous job of rescuing mariners and others in distress or the more mundane tasks (often shared by their wives): maintaining the equipment, monitoring the weather and ship traffic, keeping the daily log, maintaining the boat, and making sure the lighthouse and living quarters were orderly and immaculate for unannounced inspections.[20] From sunset to sunup, and especially during storms, the keeper was on duty. He could not let the light fail, and he could not leave his station without permission (or a substitute) for any reason, as long as he could walk.

Nevertheless, there was time for keepers and their wives to develop other interests. Salaries were not generous, and keepers were allowed to take on other work, as long as it didn't interfere with their duties. Some keepers were skilled shoemakers or tailors; others were teachers, justices of the peace, or ministers.[21] Keepers' wives, too, found useful ways to fill their time. At Seguin Light, Connie Small kept chickens, took "cooking lessons by mail from Betty Crocker," started a Sunday school for children at the station, quilted, and painted. She developed an interest in classical music when two dozen fishermen from a passing trawler turned up at Seguin Light and asked if they might listen to the opera on the station's radio.[22]

Painting became a pastime and sometimes an avocation for lighthouse keepers. At Latimer Reef Lighthouse, two miles from shore in New York's Fishers Island Sound, one keeper introduced another to painting. Frank Jo Raymond had "never seen a painting before in my life." The other keeper, Dick Fricke, tacked some spare canvas to a frame and, using whatever house paint was at hand, "made a nice painting of a square rigged ship. I was amazed, I'd never seen it done, it never occurred to me that, you know, what you saw in magazine illustrations were the result of a painter's work." He, too, began to paint. When Fricke asked him whether he had ever been to a museum, he asked, "What's a museum?" "So I started a trek every month, I went to Providence, New York, Boston." He worked as an artist for the Works Progress Administration during the Depression and painted posters during World War II. In 1961, at the age of fifty-five, he spent a year in museums in Europe, sketching and copying paintings to improve his technique.[23]

Arthur Small, too, became a recognized painter of ships and seascapes. He had begun painting while at sea, using scraps of sail canvas. His first efforts were detailed paintings of square-riggers, but he went on to use what he had seen on his voyages to tackle larger subjects. When he was at Palmer Light, he attended art school for the first time, taking classes at the Swain Free School of Design in New Bedford. His paintings were precise and accurate, based not only on his own observations but on research using his library of several hundred volumes. Although he was best known in New Bedford and Fairhaven, the Spanish Historical Society of St. Augustine, Florida, commissioned him to paint a mural of Columbus's arrival in America.[24] The best-known photograph of Arthur Small shows a handsome man in front of a painting he is working on, sleeves rolled up, corncob pipe in his mouth, and brushes in his hand.[25]

Arthur and Mabel were the opposite of the stereotypical reclusive lighthouse dwellers. In fact, the stereotype bears little resemblance to any of the keepers of their era. Connie Small remembered that when one team of workmen came to do some repairs at Seguin Light, they formed a small orchestra—violin, banjo, accordion, guitar, harmonica, and piano—and sang and danced.[26] Martin Thompson, keeper of the Sandy Point Lighthouse in Narragansett Bay from 1905 to 1932, described the socializing that went on among his colleagues: "In summertime we would have a lot of the keepers down here, . . . and we would go to their places, and there would be clambakes, good times had by all."[27] The Smalls welcomed visitors to the lighthouse. In 1938 the *Fairhaven Star* reported: "A great number of people in all walks of life have visited Captain and Mrs. Small, the noted, as well as the obscure, and have met with a sincerely cordial and generous hospitality. Mrs. Small and her husband shared their enjoyment of people and books and art with their friends." Among the visitors was an aspiring artist, Helen Cyr, who received lessons from Arthur.[28]

Arthur and Mabel were active in Fairhaven and New Bedford society. When the Mariners' Club was formed in 1927, Arthur became a member. The club met at the Peirce & Kilburn Shipyard, which had moved from New Bedford to the old Atlas Tack factory on Fort Street the year before. By 1933, according to *Motorboating* magazine, the club's membership was at capacity and they had a waiting list. All were present or former working mariners; "no yacht owner is eligible." In its "spacious clubrooms," the members traded stories, dined on chowder, and held banquets. The second

Captain Arthur Small. *Courtesy of Jeremy Burnham.*

floor exhibited photographs of sailing vessels and other art. Arthur Small gave the club several paintings, and another maritime artist, George Gale, donated paintings and etchings.[29]

Mabel Small attended the North Congregational Church in New Bedford. She had been an officer of the New Bedford chapter of the Order of the Eastern Star (a Masonic organization) and corresponding secretary of the New Bedford Woman's Club. In Fairhaven, she belonged to the Mothers' Club, a group of women who, since 1914, have raised funds for the town's children. On April 17, 1934, members of the Mothers' Club toured the Peirce & Kilburn Shipyard. After their tour, they were invited to the quarters of the Mariners' Club, where Arthur Small gave a "sage and salty" talk. He "drew an outline of the coastline of the United States, told of the various lighthouses guarding it, and described the duties of a lighthouse keeper." He answered "all sorts of questions" and invited his audience to visit the lighthouse, where he would tell them more about his experiences. Then he showed them the club's art collection, with many pieces that he had painted. At the club's April meeting the next year, Mabel was the speaker. She told the women about domestic life in a lighthouse, the difficulties of moving from one station to another, the isolation at some stations, and the pleasure of seeing ships and having frequent visitors. She told them that, despite the difficulties of getting to school, lighthouse children missed no more classes than other children.[30]

Mabel also belonged to a sewing circle in which the women met for lunch at someone's home and then worked on knitting, needlework, or other projects. At their meeting on Tuesday, September 20, 1938, her friend Stella Hay Rex looked up from the hooked rug she was working on and noticed Mabel looking out the window at the harbor. She told Mrs. Rex that "the sea is so rough, I'm afraid Arthur won't be able to row over to get me if I wait for my ride." Mrs. Rex drove her to the landing at the Peirce & Kilburn Shipyard, where Arthur was waiting to row her back to the lighthouse.[31]

A Home Destroyed

The waves that alarmed Mabel Small were signs of one of the most horrific hurricanes to strike New England in recorded history. It had been raining off and on in Massachusetts for days, and Tuesday was windy. Because of the fall equinox, the tides were unusually high. At 9:00 the next morning, a hurricane that had begun in the Atlantic Ocean near Cape Verde reached Cape Hatteras, North Carolina. The eye was 50 miles wide, it was traveling fast, and the wind speeds were terrifying—sustained winds of 121 miles per hour were recorded, with gusts as high as 186 miles per hour. At 1:00 p.m. the storm reached Atlantic City, New Jersey, tearing up the boardwalk. When it reached Bayport, Long Island, at 2:30, the impact of the tidal surge registered on seismographs as far away as Alaska. Tides of 18 to 25 feet were seen from New London east to Cape Cod. As the storm moved east, it became more and more destructive. At 5:00 the storm reached Providence. The wind blew away the anemometer at the weather bureau, and in minutes—at the height of the rush hour—the water level in the downtown streets rose to nearly 14 feet. Then the storm reached Fairhaven.[32]

On Palmer Island, the water was rising and the winds were crippling. Arthur thought the oil house would be safe because it was at the highest point of the island, so he left Mabel there and struggled against the wind to reach the lighthouse. According to one account, he reached the lighthouse; according to another, he was nearly there. In any case, an enormous wave swept him into the harbor, where the detritus of broken boats and houses filled the surface. He was badly injured, and at some point in his ordeal, he lost consciousness.[33]

Mabel saw him struggling in the harbor and did what keepers and their wives did almost automatically: she headed toward the boathouse to launch a lifeboat. Arthur saw her fighting against the wind and water, and then he saw another huge wave strike. He saw the boathouse shatter, and he lost sight of his wife. Injured and horrified, he kept swimming. He reached the lighthouse and somehow made his way up the stairs. A lighthouse keeper's duty is to keep the light burning, and Arthur Small was committed to his responsibilities. The light burned all that night, and although there was no fog, the foghorn sounded.

The next morning the storm had passed, and in the calm the people of New Bedford and Fairhaven could see the damage—houses gone, boats destroyed, trees uprooted. At 7:45, two of Small's friends—William D. Raymond and Fred W. Phillips, president of the Mariners' Club—rowed out to the island. They immediately saw that Arthur needed medical treatment, but he refused to leave the island until the Lighthouse Service gave him official permission. They rowed him back to Fairhaven and, with a police escort, drove him over the damaged bridge to New Bedford's St. Luke's Hospital. There was no sign of Mabel. Her body was found several days later. On September 29, the *Fairhaven Star* reported her death: "A happy and courageous companion through thirty years of married life in the Lighthouse Service, in Wednesday's storm, she abandoned her refuge in an attempt to help her valiant husband, struggling for his life, to reach his post of duty and thereby lost her own."

From the hospital, on September 23, Small dictated a letter to his son Wesley, to be sent to the Lighthouse Service, reporting what had happened. In October, he visited the island briefly. He then listed the personal property that he had lost: his library of several hundred volumes, which he valued at $75, and his "personal records and data of sailing ships [which] were sketches and notes, the result of thirty years' work and used for reference in painting the history of sailing ships, a spare-time hobby, $100." He did not include his paintings or the couple's life savings: $7,500 in a leather pouch that Mabel was wearing when she drowned.

The house that the Smalls had lived in for sixteen years was gone, but more devastating to her husband and the community was the loss of Mabel. "Those who have been welcomed to the home circle and who enjoyed their company will grieve that, with the gracious mistress gone, the home is no more."[34]

Notes

Introduction

1. Leonard Bolles Ellis, *History of New Bedford and Its Vicinity, 1602–1882* (Syracuse: D. Mason, 1892), 128.

1. The Minister and the Maid

SOURCES

The records of the Fairhaven Congregational Church are the vital source here. Without them, this story would have vanished. But other local history sources—property records, newspapers, and genealogies—were also helpful. Researching a story like this does show how difficult it is to find out what women were doing and thinking unless they kept diaries or wrote letters that someone saved.

Two excellent guides to using the basic sources for local history are David E. Kyvig and Myron A. Marty, *Nearby History: Exploring the Past around You*, 3rd edition (Lanham, Md.: Alta Mira Press, 2010), and Thomas A. Mason and J. Kent Calder, *Writing Local History Today: A Guide to Researching, Publishing, and Marketing Your Book* (Lanham, Md.: Alta Mira Press, 2013). A thorough guide to researching the history of an individual house is Sally Light, *House Histories: A Guide to Tracing the Genealogy of Your Home* (Spencertown, N.Y.: Golden Hill Press, 1989). In *If These Walls Had Ears: The Biography of a House* (New York: Warner Books, 1996), James Morgan has written the history of eight families who lived in the same house.

1. The 1790 U.S. census listed 582 families in New Bedford, which included Bedford, Fairhaven, and Oxford villages as well as Acushnet. Bedford was by far the largest of these settlements. On the early history of the area see Daniel Ricketson, *The History of New Bedford, Bristol County, Massachusetts* (New Bedford: published by the author, 1858). On Briggs, see Mary Balch Briggs, *We and Our Kinfolk: Ephraim and Rebekah Waterman Briggs, Their Descendants and Ancestors* (Boston: Beacon Press, 1887), 17.

2. William Herbert Hobbs, *The American Ancestry and Descendants of Alonzo and Sarah (Weston) Kimball* (Madison, Wis.: privately printed, 1902), 53–56; Thomas Weston Jr., "The Descendants of Edmund Weston of Duxbury, Massachusetts," *New England Historical and Genealogical Register* 41 (July 1887): 291–92; Fairhaven deed book, 13-378, Jan. 23, 1795, Fairhaven Archives, Millicent Library. Hobbs gives Weston's birth date

as 1770, but this is contradicted by his tombstone. The *Mercury* article appeared on Aug. 26, 1808; the poem is *The Task* (Philadelphia: Dobson, 1787), 3. The New Bedford Free Public Library holds back issues of the *Mercury* and has indexed them. For Dean, see Hobbs, *American Ancestry*, 62; *Biographical Directory of the U.S. Congress*, www .bioguide.congress.gov, s.v. Dean.

3. Hobbs, *American Ancestry*, 44; Fairhaven deed book, 15-476. My husband and I have owned 31 Middle Street since 2005.

4. Bertha W. Clark, Susan C. Tufts, and Judith Jenney-Burney, *The Jenney Book* (Baltimore: Gateway Press, 1988), 81; Rufus Babcock Tobey and Charles Henry Pope, *Tobey (Tobie, Toby) Genealogy* (Boston: Charles H. Pope, 1905), 137. Franklin was the son of William (1740/1–1798) and Maria Tobey; Elisha was the son of Thomas (1745–1782) and Patience Wing Tobey.

5. Natalie Sylvia Hemingway, *North Fairhaven Historical Tour* (Fairhaven: North Fairhaven Improvement Association, 2006), 6–8. Research in 2015, when the bell was to be moved again, confirmed that Revere had cast it (*New Bedford Standard-Times*, Aug. 24, 2015). It is inscribed "The Living to the Church I call and to the Grave I summon All."

6. All information about the Fairhaven Congregational Church comes from the first of its record books, in the collections of the Old Dartmouth Historical Society, New Bedford Whaling Museum Research Library. Unless otherwise noted, all quotations are from this source and can be found at the entries corresponding to the dates in the text.

7. Isaiah Weston to Thomas Jefferson, Dec. 6, 1804; Josiah Dean to Thomas Jefferson, Dec. 12, 1804. These letters and the one cited below can be found in the Jefferson Papers section of *Founders Online*, www.founders.archives.gov (search by author's name or exact date).

8. Josiah Dean to Thomas Jefferson, July 7, 1808. The appointment is noted as being made on Aug. 8, 1808, in *Calendar of the Correspondence of Thomas Jefferson*, Part 1 (Washington, D.C.: Department of State, 1894), 437.

9. Ricketson, *History*, 107.

10. *New Bedford Mercury*, July 29, 1813; Weston to Madison, June 5, 1813, Madison Papers, American Memory Project, Library of Congress, www.loc.gov; Weston, "Descendants," 291–92.

11. Tobey and Pope, *Tobey Genealogy*, 137.

2. Mister Rogers' Neighborhood

SOURCES

Both admirers and detractors have written a great deal about Rogers. Avoiding the admirers' apocryphal stories and the detractors' hyperbole has been essential. For the Fairhaven side of the story, Mabel Hoyle Knipe's short booklets, based on the town archives and newspaper reports, are extremely useful. They are hard to find in print but are available, unpaginated, on the Millicent Library website: www.millicentlibrary.org. Earl Dias's biography, *Henry Huttleston Rogers: Portrait of a "Capitalist,"* is balanced. On Rogers' career, Ida Tarbell's *History of the Standard Oil Company* remains a model of investigative journalism, and she was candid about her ambivalence toward Rogers in her autobiography, *All in the Day's Work*. It is a measure of Rogers' national importance that his activities were covered extensively in the *New York Times,* and their online archive was essential. Town archivist Debbie Charpentier and her volunteers provided hard-to-find material and exceptional insight into Rogers and his contemporaries in Fairhaven. I have included some stories about Rogers that cannot be verified, but since all sources are cited readers can decide which of those to take with a grain of salt.

1. "In Memory of Dear Old Days," *Boston Globe,* Jan. 28, 1902.

2. Earl J. Dias, *Henry Huttleston Rogers: Portrait of a "Capitalist"* (Fairhaven: Millicent Library, 1974), 20–21, 102; Elbert Hubbard, *Little Journeys to the Homes of Great Business Men* (1909; repr., East Aurora, N.Y.: The Roycrofters / New York: W. H. Wise, 1916), 396.

3. Dias, *Portrait,* 22, 30, 37–38; "In Memory of Dear Old Days"; Hubbard, *Little Journeys,* 367; Barnard Powers, "Henry H. Rogers—The Great Monopolist," *The Magazine of Wall Street and Business Analyst* 22, no. 6 (June 22, 1918): 397. These figures are probably exaggerated; they are much higher than the average earnings of skilled workers at the time. Clarence D. Long, *Wages and Earnings in the United States, 1860–1890* (Princeton: Princeton University Press, 1960), 94, 99.

4. "Henry H. Rogers: A Great Actor in the Present World Drama," *The Gateway: A Magazine Devoted to Literature, Economics, and Social Service* 4, no. 5 (June 1905): 29–30.

5. Ida M. Tarbell, *All in the Day's Work: An Autobiography* (1939; Urbana-Champaign: University of Illinois Press, 2003), 213–14.

6. Powers, "Great Monopolist," 397; Hubbard, *Little Journeys,* 377. Pratt became the founder of the Pratt Institute in Brooklyn.

7. Ida M. Tarbell, *The History of the Standard Oil Company,* 2 vols. (New York: McClure, Phillips, 1904), 1:88.

8. Andrea Mays, *The Millionaire and the Bard: Henry Folger's Obsessive Hunt for Shakespeare's First Folio* (New York: Simon & Schuster, 2015), 84.

9. Powers, "Great Monopolist," 398.

10. Dias, *Portrait,* 101, 119–23; *Century Association Yearbook* (New York: Century Association, 1904), 5. Around 1900 Rogers moved to 3 East 78th Street, a five-story, thirty-five-foot-wide limestone mansion guarded by griffins and winged lions of stone. Tom Miller, "The 1899 Edmund C. Converse Mansion" (Mar. 24, 2012), daytonianinmanhattan .blogspot.com.

11. Dias, *Portrait,* 99, 102.

12. Mabel Hoyle Knipe, "The First Gift: The Story of the Rogers Grammar School" (1977), www.millicentlibrary.org.

13. *New York Times,* July 9, 1885; Dias, *Portrait,* 103; "Henry H. Rogers: Captain of Industry," *Harper's Weekly* 53 (May 29, 1909): 9, quoted in *Mark Twain's Correspondence with Henry Huttleston Rogers, 1893–1909,* ed. Lewis Leary (Berkeley: University of California Press, 1969), 189n1; *Fairhaven Star,* Mar. 29, May 10, 1890; Knipe, "First Gift."

14. Mabel Hoyle Knipe, "Under a Bushel: Some Little Known Philanthropy of Henry Huttleston Rogers" (1983), www.millicentlibrary.org; Dias, *Portrait,* 149, 150.

15. S. L. Clemens to Mrs. H. H. Rogers, Nov. 1896, in Albert Bigelow Paine, "Mark Twain's Letters," *Harper's Magazine* 135 (Oct. 1917): 645; Amy Chambliss, "The Friendship of Helen Keller and Mark Twain," *Georgia Review* 24, no. 3 (Fall 1970): 306–8; Helen Keller, *The World I Live In* (New York: Century, 1908): "To Henry H. Rogers, My Dear Friend of Many Years."

16. Booker T. Washington, "H. H. Rogers as a Cash Giver," *New York Evening Post,* May 29, 1909, reprinted in *The Booker T. Washington Papers,* 14 vols. (Champaign-Urbana: University of Illinois Press, 1981), 10:123; Washington to Henry Huttleston Rogers Jr., June 7, 1909, *Booker T. Washington Papers,* 10:134, quoted in Hubbard, *Little Journeys,* 389.

17. Hubbard, *Little Journeys,* 390–91.

18. Rogers' speech at the dedication of the Millicent Library, Jan. 30, 1893, quoted in Mabel Hoyle Knipe, "The Girl in the Window: The Story of the Millicent Library" (1979), www.millicentlibrary.org; *Fairhaven Star,* May 16, 1891. On the Carnegie libraries, see Abigail Van Slyck, *Free to All: Carnegie Libraries and American Culture, 1890–1920* (Chicago: University of Chicago Press, 1995).

19. Knipe, "Girl in the Window"; *Fairhaven Star,* Feb. 17, 1894.
20. *Fairhaven Star,* Mar. 14, 1889.
21. *Fairhaven Star,* Mar. 14, May 9, 1891.
22. Charles A. Harris, *Old-Time Fairhaven,* 3 vols. (New Bedford: Reynolds, 1947–1954), 2:214–15; *Fairhaven Star,* Feb. 28, Mar. 14, Apr. 25, May 23, Dec. 5, 1891.
23. Mabel Hoyle Knipe, "The Story of a 'Town House': Fairhaven Town Hall" (1977), www.millicentlibrary.org.
24. Knipe, "Story of a 'Town House'"; *Fairhaven Star,* Feb. 17, 1894. The manuscript of Twain's speech is exhibited in the Millicent Library.
25. Tarbell, *All in the Day's Work,* 218.
26. Quoted in Thomas W. Lawson, *Frenzied Finance: The Crime of Amalgamated,* vol. 1 (New York: Ridgeway-Thayer, 1905), 291.
27. Powers, "Great Monopolist," 398; Hubbard, *Little Journeys,* 360; Lawson, *Frenzied Finance,* 15.
28. *Fort Worth Telegram,* January 7, 1906. Standard Oil was broken up in 1911, after Rogers' death, under the Sherman Antitrust Act: *Standard Oil Co. of New Jersey v. United States, 221 U.S. 1.*
29. Tarbell, *All in the Day's Work,* 212, 215, 218.
30. Lawson. *Frenzied Finance,* 17–19, 21; Mark Twain, *Autobiography,* vol. 3, ed. Benjamin Griffin and Harriet Elinor Smith (Berkeley: University of California Press, 2015), 232.
31. "In Memory of Dear Old Days."
32. Joseph D. Thomas and Jay Avila, *A Picture Postcard History of Fairhaven* (New Bedford: Spinner, 2003), 10–11; *New York Times,* Sept. 27, 1901, and July 25, 1903.
33. *Poor's and Moody's Manual Consolidated,* 2 vols. (New York: Moody Manual Co., 1921), 1:46; M. I. Baron, "Atlas Tack: A Look Inside an Abandoned Factory," video, www.youtube.com; Knipe, "Under a Bushel." In 1908 Rogers had plans drawn up for cottages for factory workers, with nominal rents that could go toward purchase, but he died before building them. *New York Times,* Aug. 24, 1908.
34. *New York Times,* Dec. 14, 1905.
35. *Representative Men and Old Families of Southeastern Massachusetts,* 3 vols. (Chicago: J. H. Beers, 1912), 1:436; *New York Times,* Sept. 18, 1907.
36. Mabel Hoyle Knipe, "Thee Will Fill It Up! The Story of the Robert Cushman Park" (1979), www.millicentlibrary.org; Harris, *Old-Time Fairhaven,* 3:124.
37. For a full description of the church buildings, see *The Memorial Church and Buildings, Fairhaven, Massachusetts: A Record of the Dedication Exercises and a Description of the Buildings* (privately printed, 1906), 48–61.
38. *Memorial Church and Buildings,* 61–63; Julie L. Sloan, "Stained Glass Condition Analysis: Unitarian Memorial Church, Fairhaven" (2005), Unitarian Memorial Church archives.
39. *Memorial Church and Buildings,* 60–63; Sloan, "Stained Glass," 4.
40. *Memorial Church and Buildings,* 46.
41. Mabel Hoyle Knipe, "House of Transition: A Compilation of Fact and Legend concerning the Tabitha Inn" (1977), www.millicentlibrary.org.
42. "An Intimate Portrait of Henry H. Rogers" (interview), *New York Times,* Sept. 22, 1907.
43. *Representative Men and Old Families,* 3:1521.
44. Thomas and Avila, *Picture Postcard History,* 14–17; Dias, *Portrait,* 152.
45. *New York Times,* July 26, 1905.
46. *New York Times,* June 19, 1905.
47. *Fairhaven Star,* Sept. 12, 1908, and May 7, 1910. It is generally believed that the houses were built for teachers at the high school, but there is no evidence that this was true. The two sales reported in the *Star* were to Clinton W. Kinsella of New York and Walter

C. Sherman, a salesman at the Kilburn Mill. *Fairhaven Star,* Oct. 30, 1909, and Mar. 26, 1910.
48. *New York Times,* Mar. 6, 1906; *Boston Globe,* Oct. 19, 1906.
49. Knipe, "Thee Will Fill It Up!"
50. Knipe, "Thee Will Fill It Up!"
51. Nathaniel Philbrick, *Mayflower: A Story of Courage, Community, and War* (New York: Viking, 2006), 19–22, 26–27, 125–26.
52. Thomas and Avila, *Picture Postcard History,* 37. The library addition was built in 1968, with town and federal funds and support from the Rogers family and friends. On James M. Curley's Jamaica Plain mansion, see Keith N. Morgan, ed., *Buildings of Massachusetts: Metropolitan Boston,* Buildings of the United States (Charlottesville: University of Virginia Press, 2009), 269.
53. *New York Times,* Jan. 24, 1926.

3. The Apple and the Tree

SOURCES

Ed Parr's *The Last American Whale-Oil Company: A History of Nye Lubricants, Inc., 1844–1994* is an excellent history of the business and the best place to start tracking down information about the Nyes. Because the industries Joe invested in were regulated by Massachusetts, his involvement in water companies and railroads can be traced in state documents. Magazines published by the Spiritualist, Methodist, and Adventist churches were also useful. Some information about Nye oils, the Onset Bay Grove Association, and the Attleboro sanitarium came from advertisements and postcards. Industry magazines and directories were also helpful.

1. Henry B. Worth, "Oxford Village," *Old Dartmouth Historical Sketches,* no. 43 (New Bedford: Old Dartmouth Historical Society, 1915); Duane Hamilton Hurd, ed., *History of Bristol County, Massachusetts* (Philadelphia: J. W. Lewis, 1883), 280. On the history of the Academy building, see Charles A. Harris, *Old-Time Fairhaven,* 3 vols. (New Bedford: Reynolds, 1947–1954), 3:118–25.
2. Leonard Bolles Ellis, *History of New Bedford and Its Vicinity, 1602–1892* (Syracuse: D. Mason, 1892), 93; Robert Glen Nye and Luther Bert Nye, *A Genealogy of the Nye Family,* 4 vols. (Cleveland: Nye Family of America Association, 1907), 1:423.
3. *Representative Men and Old Families of Southeastern Massachusetts,* 3 vols. (Chicago: J. H. Beers, 1912), 1:407; "Who Lies Here? William Mason," *Taunton Daily Gazette,* Sept. 23, 2012; *The Mason Machine Works, Taunton, Massachusetts, U.S.A.* (Taunton: Mason Machine Works, 1898), 5.
4. Allen Hughes, "An American Treasure Finds a New Home," *New York Times,* Nov. 14, 1982; Douglas Bush and Richard Kassel, eds., *The Organ: An Encyclopedia* (New York: Routledge, 2006), 33.
5. Henry David Thoreau, *Walden* (1854; New York: Crowell, 1910), 393–94; Reid Mitenbuler, "The Stubborn American Who Brought Ice to the World," *The Atlantic,* www .atlantic.com, Feb. 5, 2013.
6. Henry G. Pearson, "Frederic Tudor, Ice King," *Proceedings of the Massachusetts Historical Society,* 3rd ser., vol. 65 (Oct. 1932–May 1936): 178, 198–99.
7. David G. Dickason, "The Nineteenth-Century Indo-American Ice Trade," *Modern Asian Studies* 25, no. 1 (Feb. 1991): 69, 76; Linda H. Kistler, Clairmont P. Carter, and Brackston Hinchey, "Planning and Control in the 19th Century Ice Trade," *Accounting Historians Journal* 11, no. 1 (Spring 1984): 21–28, quotation on 25.

8. Kistler, Carter, and Hinchey, "Planning and Control," 19, 26.
9. Ellis, *History of New Bedford,* 93; George H. Tinkham, *A History of Stockton* (San Francisco: W. M. Hinton, 1880), 155, 158, 394.
10. Nye and Nye, *Genealogy,* 1:423–24; Ellis, *History of New Bedford,* 94.
11. Nye and Nye, *Genealogy,* 1:423; Alfred J. Tapson, "The Sutler and the Soldier," *Military Affairs* 21, no. 4 (Winter 1957): 176, 177–79; Ellis, *History of New Bedford,* 94.
12. *New York Times,* Dec. 10, 1861.
13. "Lubricating Watches and Clocks," *American Machinist* 31 (Feb. 6, 1908): 225; David S. Landes, *Revolution in Time: Clocks and the Making of the Modern World* (Cambridge: Harvard University Press, 1983), 314–20.
14. Nye Lubricants, "History," www.nyelubricants.com/170-years.
15. Nye Lubricants, "History."
16. Ed Parr, *The Last American Whale-Oil Company: A History of Nye Lubricants, Inc., 1844–1994* (Fairhaven: Nye Lubricants, Inc., 1996), 21–23, 29, 33–34; Nye Lubricants, "History."
17. Ellis, *History of New Bedford,* 95.
18. Parr, *Last American Whale-Oil Company,* 27; Belva A. Lockwood, "How I Ran for the Presidency," *National Magazine* 17 (Mar. 1903): 731, 733.
19. *Fairhaven Star,* 1903, quoted in Parr, *Last American Whale-Oil Company,* 27.
20. Nye Family of America Association, *Proceedings at the Second Reunion at Sandwich, Massachusetts, August 17, 18, and 19, 1904* (New Bedford: E. Anthony & Sons, 1904), 71.
21. Quoted in Parr, *Last American Whale-Oil Company,* 58.
22. William D. Moore, "'To Hold Communion with Nature and the Spirit-World': New England's Spiritualist Camp Meetings, 1865–1910," in *Exploring Everyday Landscapes: Perspectives in Vernacular Architecture VII,* ed. Annmarie Adams and Sally Ann McMurray (Knoxville: University of Tennessee Press, 1997), 230–48, quotations on 236, 241.
23. Flora B. Cabell, letter to *Banner of Light,* 1885, quoted in Moore, "To Hold Communion," 239.
24. Moore, "To Hold Communion," 236, 243.
25. Russ H. Gilbert, *The Story of a Wigwam* (Onset: n.p., 1904), 37.
26. Bernadine Rose Angelo, "Beckoning the Red Man's Spirit" (M.A. thesis, University of Massachusetts Boston, 2010), quoted in Michael J. Vieira, *A Brief History of Wareham: The Gateway to Cape Cod* (Charleston, S.C.: History Press, 2014), 94.
27. C. B. Vaughan, "Onset, a Famous Camping Ground," *New England Magazine* 32, no. 6 (Aug. 1905): 620–22.
28. Gilbert, *Story of a Wigwam,* 6, 50.
29. "The New Bedford & Onset Street Railway," *Street Railway Review,* Dec. 15, 1901, 879.
30. *Boston Sunday Post,* June 17, 1894.
31. Vaughan, "Onset, a Famous Camping Ground," 625.
32. Moore, "To Hold Communion," 238.
33. Moore, "To Hold Communion," 237 (illustration); Vaughan, "Onset, a Famous Camping Ground," 619; Vieira, *Brief History of Wareham,* 91.
34. Parr, *Last American Whale-Oil Company,* 35.
35. MIT, *Twelfth Annual Catalogue, 1876–1877* (Boston: A. A. Kingman, 1876), 16, 21.
36. Nye Lubricants, "History."
37. Parr, *Last American Whale-Oil Company,* 38, 39, 42, 44; Mabel Hoyle Knipe, "The Girl in the Window: The Story of the Millicent Library" (1979), www.millicentlibrary.org.
38. *Journal of the House of Representatives of the Commonwealth of Massachusetts,* vol. 116 (1895), 212, 242; *Private & Special Statutes of the Commonwealth of Massachusetts,* vol. 16 (1892), 1004.
39. *Public Documents of Massachusetts: Annual Reports of Various Public Officers and Institutions,* vol. 5 (1902), 522, 533; *Poor's Directory of Railway Officials* (New York, 1892), 285.

40. Parr, *Last American Whale-Oil Company*, 37, 47–50. On the Mill Pond project, see chapter 2.

41. *Fairhaven Star*, Nov. 21, Dec. 19, 1891; Parr, *Last American Whale-Oil Company*, 35.

42. *Boston Daily Globe*, Sept. 18, 1889; *Massachusetts Year Book for 1907*, 126, and *Massachusetts Year Book for 1908*, 127 (Worcester: F. S. Blanchard, 1907, 1908); Parr, *Last American Whale-Oil Company*, 36; *Boston Daily Globe*, Aug. 23, 1901, Aug. 1, 1903, and Jan. 31, 1889; *Boston Sunday Post*, May 23, 1909.

43. *Boston Daily Globe*, July 12, 1885, and Oct. 13, 1903; "Boats for Sale," *The Rudder* 19, no. 3 (Mar. 1908): 200; Parr, *Last American Whale-Oil Company*, 38, 59.

44. Parr, *Last American Whale-Oil Company*, 35.

45. *New York Times*, July 17, 2014, Mar. 18, 1909, Dec. 18, 1892, Feb. 3, 1907, and Jan. 8, 1899.

46. Nina Mikhalevsky, *Dear Daughters: A History of Mount Vernon Seminary and College* (Washington, D.C.: Mount Vernon Seminary and Alumni Association, 2001), chap. 1; email correspondence with Betty Calder and Susan T. Block of Wilmington, North Carolina; William K. Selden, *Women of Princeton, 1746–1969* (Princeton: Princeton University, 2000), 48, provided by Kenneth Henke, Archives and Special Collections, Princeton Theological Seminary Library; *Fairhaven Star*, Oct. 29, 1923, and Mar. 7, Apr. 4, 1924. In 1901 W. F. Roberts, a publisher in Washington, issued Calder's *Art History in Outline*, which was used as a textbook at Mount Vernon. She traveled in the summers, studying ancient and Byzantine art, and had an article, "Some Economical Experiences in Foreign Travel," published in *Travel* magazine in 1908. She also published articles in scholarly journals. Phila Calder studied art with the founder of the Princeton University Art Museum, Allan Marquand, for six years. In 1918 she became the editor of Princeton's Index of Christian Art project and remained in that position until 1933. She then lived in Princeton (with Marquand's widow and daughter) and Washington. She returned to Wilmington in 1958. Joe's will left her only $5,000 from a probate estate of $217,795. Under Massachusetts law, she was entitled to a 20 percent interest in the estate or a cash settlement of $10,000 plus a life interest in the remainder of the estate. She accepted an undisclosed cash settlement in 1924.

47. Parr, *Last American Whale-Oil Company*, 55–56, 58–59.

48. *New York Times*, Nov. 16, 1913; Parr, *Last American Whale-Oil Company*, 53; email from Janice Hodson, Curator of Art, Special Collections Dept., New Bedford Free Public Library, Sept. 2, 2015.

49. Parr, *Last American Whale-Oil Company*, 60; Victor Bonneville and Paula T. Sollitto, *Attleboro* (Charleston, S.C.: Arcadia, 1999), 27; Denis Fortin and Jerry Moon, *The Ellen G. White Encyclopedia* (Washington, D.C.: Review and Herald Press, 2014), s.v. Nicola; www.asylumprojects.org; *New York Times*, Feb. 7, 1911.

50. "Ministry of Health Annexed to Centenary," *The Christian Advocate* 93, no. 42 (Oct. 17, 1918): 1318; Commonwealth of Massachusetts, death certificate, Sept. 19, 1923.

4. A Home Above

SOURCES

The main source for biographical material in this chapter is Joseph Bates's *Autobiography*, first published in 1868 by the Adventist Publishing Association and reprinted many times since then. Like any autobiography, it is often the only source of information for his early life and for his private experiences. I have checked the facts in it against other sources whenever possible. I have noted inconsistencies when they appear, and the additional sources appear in the notes. The biographies of Bates, which draw heavily on his *Autobiography*, were published by the Adventist publishing house and tend to be worshipful rather than analytical. There is a small amount of scholarly discussion of Bates, and I have consulted and cited it when relevant.

1. The house at 191 Main Street is owned by the Adventist Heritage Society, which is restoring it to its appearance at the time Bates lived there. The description is drawn from my own visits. The Fairhaven Academy, called the New Bedford Academy until Fairhaven's incorporation in 1812, was moved to the northeast corner of Main Street and Huttleston Avenue (Route 6) in 1907. When Bates attended, it was on the west side of Huttleston Avenue, closer to the harbor. On Joseph Bates Sr. and the Academy, see Charles A. Harris, *Old-Time Fairhaven*, 3 vols. (New Bedford: Reynolds, 1947–1954), 3:118–25.

2. Joseph Bates, *The Autobiography of Joseph Bates* (Battle Creek, Mich.: Steam Press of the Seventh-day Adventist Publishing Assoc., 1868), 25–26, 28–31, 32–35.

3. Bates, *Autobiography*, 35.

4. Bates, *Autobiography*, 36–49, quotation on 43.

5. Bates, *Autobiography*, 50–53; Massachusetts Office of the Secretary of State, *Massachusetts Soldiers and Sailors of the Revolutionary War*, vol. 1 (Boston: Wright & Potter, 1896), 793; Bates, *Autobiography*, 52–85, quotation on 84–85. For a detailed first-person account of American prisoners' experiences at Dartmoor during this period, including the massacre and documents related to it, see Charles McLean Andrews, *The Prisoner's Memoirs* (New York: published for the author, 1852). Andrews does not list Bates among the prisoners, but there is no reason to doubt that he was there.

6. Bates, *Autobiography*, 85–95.

7. Bates, *Autobiography*, 96.

8. Bates, *Autobiography*, chaps. 8–19.

9. *Representative Men and Old Families of Southeastern Massachusetts*, 3 vols. (Chicago: J. H. Beers, 1912), 2:785.

10. Bates, *Autobiography*, 143, 150, 168, 172, 173–74, 179.

11. Bates, *Autobiography*, 116, 184.

12. Bates, *Autobiography*, 193.

13. Bates, *Autobiography*, 193, 201.

14. Bates, *Autobiography*, 204–5.

15. Bates, *Autobiography*, 204–8; T. Abbot, *Cold Water Melodies* (Boston: Theodore Abbot, 1842), 33.

16. George Knight, *Joseph Bates: The Real Founder of Seventh-day Adventism* (Hagerstown, Md.: Review and Herald Publishing Assoc., 2004), 48; Bates, *Autobiography*, 209–13; photocopy of the original holograph log book of Captain Joseph Bates's voyage on the bark *Empress* of New Bedford, Mass., Aug. 9, 1827–June 16, 1828, New Bedford Whaling Museum Research Library, entries for Nov. 24 and Dec. 25, 1827.

17. Bates, *Autobiography*, 227, 231; *Ship Registers of New Bedford*, vol. 1 (Boston: WPA, 1940), 91–92.

18. The Bateses had five children: Anson Augustus (1819–1821), Helen (b. ca. 1822), Eliza (b. 1824), Joseph (1830–1865), and Mary (b. 1834), who cared for her parents in their old age (Knight, *Joseph Bates*, 21). Merlin D. Burt, *Adventist Pioneer Places: New York and New England* (Hagerstown, Md.: Review and Herald Publishing Assoc., 2011), 58, 64; Arthur Whitefield Spalding, *Origin and History of Seventh-day Adventists*, vol. 1 (1949; repr., Washington, D.C.: Review and Herald Publishing Co., 1961), 400, note to p. 123.

19. Bates, *Autobiography*, 232–33; Knight, *Joseph Bates*, 49.

20. *Laws of the Commonwealth of Massachusetts [May 1831–March 1833]*, vol. 12 (Boston: Dutton and Wentworth, 1833), 627.

21. Bates, *Autobiography*, 243–54. Miller's volume, a collection of nineteen lectures, was first

published in 1936 by Kemble and Hooper of Troy, N.Y., and was reprinted numerous times over the next few years. The first edition is distinguished by a typographical error in the title: *Scirpture* for *Scripture*.

22. Ronald D. Graybill, "The Abolitionist-Millerite Connection," in *The Disappointed: Millerism and Millenarianism in the Nineteenth Century,* ed. Ronald L. Numbers and Jonathan M. Butler (Bloomington: Indiana University Press, 1987), 143, 149; Arthur Whitefield Spalding, *Captains of the Host: A History of the Seventh-day Adventists,* Part 1 (Washington, D.C.: Review and Herald Publishing Assoc., [1949]), 32–33.

23. Bates, *Autobiography,* 277; Graybill, "Abolitionist-Millerite Connection," 142; Burt, *Adventist Pioneer Places,* 64, 65.

24. Graybill, "Abolitionist-Millerite Connection," 145–46; Eugen Weber, *Apocalypses: Prophecies, Cults, and Millennial Beliefs through the Ages* (Cambridge: Harvard University Press, 1999), 231.

25. Spalding, *Origin and History,* 1:27–28; Bates, *Autobiography,* 258–59.

26. Bates, *Autobiography,* 274, 276.

27. Bates, *Autobiography,* 300.

28. Conversation with J. O. Corliss, quoted in Knight, *Joseph Bates,* 71.

29. Jonathan M. Butler, "The Making of a New Order: Millerism and the Origins of Seventh-day Adventism," in Numbers and Butler, *The Disappointed,* 200–201.

30. Graybill, "Abolitionist-Millerite Connection," 149; Joseph Bates, *The Seventh Day Sabbath, a Perpetual Sign,* pamphlet (New Bedford: Press of Benjamin Lindsey, 1846); quotations from Spalding, *Captains of the Host,* 411, and *Origin and History,* 1:130n15.

31. Spalding, *Origin and History,* 1:123–24, quotation on 124.

32. Spalding, *Origin and History,* 1:124–25.

33. Knight, *Joseph Bates,* 173, 183, 198, quotation on 183.

34. Knight, *Joseph Bates,* 185–87, quotation on 186–87.

35. Knight, *Joseph Bates,* 191; Spalding, *Captains of the Host,* 43, 305–14; Butler, "Making of a New Order," 204.

36. Knight, *Joseph Bates,* 199, 208. An image of the grave is available at www.findagrave .com. There is some disagreement about the cause of Bates's death. Knight, working from a newspaper obituary, reports it as "diabetes and putrid erysipelas" (*Joseph Bates,* 208), but Spalding questions whether Bates could have remained as active and healthy as he was until shortly before his death had he been diabetic (*Origin and History,* 1:407–8, note to p. 355).

5. Home Is Not a House

SOURCES

The accounts by Joshua Slocum and his son Victor provide the basic information about the captain's life and voyages, as well as Victor's own memories of his childhood. Victor's book, *Capt. Joshua Slocum: The Adventures of America's Best Known Sailor,* first published in 1950 in the United States and in 1952 in the United Kingdom, was revised in 1972.

Walter Teller interviewed Hettie Slocum shortly before she died and corresponded with Ben Aymar Slocum, Garfield Slocum, and Jessie Slocum Joyce. He consulted Slocum's correspondence with his publishers at the Peabody Essex Museum and the New York Public Library. Unfortunately Hettie burned most of Joshua's correspondence. Ann Spencer's biography, for which she consulted Teller's archive, is especially useful for family relationships. Geoffrey Wolff's biography is superb—thorough, insightful, and elegantly written.

Online collections of historical newspapers proved invaluable: *America's Historical Newspapers,* collected by the American Antiquarian Society, published by Readex, and available through many libraries; *Newspaperarchive.com,* accessed through the Boston Public Library; and *Chronicling America,* available free from the Library of Congress (www .chroniclingamerica.loc.gov). The *New York Times* maintains its own archive.

1. Victor Slocum, *Capt. Joshua Slocum: The Adventures of America's Best Known Sailor* (Dobbs Ferry, N.Y.: Sheridan House, 1972; repr., 1993), 273–74; Duane Hamilton Hurd, ed., *History of Bristol County, Massachusetts* (Philadelphia: J. W. Lewis, 1883), 274.
2. Walter Teller, *Joshua Slocum* (New Brunswick, N.J.: Rutgers University Press, 1971), 61; Joshua Slocum, *Sailing Alone Around the World* (1900; repr., New York: Dover Publications, 1956), 4–10.
3. Teller, *Joshua Slocum,* 5; Victor Slocum, *The Life and Voyages of Captain Joshua Slocum* (London: Rupert Hart-Davis, 1952), 32, 35–37, 41.
4. Victor Slocum, *Capt. Joshua Slocum,* 47–51.
5. Victor Slocum, *Capt. Joshua Slocum,* 54–55. This edition substitutes "orphan" for "widow," but the reading from the 1952 edition makes more sense.
6. Victor Slocum, *Capt. Joshua Slocum,* 56–57, 59.
7. Victor Slocum, *Capt. Joshua Slocum,* 68.
8. Victor Slocum, *Life and Voyages,* 76–79; *Capt. Joshua Slocum,* 81–90.
9. Victor Slocum, *Capt. Joshua Slocum,* 102, 104, 110.
10. Victor Slocum, *Capt. Joshua Slocum,* 113, 114–16, 119–28.
11. Geoffrey Wolff, *The Hard Way Around: The Passages of Joshua Slocum* (New York: Knopf, 2010), 79–80; *New-York Daily Tribune,* June 26, 1882.
12. Victor Slocum, *Capt. Joshua Slocum,* 146–47.
13. Victor Slocum, *Capt. Joshua Slocum,* 146–47.
14. Wolff, *Hard Way Around,* 94–97.
15. *New York Sun,* "Boarding Up a Mutineer," Nov. 24, 1883.
16. "Boarding"; *New-York Tribune,* Nov. 24, 28, Dec. 12, 14, 23, 1883.
17. *New York Sun,* Jan. 13, 1884. Slater had also sued Mitchell and was awarded $25 in damages in that suit. *New-York Tribune,* Dec. 5, 1883.
18. *New-York Tribune,* Jan. 18, 1884.
19. Wolff, *Hard Way Around,* 111, 113, 114; Victor Slocum, *Capt. Joshua Slocum,* 179–80.
20. Quoted in Teller, *Joshua Slocum,* 30.
21. Wolff, *Hard Way Around,* 116–17.
22. Wolff, *Hard Way Around,* 120–32, 140; Slocum to Capt. Hubbard, Nov. 1, 1888, quoted in *Boston Daily Globe,* Nov. 14, 1888.
23. Wolff, *Hard Way Around,* 144; *Boston Daily Globe,* Nov. 14, 1888; Ann Spencer, *Alone at Sea: The Adventures of Joshua Slocum* (Toronto: Doubleday Canada, 1998), 77.
24. Dexter Marshall, "Our New York Letter," *Copper Country Evening News* (Calumet, Mich.), July 6, 1898.
25. Spencer, *Alone at Sea,* 77; Wolff, *Hard Way Around,* 145–46.
26. Joshua Slocum, *Sailing Alone,* 10.
27. *Boston Daily Globe,* Nov. 9, 1893, and Nov. 28, 1891.
28. Victor Slocum, *Capt. Joshua Slocum,* 363.
29. Guy Bernardin, *Sur les traces de Joshua Slocum* (Cenon: Editions Loisirs Nautiques, 2000), 7 (my translation).
30. Victor Slocum, *Capt. Joshua Slocum,* 18; *America's Historical Newspapers* (online database); *New York Sun,* June 28, 1898.
31. *Omaha World Herald,* July 17, 1898.
32. *New York Times,* Aug. 5, 1898.
33. Victor Slocum, *Capt. Joshua Slocum,* 364–65; Wolff, *Hard Way Around,* 197, 198n, 203; *Fairhaven Star,* July 9, 1898; *Boston Globe,* Jan. 17, 1899. The booklet is very difficult

to find, but the Millicent Library in Fairhaven has put it online: millicentlibrary.org /fairhaven-history (click on "Joshua Slocum Page").

34. Clifton Johnson, "Captain Joshua Slocum," *Outing*, Oct. 1902, 38; Spencer, *Alone at Sea*, 208.

35. Quoted in Teller, *Joshua Slocum*, 231.

36. Quoted in Teller, *Joshua Slocum*, 222.

37. Wolff, *Hard Way Around*, 206–8; *Philadelphia Inquirer*, May 27, June 1, 1906.

38. *Boston Post*, Aug. 7, 1906.

39. Wolff, *Hard Way Around*, 212.

6. A House for Friends

SOURCES

All the genealogical information in this chapter—vital records, census records, street directories, deeds, and the like—is derived from the extensive research files compiled by Cynthia McNaughten, which she graciously donated to the Colonial Club in 2014. The club's archives, including secretaries' and treasurers' reports, can be consulted at the town archives in the Millicent Library.

1. Mattie Coggeshall's death certificate, dated April 16, 1916, gives the duration of her illness as two years, two months, and two days. Her will, dated Feb. 19, 1914, can be found in the Colonial Club archives (hereafter CC archives), box 14.

2. Cynthia McNaughten research notes, CC archives, box 15.

3. News item quoted in Charles A. Harris, *Old-Time Fairhaven*, 3 vols. (New Bedford: Reynolds, 1947–1954), 1:173; wedding invitation, CC archives, box 14; Bradford Hammond Coggeshall obituary, *New Bedford Mercury*, Feb. 14, 1880; McNaughten research notes, CC archives.

4. New York censuses, 1890, 1895, 1900; McNaughten research notes, CC archives.

5. New York censuses, 1900, 1905; current online real estate listings provide dimensions and photographs of the Carlton Avenue houses. Francis Morrone, *Fort Greene and Clinton Hill* (New York: Brooklyn Historical Society, 2010); "Fort Greene Park," www .nycgovparks.org.

6. New York censuses, 1895, 1900, 1905; online real estate listings provide dimensions and photographs for George's Brooklyn Heights home. New York censuses, 1875, 1880; George Coggeshall obituary, *New York Times*, Jan. 10, 1907; Martha Coggeshall's will, CC archives; inscription in *The Narrow Way*, CC archives.

7. McNaughten research notes, CC archives; *Brooklyn Eagle*, June 27, 1894, and June 27, 1895; Brooklyn Historical Society, "Guide to the Boys' High School Register and Publications," "Girls' High School Collection," www.brooklynhistory.org/library; *Brooklyn Eagle*, Sept. 9, 1900.

8. New York City marriage certificate no. 7173, Oct. 22, 1903; New York City births, July 8, 1904; *Brooklyn Eagle*, July 7, 1905; New York censuses, 1900, 1905; Colorado State Board of Horticulture, *Annual Report* 18 (1907), 4.

9. Denver, Colorado, marriage license no. 31706, July 8, 1903. Their marriage license presents a mystery. Edward indicated that he had been married before and divorced in 1891 in Chicago, on grounds of desertion. Since he was about to enter high school in Brooklyn at the time, this is impossible. Perhaps the error is the date, or perhaps it was Mary who had been married before. For their daughter's birth and death, Denver Birth Book, Mar. 14, 1907; Denver Death Book, Oct. 9, 1908. Edward's paintings are *Rousseau and Desdemona* and *Whalers*. The model is of the brig *Lily Pond*.

10. George Coggeshall obituary, *New York Times*, Jan. 10, 1907; reports of gas accident and subsequent deaths, *Brooklyn Eagle*, May 6, 1898, and Oct. 6, 1898; deaths of Edward and Kate, Denver Death Book, Oct. 4, 1907; New York State death certificate no. 4871, July 24, 1907; *Brooklyn Eagle*, July 25, 1907; Elizabeth's death, *Painesville (Ohio) Evening Telegram*, June 7, 1904.

11. The property records can be found in Cynthia McNaughten's research notes in the CC archives; the builder's invoices are also available in the CC archives, box 14. The fact that Mattie was able to build such an expensive home has led to some curiosity—and misunderstandings—about the origins of her wealth. Neither she nor John was born into a wealthy family, and John's income, though respectable, was not large enough for extravagance. Most likely, the source of her grief was also the source of her wealth: she and John were the only heirs of many relatives on her side, and John would have shared inheritances only with his sister, Mary. A large source of wealth, I suspect, was the estate of John's brother, George, who was a very successful businessman. His *New York Times* obituary (Jan. 10, 1907) noted that he had worked for Mitchell Vance, a gas fixture company, for forty years: "Beginning in an humble capacity he worked with untiring energy until at the time of his death he was a member of the firm and a large stockholder." His Brooklyn Heights home was in a far more stylish neighborhood than Fort Greene, and it was nearly three times as large as John's house. With his wife and daughter dead, he likely left his fortune to his brother and sister.

12. *Fairhaven Star*, Aug. 30, Nov. 8, 1913. The CC archives include a photograph of the attendees, oversize photo box, folder 2; a copy of the photograph labeled with the names of the attendees can be found in Cynthia McNaughten's research notes in the CC archives; a colorized photo was displayed in the front hall (inventory no. Doc-P0075). On the King's Daughters, see www.iokds.org/history.html.

13. "By-Laws of the Fairhaven Colonial Club, Organized April 12, 1912," printed by Fairhaven Star Print, 1914, CC archives, box 6A. The archives also hold photographs of the antique show.

14. On the history of the Academy building, see Charles A. Harris, *Old-Time Fairhaven*, 3 vols. (New Bedford: Reynolds, 1947–1954), 3:118–25. The Colonial Club remained responsible for the interior of the building until 1975, when the town took over its maintenance. In 1992 the Fairhaven Historical Society opened the Museum of Fairhaven History there. The Colonial Club gave part of its collection to the Society, and those items remain at the Academy. The secretary's minutes for 1912–16, CC archives, box 1, detail the many repairs to the building and their costs.

15. All accounts of club activities are drawn from the CC archives, which contain the minutes of the secretaries and treasurers, reports of various committees, financial records, publicity, and other documents.

16. For an account of women's clubs from 1896 to 1906, see May Alden Ward, "The Influence of Women's Clubs in New England and in the Middle-Eastern States," *Annals of the American Academy of Political and Social Science* 28, no. 2 (Sept. 1906): 7–28. It is noteworthy that the journal devoted an entire issue to women's clubs at this early date. A more recent scholar explains that a "significant impact of the clubs was their contribution to the civic education and development of their members—their leadership, political, research, and public speaking skills." Teva J. Scheer, "The 'Praxis' Side of the Equation: Club Women and American Public Administration," *Administrative Theory and Practice* 24, no. 3 (Sept. 2002): 529–50.

17. Secretary's report, Oct. 4, 1915, CC archives, box 1.

18. As noted earlier, Mattie Coggeshall's will is in the CC archives. When Mary E. Coggeshall (Mattie's sister-in-law) died, some distant relatives contested the disposition of her estate and, on the advice of their lawyers, the club agreed to settle with them for $10,000 in 1920. Secretary's report, June 28, 1920, CC archives, box 1.

19. Report of the Gifts and Loans Committee at the annual meeting, June 5, 1916, CC archives, box 1. The research for this chapter was initially undertaken as preparation for a talk to be given from time to time at the Coggeshall Memorial as a way of making Mattie's story known to later generations.

20. Secretary's reports, July 31, Aug. 21, 1916, CC archives, box 1.

21. Secretary's report, Sept. 11, 1916, CC archives, box 1.

22. Secretary's reports, Jan. 6, Mar. 3, Apr. 7, May 5, June 2, 1913, and Feb. 4, Mar. 2, Apr. 6, May 4, June 1, Sept. 4, Oct. 5, 1914, CC archives, box 1.

23. Annual report, June 4, 1917, CC archives, box 1.

24. The inventory of the club's holdings created between 2013 and 2016 provides information about when items were created and by whom, when they were donated and by whom, and information about the item's history and provenance, when these facts are known.

25. Secretary's reports, Dec. 14, 1914; Feb. 5, 1915; Jan. 20, Apr. 15, May 7, 18, June 4, Oct. 1, Nov. 19, 1917; June 3, 1918; Mar. 18, Oct. 6, 1919; all in CC archives, box 1.

26. Interview with Nancy Perry, former president of the Colonial Club, Sept. 29, 2014; notarized letter from Fairhaven Board of Health, Oct 2, 1918; secretary's minutes, Oct. 7, 31, 1918, CC archives, box 1.

27. Secretary's minutes, Nov. 1, 1918, CC archives, box 1; annual report, June 2, 1919, CC archives, box 1.

28. Secretary's report, June 5, 1922; annual report, June 1, 1925; minutes, Apr. 4, 1927; all in CC archives, box 1. The "Record of Service" is in the CC archives, box 14.

29. Minutes, Nov. 2, Dec. 7, 1925; Apr. 5, June 7, 1926; Oct. 1, 1928, all in CC archives, box 1; doorway photographs, CC archives, box 16; hurricane photographs, CC archives, Doc-P0027; hurricane essays, CC archives, box 6; minutes, May 7, 1940, CC archives, box 2; *New Bedford Standard-Times,* May 11, 2014.

30. Minutes, Oct. 10, 1921; Jan. 10, Feb. 6, 1922; July 7, Sept. 7, 1926; all in CC archives, box 1.

31. Entertainment Committee annual reports, June 1925, June 1926, CC archives, box 1; minutes, Dec. 11, 1928, CC archives, box 1.

32. Christopher J. Richard, "The Academy: Old Fairhaven's Civic Center," www .fairhavenhistory.blogspot.com.

33. Secretary's minutes, Apr. 7, Sept. 2, 1941; Jan. 5, Feb. 2, Mar. 2, May 4, 1942; annual reports, June 1942, 1943; all in CC archives, box 2.

7. You Can't Go Home Again

SOURCES

The most important source for Manjiro's story is the text of his interrogation at Kochi, transcribed and illustrated by Kawada Shoryo in 1852. The Japanese title is *Hyōson Kiryaku,* or "A Brief Account of Drifting Toward the Southeast." There are fewer than ten known copies, and only two of those are outside Japan. One is in the Millicent Library in Fairhaven, a gift of the Japanese government; another is at the Rosenbach Museum and Library in Philadelphia. Each manuscript differs from the others in some ways. The complete text of his Nagasaki interrogation has not been published.

In 2003 Spinner Publications in New Bedford published *Drifting Toward the Southeast: The Story of Five Japanese Castaways Told in 1852 by John Manjiro,* translated by Junya Nagakuni and Junji Kitadai. The translators were able to consult several of the manuscripts. *Drifting* includes illustrations by Kawada Shoryo and Manjiro as well as photographs of relevant paintings and Fairhaven sites. A foreword by Stuart Frank, a preface by Junya Nagakuni, and an epilogue by Junji Kitadai provide context as well as information about

Manjiro's life after 1852. It is an invaluable source. *Hyōsen Kiryaku* has the advantage of recording Manjiro's testimony as it was delivered, but it is important to remember that it was given during an interrogation on which his life depended. Manjiro would have omitted dangerous evidence, such as church attendance and religious beliefs, for example.

The Rosenbach Museum and Library presented an exhibit based on their copy of *Hyōsen Kiryaku* from October 1999 through January 2000 and published *Nakahama Manjirō's "Hyōsen kiryaku": A Companion Book.* It includes translated excerpts, illustrations, and excellent essays by Derick Dreher, Elizabeth E. Fuller (on the provenance of the manuscript), Pamela D. Winfield ("Visual Text and Historical Context"), Judith M. Guston, ("Form and Meaning in Manjiro's Hyōsen kiryaku"), and a reprinting of "John Manjirō: Whaler, Navigator, and Interpreter," by Fumiko Mori Halloran. It, too, is essential.

Katherine Plummer's *The Shogun's Reluctant Ambassadors: Sea Drifters* provides accounts of other shipwrecked Japanese sailors (Manjiro was not the first to arrive on U.S. shores) and adds to our knowledge of Manjiro in Japan. It is based on her unpublished translation of Nakahama Akira's biography of his grandfather and includes letters by officials of the shogunate.

Honolulu was also an important place for Manjiro, and his activities there were recorded in issues of *The Friend,* Samuel Chenery Damon's quarterly journal. It is not easy to find, but the October 1884 issue is available through Google Books and includes the material about Manjiro that had been published in January 1852, November 1852, and June 1860.

Donald Bernard's *Life and Times of John Manjiro* brings together material on the Fairhaven years from the *Fairhaven Star,* the *New Bedford Mercury,* and other local publications.

Emily V. Warinner, *Voyager to Destiny,* contains material not found elsewhere, including translated excerpts from the Nagasaki testimony and Toichiro Nakahama's biography of his father, but because it contains no notes some of the sources cannot be identified or verified.

1. *New Bedford Evening Standard,* Aug. 1924, quoted in Donald R. Bernard, *The Life and Times of John Manjiro* (New York: McGraw-Hill, 1992), 228; Fumiko Mori Halloran, "John Manjirō: Whaler, Navigator, and Interpreter," in *Nakahama Manjirō's "Hyōsen kiryaku": A Companion Book* (Philadelphia: Rosenbach Museum and Library, 1999), 18, reprinted from *Humanity Above Nation: The Impact of Manjirō and Heco on America and Japan* (Honolulu: Japanese Cultural Center of Hawaii, 1995).

2. Rosenbach Library, *Companion Book,* 52–54.

3. Marius B. Jansen, *The Making of Modern Japan* (Cambridge: Belknap Press of Harvard University Press, 2000), 66–68, 75, 77–79.

4. Jansen, *Making of Modern Japan,* 81.

5. Jansen, *Making of Modern Japan,* 266.

6. Halloran, "John Manjirō," 18.

7. Rhys Richards, "Pacific Whaling 1820–1840," *The Great Circle* 24, no. 1 (June 2002): 27; Gavan Daws, "Honolulu in the 19th Century: Notes on the Emergence of Urban Society in Hawaii," *Journal of Pacific History* 2 (1967): 77; James Farr, "A Slow Boat to Nowhere: The Multi-Racial Crew of the American Whaling Industry," *Journal of Negro History* 68, no. 2 (Spring 1983): 159–64.

8. Shoryo Kawada, *Drifting Toward the Southeast: The Story of Five Japanese Castaways,* trans. Junya Nagakuni and Junji Kitadai (New Bedford: Spinner, 2003), 52; Hawaiian Mission Children's Society, *Portraits of American Protestant Missionaries to Hawaii* (Honolulu, 1901), 25.

9. Kawada, *Drifting,* 52; Halloran, "John Manjirō," 18; Katherine Plummer, *The Shogun's Reluctant Ambassadors: Sea Drifters* (Tokyo: Lotus Press, 1985), 186–88. Manjiro is known by several names. At the time of his shipwreck, he had only the name Manjirō; he was later permitted a surname, and he added "Nakahama." On board the *John Howland* and in Fairhaven, he was known as "John Mung," and "John" was sometimes used

as a first name with "Manjiro." "Manjiro" is sometimes spelled "Munjero" or "Mungero." I have used "Manjiro" in its English form, without the diacritical, throughout.

10. Kawada, *Drifting*, 85–88; Plummer, *Shogun's Ambassadors*, 188; Manjiro's Nagasaki testimony, in Emily V. Warinner, *Voyager to Destiny: The Amazing Adventures of Manjiro, the Man Who Changed Worlds Twice* (New York: Bobbs-Merrill, 1956), Appendix IV, 250. The Old Stone School on North Street is maintained by the Fairhaven Historical Commission and is open to visitors.

11. Kawada, *Drifting*, 88; Plummer, *Shogun's Ambassadors*, 190; Rosenbach Library, *Companion Book*, 90; Halloran, "John Manjirō," 19. William Henry died in 1846, and subsequent references to Whitfield's son are to Marcellus (1849–1926).

12. Bernard, *Life and Times*, 56; FDR to Dr. Toihiro Nakahama, June 8, 1933, reprinted in Plummer, *Shogun's Ambassadors*, 189.

13. Quoted in Plummer, *Shogun's Ambassadors*, 193.

14. Halloran, "John Manjirō," 19; Hawaiian Mission Children's Society, *Portraits*, 79.

15. Halloran, "John Manjirō," 19; Plummer, *Shogun's Ambassadors*, 192.

16. Kawada, *Drifting*, 99.

17. Halloran, "John Manjirō," 20; Kawada, *Drifting*, 107.

18. Plummer, *Shogun's Ambassadors*, 195; *The Polynesian*, Dec. 14, 1850, quoted in *The Friend*, Oct. 1884, 68. The captain was either Jacob D. Whitmore (1825–1860) or his brother James N. W. (1830–1856). Both died at sea; see *New England Historical and Genealogical Register* 15 (1861): 362; 10 (1856): 295.

19. Quoted in *The Friend*, Oct. 1884, 73.

20. *The Friend*, Jan. 1851, quoted in Oct. 1884 issue, 74.

21. Rosenbach Library, *Companion Book*, 112.

22. Kawada, *Drifting*, 112–14.

23. Kawada, *Drifting*, 116–20.

24. Kawada, *Drifting*, 120.

25. Kawada, *Drifting*, 86; Manjiro's Nagasaki testimony, quoted in Plummer, *Shogun's Ambassadors*, 198.

26. Kawada, *Drifting*, 44–48, 80, 91, 103–6; Rosenbach Library, *Companion Book*, 52–53, 56–57, 65, 67, 101–4.

27. Manjiro's Nagasaki testimony, in Warinner, *Voyager*, 250.

28. Nagasaki testimony in Warinner, *Voyager*, 251, 253.

29. Kawada, *Drifting*, 11, 121–23.

30. *The Friend*, June 1, 1860, quoted in Oct. 1884 issue, 75; Kawada, *Drifting*, 123.

31. Junya Nagakuni, "Preface," in Kawada, *Drifting*, 11; Junji Kitadai, "Epilogue: The Legacy of Manjiro," in Kawada, *Drifting*, 125.

32. Kitadai, "Epilogue," 127.

33. Tokugawa Nariaki, Lord of Mito, to Egawa Tarozaemon, quoted in Kitadai, "Epilogue," 128; Abe Ire-no-Kami to Egawa Tanan, quoted in Plummer, *Shogun's Ambassadors*, 201; Warinner, *Voyager*, 167 and note on Manjiro's role, 159–61. The treaty is available at www.archives.gov/exhibits.

34. Plummer, *Shogun's Ambassadors*, 190; *The Friend*, June 1, 1860, reprinted in Oct. 1884 issue, 75; Kitadai, "Epilogue," 129.

35. Kitadai, "Epilogue," 130; John M. Brooke and George M. Brooke, *John M. Brooke's Pacific Cruise and Japanese Adventure, 1858–1860* (Honolulu: University of Hawaii Press, 1986), quoted in Kitadai, "Epilogue," 133.

36. *The Friend*, June 1, 1860, quoted in Oct. 1884 issue, 75; Warinner, *Voyager*, 186, 202–3.

37. *The Friend*, June 1, 1860, quoted in Oct. 1884 issue, 75; Warinner, *Voyager*, 193.

38. Quoted in Bernard, *Life and Times*, 204. The prohibition against correspondence abroad was not limited to Manjiro but was general policy.

39. Halloran, "John Manjirō," 23.

40. *The Friend,* Oct. 1884, 75; Kitadai, "Epilogue," 135. Manjiro had married Danno Tetsu in 1854, and they had one son and two daughters before she died in 1862. He married twice more and had two sons from each marriage. In 1884, when Father Damon visited Japan, he reported that Manjiro had four sons and one daughter. His oldest son, Toichiro, from the first marriage, was a physician; Nishijiro was an architect and professor; and Keizaburo became chief paymaster of the Japanese Navy. Halloran, "John Manjiro," 23–24; *The Friend,* Oct. 1884, 75; *Japan Weekly Mail* 30 (Nov. 19, 1898), 505. The children's book was issued by Hakubunkan Publishing as one of their widely read books for new readers (email from Ian Jared Wilson, professor of history, Harvard University, July 23, 2015).

41. Mito clan official quoted in Plummer, *Shogun's Ambassadors,* 201–2; Halloran, "John Manjiro," 23; Kawada, *Drifting,* 133.

42. Bernard, *Life and Times,* 218–19.

43. Millicent Library, "The Presentation of a Samurai Sword" (pamphlet; Fairhaven, 1918), 16.

44. Millicent Library, "Presentation," 16; Bernard, *Life and Times,* 221–22. The sword was stolen in 1977, but Dr. Tedashi Kikuoka, a professor at Seton Hall University, raised money from Japanese businesses to buy a replacement. *New Bedford Standard-Times,* Aug. 19, 2012.

45. *New Bedford Morning Mercury,* Feb. 13, 1920, reprinted in Bernard, *Life and Times,* 226–28.

46. Tsutomu Himeno, Consul General of Japan in Boston, open letter to the 2015 John Manjiro Festival.

47. *New Bedford Evening Standard,* Dec. 2, 1924, in Bernard, *Life and Times,* 233.

48. Minutes, trustees of the Millicent Library, June 2, 1944, reprinted in Bernard, *Life and Times,* 240–41.

49. Bernard, *Life and Times,* 248–52.

50. For news coverage of the establishment of the museum, the gift of cherry trees, and the annual Cherry Blossom Festival, see, for example, the *New Bedford Standard-Times,* May 7, 2008, Oct. 28, 2010, Oct. 2, 2011, Aug. 10, 2012, and Apr. 29, 2013.

8. The Biggest House in Town

SOURCES

The Zeitz Papers, held by the New Bedford Whaling Museum Research Library, are mostly business records and are useful for anyone interested in the history of movies and movie theaters. The *Fairhaven Star* and *New Bedford Standard-Times* were useful. Conversations with Sharon Challingsworth and Vanessa Gralton were also helpful; both of them had spoken to now-deceased family members and neighbors who remembered events that took place in the house. Barney Zeitz, Harry's grandson, kindly shared some family memories and photographs.

1. Thomas Tripp, "The Story of Fairhaven" (1929), millicentlibrary.org; Fairhaven Office of Tourism, "Riverside Cemetery Map and Guide" (2011), and visit to Riverside Cemetery; Zephaniah W. Pease, *History of New Bedford,* 3 vols. (New York: Lewis Historical Publishing, 1918), 1:232; "109 Green Street," street files, Fairhaven Archives, Millicent Library.

2. Editorial, *New Bedford Morning Mercury,* Dec. 11, 1911; *Representative Men and Old Families of Southeastern Massachusetts,* 3 vols. (Chicago: J. H. Beers, 1912), 1:116; Elbert Hubbard, *Little Journeys to the Homes of Great Business Men* (1909; repr., East Aurora, N.Y.: The Roycrofters / New York: W. H. Wise, 1916), 390–91.

3. *Fairhaven Star,* Oct. 18, 1879; interview with Sharon Challingsworth, Apr. 23, 2016.

4. *Fairhaven Star,* Oct. 18, 1879; *Transactions of the Massachusetts Horticultural Society for the Year 1903,* pt. 1, 161, 188, and *Transactions . . . 1904–1905,* 161; *The American Florist* 16 (March 2, 1901): 1039; Thomas White, "Winsor and Its Birthplace," *Horticulture,* Jan. 19, 1907, 64–65. Murray's greenhouses were at Washington and Temple Streets.

5. Irving Howe, *World of Our Fathers* (New York: Harcourt Brace Jovanovich, 1976), 5–7, 26, 36, 29–42.

6. William Toll, "Jewish Families and the Intergenerational Transition in the American Hinterland," *Journal of American Ethnic History* 12, no. 2 (Winter 1993): 5–6, 24. In determining birth dates, I used census data, birth and death records, obituaries, and draft registration forms when they were available. When they conflicted, I chose the most likely date. The Galveston immigration records have no information about the Zeitzes, but those records are incomplete.

7. On the Genensky family in New Bedford, see Ann Rubin, "A Lifetime of Memories," *The Ser-Charlap Family Newsletter* 8, no. 2 (Apr. 1997): 2; "South End Jewish Community," www.lib.umassd.edu/archives/jewish-tour.

8. New Bedford City Directories; Andrew F. Smith, *Oxford Companion to Food and Drink* (New York: Oxford University Press, 2007), 546; interview with Barney Zeitz, Harry's grandson, Mar. 30, 2016.

9. New Bedford City Directories; Zeitz Papers, New Bedford Whaling Museum Library.

10. New Bedford City Directories; for the first of several ads placed by Zeitz see *American Bottler* 35, no. 1 (January 1, 1915): 88; House Select Committee on Expenditures in the War Department, Subcommittee No. 4, *Hearings . . . on War Expenditures,* 66th Cong., 1st and 2d sess., July 8, 1919–Feb. 26, 1920, 576.

11. Executive Office of Energy and Environmental Affairs, "Port Hunter," www.mass.gov/eea/agencies/czm/buar/shipwrecks/.

12. Interview with Stan Lair, "The 1918 Wreck of the *Port Hunter*" (1979), transcribed by C. Baer, 1995, http//history.vineyard.net/porthunt.htm.

13. Select Committee, *Hearings,* 577–80.

14. Select Committee, *Hearings,* 581–86, 593.

15. Select Committee, *Hearings,* 585, 583.

16. Lair, "1918 Wreck."

17. Select Committee, *Hearings,* 595.

18. Select Committee, *Hearings,* 589–92, 595.

19. New Bedford City Directories; *Fairhaven Star,* Nov. 12, 1926.

20. New Bedford City Directories, Fairhaven section; for Harry, Cecile and their children, see John Fass Morton, *Backstory in Blue: Ellington at Newport '56* (New Brunswick, N.J.: Rutgers University Press, 2008), 161.

21. "109 Green Street," street files, Fairhaven Archives, Millicent Library; New Bedford City Directories, Fairhaven section; interview with Sharon Challingsworth.

22. Mabel Hoyle Knipe, "House of Transition: A Compilation of Fact and Legend concerning the Tabitha Inn" (1977), millicentlibrary.org.

23. On the Zeitz business empire generally, see the Zeitz Papers, New Bedford Whaling Museum Research Library. The Zeiterion has been restored and is in full operation. For a description and history, see http://zeiterion.org/history/.

24. There are many well-illustrated architectural histories of the movie theaters of the 1920s through the 1940s: Ben M. Hall, *The Golden Age of the Movie Palace: The Best Remaining Seats* (New York: Clarkson Potter, 1971); John Margolies and Emily Gwathmey, *Ticket to Paradise: American Movie Theaters and How We Had Fun* (Boston: Little, Brown, 1991); David Naylor, *American Picture Palaces: The Architecture of Fantasy* (New York: Van Nostrand Reinhold, 1981); and Dennis Sharp, *The Picture Palace and Other Buildings for the Movies* (New York: Praeger, 1969).

25. Hall, *Golden Age,* 17.

26. Margolies and Gwathmey, *Ticket to Paradise*, 10, 11.

27. Carmen Maiocco, *The Center: Downtown New Bedford in the 1950s* (New Bedford: n.d.), 9.

28. Quoted in Naylor, *American Picture Palaces*, 31.

29. Maiocco, *The Center*, 10.

30. Maiocco, *The Center*, 63.

31. Hall, *Golden Age*, 246; Zeitz Papers.

32. *Fairhaven Star*, Nov. 6, 1925, and Apr. 27, 1928.

33. Interview with Barney Zeitz., Mar. 30, 2016.

34. Morton, *Backstory*, 163; for Elaine's obituary, see the *Boston Globe*, Apr. 21, 2004.

35. Maiocco, *The Center*, 64–65; James Barron, "A Jazz Mystery, a Sultry Memory," *New York Times*, May 27, 1999; interview with Barney Zeitz.

36. *Fairhaven Star*, Apr. 27, 1928, May 22, 1931, and Aug. 31, 1928.

37. *Fairhaven Star*, Feb. 25, 1932 (the house was sold to St. Luke's Hospital in 1967; Zeitz Papers); Morton, *Backstory*, 161; interview with Barney Zeitz.

38. Zeitz Papers; interview with Sharon Challingsworth.

39. *Fairhaven Star*, May 16, 1930, Nov. 12, 1953, and June 18, 1959; New Bedford City Directory (1935, 1947), Deaths, 1934, 1946; interview with Barney Zeitz; Knipe, "House of Transition."

40. Interview with Sharon Challingsworth.

41. Scott Harshbarger, Attorney General, Commonwealth of Massachusetts, "Fraud Detection and Prosecution: Combatting the 'Fraud Tax,'" Boston, Feb. 9, 1993, unpaginated; *Boston Globe*, Dec. 14, 1993; interview with Sharon Challingsworth.

42. Interview with Sharon Challingsworth.

43. Interview with Vanessa Gralton, Apr. 11, 2016.

9. Homeward Bound

SOURCES

Alexander Winsor's journals and letters can be found at the Rhode Island Historical Society, the G. W. Blunt White Library at Mystic Seaport, and the Bancroft Library, University of California, Berkeley. Some of the journals are available only as transcriptions by Bradford Swan, a descendant. The letters are essential: Winsor did not record in his journals that his second wife sailed with him, but he mentions her in two letters to Thatcher Magoun. Emily Pope Winsor's diary exists in two versions, both at Mystic Seaport's White Library. I was unable to determine the relationship between the two. I have designated the version with very faint handwriting as I, and the slightly more ornate (and legible) one as II, but this should not be taken as a judgment on the order in which they were written. They do not contradict each other, but despite a great deal of overlap, each has material absent from the other. They are best read together, interpolating as you read. The Thatcher Magoun business records are available at Mystic Seaport, Coll. 230, Manuscripts Collection, G. W. Blunt White Library.

1. Zephaniah W. Pease, *History of New Bedford*, 3 vols. (New York: Lewis Historical Publishing, 1918), 3:483.

2. Bradford F. Swan, "The Vicissitudes of a Clipper Ship Captain," typescript, Bradford Swan Papers, Rhode Island Historical Society, MSS 744, box 2.

3. Alexander Winsor to Thatcher Magoun, Nov. 11, 1836, Swan Papers.

4. Bradford Swan, "Captain Alexander Winsor," *Old Dartmouth Historical Sketches*, no. 72 (New Bedford: Old Dartmouth Historical Society, 1940), unpaginated.

5. "The Winsor Family," *The Navigator,* Sept. 2007, 10. The house remains a private residence.

6. *New York Express,* reprinted in *Savannah Republican,* May 14, 1851; *Boston Daily Atlas,* Sept. 6, 1854; Alexander Winsor, *Flying Cloud* journal, May 21, Aug. 8, 1860, transcribed by Bradford Swan, Swan Papers.

7. Winsor to Magoun, Sept. 14, 1868. The "puffs" appeared in the *San Francisco Daily Evening Bulletin,* Sept. 5, 1868, and the *Daily Alta California,* also published in San Francisco, Sept. 9, 1868. They are pasted into Emily Pope Winsor's journal at the Mystic Seaport Library.

8. *San Francisco Bulletin,* Nov. 11, 1870. The condition of the ship could not be credited to "woman's refining influence." Emily Winsor's journal makes it clear that she traveled as a passenger, with neither responsibilities nor authority. On all voyages, Winsor insisted on flawless maintenance, and the steward and crew carried out his orders.

9. Captain Alexander Winsor sea journal, 1850–1854, BANC MSS 2013/125, The Bancroft Library, University of California, Berkeley: *Audubon* journal, Jan. 10, 11, 19, 1851, and *Gertrude* journal, Aug 9, Sept. 1, 1852.

10. Winsor to Magoun, Nov. 15, 1870, and Sept. 2, 1868, Swan Papers.

11. Winsor, *Hussar* journal, Apr. 7. 1855, and Oct. 21, Dec. 27, 1854; *Sea Nymph* journal, Aug. 19, 1857; both transcribed by Bradford Swan, Swan Papers.

12. Winsor, *Sea Nymph* journal, Aug. 19, 1857; *Audubon* journal, Apr. 16, Aug. 27, Oct. 31, Nov. 6, 1851.

13. Emily Pope Winsor, journal I, "Herald of the Morning, New York to San Francisco," May 26, 1868, White Library, Mystic Seaport; Winsor, *Gertrude* journal, Feb. 10, 1854.

14. Winsor to Magoun, Sept. 16, 1870, Swan Papers.

15. Winsor, *Gertrude* journal, Sept. 27, 1853.

16. Winsor, *Gertrude* journal, Nov. 27, 31, Dec. 4, 1852, and Mar. 18, 1853; *Audubon* journal, Feb. 7, 11, 18, 1851.

17. Winsor, *Audubon* journal, Feb. 21, 1851; *Gertrude* journal, Dec. 6. 1852.

18. Winsor, *Audubon* journal, Jan. 10, 11, 1852, and Jan. 6, 1851; *Hussar* journal, Dec. 3, 1854.

19. Winsor, *Hussar* journal, Oct. 14, 1856.

20. Winsor, *Sea Nymph* journal, July 1, 2, Aug. 25, 1857.

21. Winsor, *Gertrude* journal, Aug. 15, Sept. 5, Oct. 12, 1852.

22. Winsor, *Sea Nymph* journal, July 24, Sept. 2, 18, 1857.

23. Winsor, *Flying Cloud* journal, Dec. 30, 1861, Jan. 2, 18, 21, 1862, and Mar. 12, 28, 29, 1862.

24. Louis J. Rasmussen, *San Francisco Ship Passenger Lists,* vol. 2 (1850–1851), 132–33; Winsor, *Audubon* journal, Jan. 6, 1851.

25. Winsor, *Audubon* journal, Feb. 25, 22, 1851.

26. Winsor *Audubon* journal, Feb. 26, 28, 1851.

27. For shipowners see, for example, the letter books of merchant and shipowner Jonathan Avery Parker, New Bedford Whaling Museum Library. Lorraine McConaghy, "The Old Navy in the Pacific West: Naval Discipline in Seattle, 1855–1856," *Pacific Northwest Quarterly* 98, no. 1 (Winter 2006/2007): 18. Joshua Slocum had similar problems with crews; see chapter 7, "Home Is Not a House."

28. Lance S. Davidson, "Shanghaied! The Systematic Kidnapping of Sailors in Early San Francisco," *California History* 64, no. 1 (Winter 1985): 10–17.

29. Winsor to Magoun, Oct. 4, 1868, Swan Papers.

30. Winsor, *Audubon* journal, Jan. 8, 1851, and Jan. 1, 1852.

31. Winsor, *Audubon* journal, Jan. 27–30, Feb. 17, 1852.

32. Winsor, *Sea Nymph* journal, July 8, Aug. 25, 1857, and May 19, 1858, in Swan, "Captain Alexander Winsor."

33. Winsor to Magoun, Sept. 2, 1868, and Nov. 15, 1870, Swan Papers.

34. Emily Pope Winsor journal II, June 19, 1868; Winsor to Magoun, Sept. 2, Oct. 9, 1868, Swan Papers.
35. Winsor to Magoun, Sept. 16, 1870, Swan Papers.
36. Winsor to Magoun, Apr. 26, 1871.
37. Winsor, *Sea Nymph* journal.
38. *Representative Men and Old Families of Southeastern Massachusetts,* 3 vols. (Chicago: J. H. Beers, 1912), 1:543.
39. *San Francisco Bulletin,* Feb. 16, Mar. 17, June 29, 1865; *New York Herald,* Sept. 30, Nov. 25, 1865; Winsor's copy of Bowditch, Swan Papers.
40. Emily Winsor journal II: Apr. 29 1868; I: May 1, 13, Aug. 3, June 18, 1868.
41. Emily Winsor journal II: Aug. 24, 26, June 5, 1868.
42. Emily Winsor journal II: May 26, 1868.
43. Emily Winsor journal I: May 16, June 1, 17, 21, 1868.
44. Emily Winsor journal II: May 17, 1868.
45. Emily Winsor journal I: Aug. 26, June 18, 1868.
46. Emily Winsor journal I: Aug. 29, Sept. 1, 1868.
47. Emily Winsor journal I: Sept. 2–Oct. 10, 1868.
48. Winsor, *Herald* journal, 1870, in Swan, "Vicissitudes."
49. Emily Winsor journal I: Sept. 1, 11, 1868.
50. Swan, "The Winsors of Fairhaven," ms., p. 8, Swan Papers.
51. A copy of the will is included in Swan, "The Winsors of Fairhaven"; Fairhaven Office of Tourism, "Riverside Cemetery Map and Guide" (2011), entries 2 and 21, and visit to Riverside Cemetery.
52. *Fairhaven Star,* June 13, 1891.

10. "Perfectly Safe"

SOURCES

The basic source on New England lighthouses is Edward Rowe Snow's *The Lighthouses of New England,* first published in 1945 and updated by Jeremy D'Entremont in 2002. Snow visited the lighthouses often and interviewed many of the keepers. The book covers history, design, mechanical details, and more, but is documented only with a bibliography. (Snow was known as the "Flying Santa" because for many years, with his wife, Anna, as copilot, he delivered Christmas gifts to the lighthouses from a twin-engine plane.) D'Entremont has also published state-by state guides to lighthouses, maintains an extremely useful website, newenglandlighthouses.net, and conducts lighthouse tours. Both the books and the website are heavily, and beautifully, illustrated. Sarah Gleason's *Kindly Lights: A History of the Lighthouses of Southern New England* provides an excellent legislative and administrative history, as well as some interviews with keepers. In 1889 Arnold Burges Johnson wrote the official administrative history: *The Modern Light-house Service.*

1. Sarah C. Gleason, *Kindly Lights: A History of the Lighthouses of Southern New England* (Boston: Beacon Press, 1991), xiii, 116.
2. Interview, Arthur Small, *American Experience,* www.pbs.org/wgbh/americanexperience.
3. For a complete history of the Lighthouses Act, see Walter J. Stewart, *The Lighthouses Act of 1789* (Washington, D.C.: U.S. Senate Historical Office, 1991).
4. Gleason, *Kindly Lights,* 97.
5. U.S. Congress, *House Reports,* 65th Cong., 1st sess. (Washington, D.C.: GPO, 1917), vol. 1, 3–5.
6. Arnold Burges Johnson, *The Modern Light-house Service* (Washington, D.C.: GPO, 1889), 103.

7. Arnold B. Johnson, "Lighthouse Libraries," *Library Journal* 10, no. 2 (Feb. 1885): 31–32. The libraries were oddly sectarian in their choice of religious reading, offering only a New Testament and Book of Psalms plus the Episcopal *Book of Common Prayer.*

8. Johnson, *Modern Light-house Service,* 104–6.

9. Connie Scovill Small, *The Lighthouse Keeper's Wife,* rev. ed. (1999; Orono: University of Maine Press, 2012), 36–37.

10. Small, *Lighthouse Keeper's Wife,* 44–49.

11. Small, *Lighthouse Keeper's Wife,* 76–78, 80–81.

12. Small, *Lighthouse Keeper's Wife,* 95–128. The couple's last posting, after World War II, was at the Portsmouth Harbor Light—their first home with electricity and a telephone (145, 150).

13. Elinor DeWire, *Guardians of the Lights: Stories of U.S. Lighthouse Keepers* (Sarasota, Fla.: Pineapple Press, 1995), 212; Edward Rowe Snow, *The Lighthouses of New England,* updated by Jeremy D'Entremont (Beverly, Mass.: Commonwealth Editions, 2002), 222–24, 228; Edward Rowe Snow, *The Romance of Boston Bay* (Dublin, N.H.: Yankee Publishing Co., 1944), 110.

14. Everett S. Allen, *A Wind to Shake the World: The Story of the 1938 Hurricane* (Boston: Little, Brown, 1976), 320–21; *Fairhaven Star,* Sept. 28, 1939; 1930 U.S. Census (Mabel's name is spelled "Mabelle" in the census and in her obituary, but I have followed other historians in using the shorter spelling); *New Bedford Mercury,* Apr. 17, 1935.

15. Jeremy D'Entremont, *The Lighthouses of Massachusetts* (Beverly, Mass.: Commonwealth Editions, 2007), 307, 309; *New Bedford Mercury,* Apr. 17, 1935.

16. Snow, *Lighthouses of New England,* 223.

17. D'Entremont, *Lighthouses of Massachusetts,* 309.

18. Snow, *Lighthouses of New England,* 305; *The Huttlestonian* (Fairhaven High School magazine and yearbook), 1931, 38, Fairhaven Archives, Millicent Library; *New Bedford Mercury,* Apr. 17, 1935.

19. Snow, *Lighthouses of New England,* 305–6.

20. Mary Ellen Chase, *The Story of Lighthouses* (New York: Norton, 1965), 140–41, 155.

21. Johnson, *Modern Lighthouse Service,* 103.

22. Small, *Lighthouse Keeper's Wife,* 83–88, 109–10. Mary Stillman Harkness (Mrs. Edward S.), an heiress and wife of a Standard Oil heir, had donated about two hundred battery-powered radios to the Lighthouse Service. See Gleason, *Kindly Lights,* 109; Edward T. James, Janet Wilson James, and Paul S. Boyer, eds., *Notable American Women,* vol. 1 (Cambridge: Harvard University Press, 1971), 135–36.

23. Gleason, *Kindly Lights,* 108–9; Steven Slosberg, "Art Dictates Path of His Life," *The Day* (New London, Conn.), Mar. 24, 1979; Jackie Fitzpatrick, "Artist's Work of 50 Years Exhibited," *The Day,* Nov. 25, 1983.

24. Mary Jean Blasdale, *Artists of New Bedford: A Biographical Dictionary* (New Bedford: Old Dartmouth Historical Society, 1990), 172; Allen, *A Wind to Shake the World,* 321, 325.

25. D'Entremont, *Lighthouses of Massachusetts,* 23. Many of Small's paintings were lost in 1938, but two are exhibited in the Millicent Library, one is in the New Bedford Whaling Museum collection, and a few are in private collections.

26. Small, *Lighthouse Keeper's Wife,* 82.

27. Gleason, *Kindly Lights,* 103.

28. *Fairhaven Star,* Sept. 29, 1938; "Portrait Shines a Light on Loyal Keeper," *New Bedford Standard-Times,* Jan. 13, 2011.

29. "Mariners' Club Closes Winter Season with Banquet and Entertainment," *Motorboating,* May 1933, 103; Federal Writers' Project of the Works Progress Administration in Massachusetts, *Fairhaven, Massachusetts* (1939), 52–53.

30. *New Bedford Standard-Times,* Apr. 22, 1934; unidentified clippings, Mother's Club

scrapbook, 1934–35, Fairhaven Archives, Millicent Library; *Fairhaven Star,* Sept. 29, 1938; *New Bedford Mercury,* Apr. 17, 1935.

31. Jack Stewardson, "On the Anniversary of the Hurricane of '38, Memories That Never Die," *New Bedford Standard-Times,* Jan. 11, 2011. Mrs. Rex (1893–1998) was a well-known creator of hooked rugs and the author of three books on the subject. She taught at the New Bedford Vocational School and wrote for the *New Bedford Standard-Times.* Stella Hay Rex obituary, *Standard-Times,* Oct. 30, 1998.

32. "The Great New England Hurricane of 1938," www.weather.gov, with information from David R. Vallee and Michael R. Dion, *Southern New England Tropical Storms and Hurricanes: A Ninety-Eight-Year Summary 1909–1997* (Taunton, Mass.: National Weather Service, 1998).

33. This paragraph and the following three are based on Allen, *A Wind to Shake the World,* 321–25; Donald W. Davidson, *Lighthouses of New England* (Secaucus, N.J.: Wellfleet Press, 1990), 88–90; Jeremy D'Entremont, "Keeper Arthur Small: Hero and Artist," *Lighthouse Digest,* Aug. 2003.

34. *Fairhaven Star,* Sept. 29, 1938. On October 18, at its regular meeting, the Fairhaven Mothers' Club read a eulogy for Mabel and observed a moment of silent prayer. They then voted to "select a book to be sent to Capt. Small as a remembrance from the Club since he lost his Library as well as his other possessions in the hurricane." Secretary's minutes, 1932–40, 214, Fairhaven Archives, Millicent Library.

After recuperating at the Chelsea Marine Hospital, Arthur visited his son in Panama and then became the keeper of Hospital Point Light in Beverly, Massachusetts. During World War II, he patrolled the shore between Boston and Salem. He died in 1958 and was buried in Arlington National Cemetery. D'Entremont, "Keeper Arthur Small."

The Palmer Island Lighthouse was automated in 1941 and deactivated in 1962. It was relit on Aug. 30, 1999. Snow, *Lighthouses of New England,* 310–12. The New Bedford–Fairhaven harbor is now protected by a hurricane barrier begun in 1962 and completed in 1966. It is 20 feet high. Whether it could protect the harbor against a storm with the strength of the hurricane of 1938 has never been tested. See "New Bedford Hurricane Protection Barrier," www.nae.usace.army.mil.

Index